The Arguments of Kant's *Critique of Pure Reason*

The Arguments of Kant's
Critique of Pure Reason

Bryan Hall

with the assistance of Mark Black and Matt Sheffield

LEXINGTON BOOKS
A division of
ROWMAN & LITTLEFIELD PUBLISHERS, INC.
Lanham • Boulder • New York • Toronto • Plymouth, UK

Published by Lexington Books
A division of Rowman & Littlefield Publishers, Inc.
A wholly owned subsidiary of The Rowman & Littlefield Publishing Group, Inc.
4501 Forbes Boulevard, Suite 200, Lanham, Maryland 20706
http://www.lexingtonbooks.com

Estover Road, Plymouth PL6 7PY, United Kingdom

British Library Cataloguing in Publication Information Available

Library of Congress Cataloging-in-Publication Data

Hall, Bryan, 1977–
  The arguments of Kant's Critique of pure reason / Bryan Hall with the assistance of
Mark Black and Matt Sheffield.
      p. cm.
  Includes bibliographical references (p.   ) and index.
  ISBN 978-0-7391-4165-6 (cloth : alk. paper) — ISBN 978-0-7391-4166-3 (pbk. : alk.
paper)
  1. Kant, Immanuel, 1724-1804. Kritik der reinen Vernunft. 2. Knowledge, Theory of.
3. Causation. 4. Reason. I. Black, Mark. II. Sheffield, Matt. III. Title.
  B2779.H33 2011
  121—dc22   2010047224

⊖™ The paper used in this publication meets the minimum requirements of American
National Standard for Information Sciences—Permanence of Paper for Printed Library
Materials, ANSI/NISO Z39.48-1992.

Printed in the United States of America

Contents

Part 3: The Transcendental Dialectic

Preface

This book is the product of several semesters of teaching Immanuel Kant's *Critique of Pure Reason* (Abbreviated *CPR*) at both the undergraduate and graduate levels. Regardless of the level at which I have taught Kant, I found that my most difficult task was not getting the student to understand *what* Kant's position is (admittedly difficult in its own right), but rather *why* Kant takes that position. Understanding the latter requires examining the arguments Kant offers for the positions that he adopts. Students generally have a terrible time reading Kant and to help them in this task I developed worksheets that defined Kant's key terms and reconstructed the arguments that Kant was offering in *CPR*. We could then take time in class to examine how these arguments are reflected in the text as well as to criticize both Kant and the reconstructions in light of what we found in the text. In other words, the reconstructions were not an end in themselves, but rather a means toward engaging Kant's text. The worksheets I developed for these classes were the inspiration for the current book and I encourage instructors to use this book in the same way as I used the worksheets in my own courses, viz., as a supplement to the text though not as a replacement for it. Given how valuable my students have been over the years in helping me hone these arguments, I asked two of my current students (Mark Black and Matt Sheffield) to aid in the writing of this book. At every stage of its development, these students insured that the book would be as accessible as possible to the students who one day would be reading it.

Again, the reconstructions of Kant's arguments in this book should not be viewed as definitive, but are best regarded as starting points for engaging Kant's arguments at a more formal level. His arguments are admittedly abstruse and there are often multiple ways in which an argument could be formalized such that each way is still consistent with the text. In addition, there may be more than one argument for a given conclusion. For example, in the First Analogy, I only reconstruct one of Kant's arguments for the principle of the First Analogy though commentators have identified at least three different lines of argument for the principle. For each argument I reconstruct, however, I have chosen a way of formalizing it so that it is maximally consistent with the text and minimally valid (except for some of the arguments in the Transcendental Dialectic which are intended to be invalid). Instructors and students alike, however, should feel free to challenge the soundness of these arguments as well as to rework them in light of Kant's text and the problems they see for the arguments as they are currently reconstructed.

Although certainly open to revision, the argument reconstructions can be useful when presenting Kant's position in class and can aid in the evaluation of Kant's arguments for validity and soundness. All that is really required for understanding the arguments is 1) a basic knowledge of propositional logic, and 2) an understanding of Kant's technical vocabulary. When it comes to the first requirement, it could be useful to review the basic rules of inference before reading the book. When it comes to the second requirement, I have included a glossary near the end of this book which defines, in plain English, all of Kant's technical terms. Since this book is written primarily for students, I thought it best to ask my students to help formulate definitions for Kant's technical terms in hopes of insuring that these definitions are comprehensible for the average philosophy student.

In addition to helping write synopses for Kant's arguments and translating his vocabulary into terms that the average philosophy student will understand, Matt and Mark have also written an appendix included at the end of the book. This appendix offers advice, from the perspective of a student, as to how one should approach *CPR* for the first time. In contrast to most pedagogical philosophical literature, this book is tailored *to* students *by* students.

The book is broken into three parts corresponding to the three parts of *CPR* that are typically covered in a course on Kant. The first part of the book deals with the Transcendental Aesthetic. The second part covers the Transcendental Analytic. The final part examines the Transcendental Dialectic. In total, the book reconstructs 36 of Kant's arguments. Generally, a chapter begins with a quote from *CPR* followed by a synopsis of the argument. Often, the synopses offer examples, metaphors, and other illustrations to aid the reader in understanding Kant's argument. Finally, each synopsis is followed by a reconstruction that presents formally what was explained informally in the synopsis. Each part of the book has both an introductory and a concluding chapter. Since the other chapters deal almost exclusively with individual arguments, it is important to read both the introductory chapter and the concluding chapter for each part of the book you are studying. The introductory chapters contain a general discussion of the arguments in individual chapters as well as how the arguments in different chapters are related to one another. The concluding chapters explain how these different arguments go to support Kant's overall theory of transcendental idealism and how the arguments in that part of the book relate to arguments in different parts of the book.

Although the main focus is on reconstructing and explaining Kant's central arguments, a proper understanding of these arguments often requires familiarity with their historical background as well as some of the central criticisms directed against them. The introduction covers much of the historical background that a student should be familiar with when approaching *CPR* as well as the central points of the Preface and Introduction to *CPR* itself. I have also included some important criticisms of Kant's arguments throughout the book. When it comes to the criticisms I discuss, I have limited myself to criticisms that might be considered *internal* to Kant, i.e., criticisms that attempt to use Kant's own claims against him (e.g., Friedrich Adolf Trendelenburg's criticism that Kant neglects the possibility that space and time might be *both* forms of intuition as well as things-in-themselves). In consideration of both length and focus, I have omitted *external* criticisms of Kant's arguments, i.e., criticisms that rely on the truth of claims external to the Critical philosophy (e.g., the problems posed by non-Euclidean geometry for the synthetic *a priori* status of Euclidean propositions concerning space). This is not a temporal distinction, however, and so I am including some common internal criticism of Kant's view from contemporary philosophers as well (e.g., W.V. Quine's objections to Kant's analytic/synthetic distinction). I believe the internal criticisms will be most helpful in understanding and evaluating Kant's arguments by his own lights. I have tried not to overburden the main text with discussions of these criticisms, however, so the reader should pay special attention to the endnotes both for further critical discussion and for references to the relevant secondary literature.

When it comes to the quoted text, I decided to use the Guyer/Wood translation of *CPR* since I believe that it is the most literal translation of Kant's German and does the best job of exposing the underlying logical syntax of Kant's arguments. Even if you are not using this translation of *CPR*, however, I believe that the reconstructions can be easily fitted to any of the standard translations. The only quote not taken from *CPR* is the one for the Argument from Incongruent Counterparts (chapter two) which was taken from the Ellington translation of the *Prolegomena to Any Future Metaphysics*. While the citations to *CPR* will refer to the standard A (1781) and B (1787) editions, all other citations to Kant's writings use the pagination in the *Akadamie* edition of Kant's collected works (29 volumes). In the bibliography, you can find other companions to Kant's *CPR* that I found useful while working on this book. My aim has been to include what is most helpful from these other books while at the same time aiding the reader in a way that these other books do not. Although there is nothing new about reconstructing Kant's arguments, I believe this book covers many more arguments than any individual companion to *CPR* has in the past. In addition, the book consistently aims to focus the reader's attention on the passages from *CPR* that support these reconstructions while at the same time explaining how the different arguments go to support Kant's overall theory of transcendental idealism. Consequently, I hope that both teachers and students of Kant will find this book a valuable addition to their libraries and classrooms.

Besides my students, former teachers as well as colleagues both past and present have helped me through various stages of the writing process. This includes my former thesis advisor Robert Hanna whose worksheets were an inspiration for my own. Thanks to Joe Pitt for suggesting I write the book and to Walter Ott and George Harvey for commenting on parts of it. Thanks also to the anonymous referee at Lexington Books whose comments were invaluable as I worked to revise the manuscript. I would also like to thank Indiana University Southeast for their support and in particular for the Faculty/Student Working Group Summer Fellowship in 2008 which made it possible for the students and me to begin work on the project. Finally, thanks to Cambridge University Press. The quotes from *CPR* were reprinted with the permission of Cambridge University Press.

Introduction

When you get a paper back from your instructor, what do you expect to see? In addition to the grade (hopefully a high one), you probably expect to see some comments justifying the grade you received. Imagine that you receive a "B" on your paper. You should expect these comments to say what you have done right and what you have done wrong. If the comments are wholly negative, you have no idea what you did right to warrant a "B," and there must be something since you did not get an "F" or even a "C" for that matter. If the comments are wholly positive, you have no idea what you can do to improve, and there must be something since you did not get an "A." In other words, a good *critique* of your paper should make clear where the paper succeeded and where the paper failed.[1]

Kant's *CPR* is similar to the above case where Kant is the instructor and pure reason is the paper he is grading. Kant is uncomfortable with the way both rationalists (philosophers like René Descartes and Gottfried Leibniz) as well as empiricists (philosophers like John Locke and David Hume) evaluated reason in the past.[2] Whereas rationalists were wholly uncritical of reason and believed that reason alone could make informative claims even beyond the bounds of sense (comments are wholly positive), empiricists believed that reason alone could not make any informative claims whatsoever (comments are wholly negative). In the Preface and Introduction to *CPR*, Kant argues that although reason is doomed to failure when used beyond the bounds of sense (negative comments), it not only succeeds but has an important and indispensible role within those bounds (positive comments).[3]

Even though rationalists and empiricists might seem to be diametrically opposed to one another, Kant points out an important similarity between them in the Preface to *CPR*. Both rationalists and empiricists agree that cognition (Kant's term for how we know objects) must conform to the object cognized.[4] In other words, it is the object that fully determines both how we come to know the object and what we come to know about it. For a rationalist like Descartes, God safeguards this relationship. In the sixth of Descartes' *Meditations on First Philosophy*, he argues that since God is not a deceiver, the latter insures not only that external objects are the cause of our sensible ideas of these objects, but also that what we clearly and distinctly perceive in these ideas must be true of the objects represented by them. What we clearly and distinctly perceive in these ideas, however, is not delivered by sensation but rather by reason itself. Sensation is only the impetus for rational reflection.[5] Leibniz does Descartes one better arguing that sensation itself is only a more confused form of intellection, and that all cognition is ultimately delivered by reason (though it is always less perfect than God's cognition).[6] In either case, however, reason grasps the nature of something which exists independently of reason itself.

Although empiricists minimize the epistemic role of reason in favor of sensation, they are still committed to the underlying assumption that our cognition must conform to the object known. An empiricist like Locke, e.g., believes our ideas of the primary qualities of objects (size, shape, motion, and rest) resemble their causes which are the primary qualities of the object itself. By *resembling* their causes, our ideas of primary qualities *conform* to the primary qualities they represent.[7] Although George Berkeley rejects Locke's resemblance thesis (how could an idea resemble anything but another idea?), he holds that our sensible ideas represent the world insofar as they are produced by God.[8] In a strange twist on Descartes' argument for the external world in Meditation Six, Berkeley argues that God is the guarantor of our cognition of the world, not by insuring that external objects cause our sensible ideas, but rather by producing the sensible ideas himself where these ideas are themselves the world that is cognized.[9] In other words, our sensible ideas adequately represent the world insofar as they conform to God's own ideas. Although Descartes would consider this tantamount to divine deception, Berkeley simply cannot understand how anything other than a mind could ever cause sensible ideas in a mind (a problem of which Descartes himself is acutely aware).[10] Hume agrees that cognition must conform to its object, but this leads him to a deep skepticism about what we can cognize. Like Locke and Berkeley, Hume is an empiricist and he believes that all of our cognition must ultimately be grounded in sensible experience. Whereas Berkeley's empiricism leads him to deny that we have any proper idea of external objects existing in themselves unperceived (contra Locke), Hume's empiricism leads him to deny that we have any proper idea of the soul or of God as the cause of our ideas (contra Berkeley).[11] Since we cannot determine whether our ideas conform to external objects or whether they conform to God's ideas, the most we can ever cognize is whether our ideas conform to one another. The world beyond our ideas is entirely shut off from us.

For Kant, this thoroughgoing skepticism is the logical result of both rationalism's and empiricism's shared commitment to the epistemological view that cognition must conform to its object. In the Preface to *CPR*, Kant suggests that instead of thinking that our cognition must conform to its object, perhaps the object must conform to our cognition of it.[12] This is a radical suggestion, one that Kant compares to Nicolaus Copernicus' own suggestion that instead of thinking that the earth is stationary and the sun revolves around the earth, perhaps the earth revolves around the sun and the sun is stationary. Just as Copernicus saw that this would solve many problems that faced sixteenth century astronomy (e.g., how to deal with the retrograde motion of the other planets), Kant saw that this could solve the problems that faced eighteenth century philosophy (e.g., how to deal with Hume's thoroughgoing skepticism). Just as our own motion has an impact on the motions we observe for Copernicus, so too do our own minds have an impact on the world that we experience for Kant. For Kant, we are not simply passive observers of the world that we experience, but have a necessary and indispensible role to play in helping to construct that world.

More specifically, Kant will argue that space and time as well as certain conceptual conditions (what Kant calls the "categories") are contributed *a priori* by the subject to her experience of objects. Things are objects of experience just in case they conform to these sensible and conceptual conditions of experience which are themselves grounded in the subject's epistemic faculties (what Kant calls our "cognitive" nature). A result of this view is that things are objects for us only insofar as they appear to us in space and time and in accordance with our concepts. We have no cognition of objects (or even ourselves) as they might be in themselves independent of the cognitive conditions of the subject. This is the core idea of Kant's theory of transcendental idealism, viz., we cannot cognize objects as they might exist in themselves but only insofar as they appear to us spatiotemporally and in accordance with our concepts of them, where not only these concepts but space and time themselves are contributions of the subject to her experience of these objects. The below diagram illustrates the basic relationship between subjects and objects according to transcendental idealism. Although we can cognize an object insofar as it appears to the subject, what lies beyond appearances may only be thought.

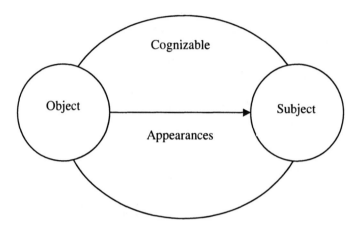

Figure 1: Relationship between Subject and Object

This dramatic shift in philosophical perspective ushers in what is called the "Critical" era of Kant's philosophy (i.e., the result of a proper *critique* of reason) and stands in sharp contrast to the pre-Critical philosophy where Kant was very much under the influence of Leibnizian rationalism (via Christian Wolff who popularized Leibniz' philosophy in Germany).[13] According to Kant, it was reading Hume that awoke him from this "dogmatic slumber."[14] Although Kant accepts Hume's devastating criticisms of prior rationalist and empiricist philosophers, he takes the resulting skepticism as tantamount to the "euthanasia of pure reason," a result Kant found unacceptable.[15]

Kant's Critical philosophy has certain distinct advantages over both rationalism as well as empiricism. Primarily, we will not misrepresent the world if we limit ourselves to the world as it appears which is partially constituted by our own minds. We avoid skepticism if we do not aim to experience something we cannot experience.[16] Although Kant rejects the rationalist's claim to cognition beyond the bounds of sense as well as the empiricist's claim that all of our concepts are grounded in sensation, he agrees with the rationalist that there are certain concepts not derived from sensation (the categories) and with the empiricist that cognition is possible only within the bounds of sense.[17]

Kant spends much time in the Introduction to *CPR* explaining the epistemic distinction between *a priori* and *a posteriori* cognition as well as the judgmental or semantic distinction between how analytic and synthetic propositions are formed.[18] Although variations of these distinctions can be found in Locke, Leibniz, and Hume, Kant is the first philosopher to spell out the relationships between the epistemic and judgmental distinctions in detail.[19] To put it simply, whereas *a priori* cognition is cognition that is logically independent of experience, *a posteriori* cognition is not.[20] All and only *a priori* cognitions will be necessary since the cognition is logically independent of experience and so will be true or false irrespective of the way the world in fact turns out. Notice the difference between the way in which you know that "Bachelors are unmarried, adult, males" and that "Steve (your swinging friend) is a bachelor." Once one has obtained the appropriate concepts, no appeal to experience is required in order to cognize the first proposition whereas the second proposition is highly contingent and appeal to experience is required to cognize it (maybe Steve finally met the right person).

Judgment can either relate concepts to other concepts, concepts to objects, or judgments to other judgments producing truth-evaluable propositions. Using the first case for illustration, whereas judgment can relate the concepts of an analytic proposition without appeal to anything beyond the concepts themselves, this is not the case in a synthetic proposition where judgment must appeal to something beyond concepts themselves in order to relate them in a proposition.[21] What this "something" might be will be explained at greater length below. Notice, however, that the above propositions also fit well with the analytic/synthetic distinction. One need only possess the requisite concepts to judge that "Bachelors are unmarried, adult, males" though one need appeal to something beyond the concepts to judge that "Steve is a bachelor." There is nothing in the concept of "Steve" that entails he must be a bachelor and it might turn out (if he finally settled down) that he is not.

Hume recognized only two possible relationships between the epistemic and the judgmental, viz., analytic *a priori* propositions (what Hume calls "relations of ideas") and synthetic *a posteriori* propositions (what Hume calls "matters of fact").[22] If a proposition is based on a relation of ideas, then relating the concepts in a proposition does not rely on experience. Of course, one might need to appeal to experience in order to acquire the concepts in question, but once they are acquired the judgment itself is logically independent of experience.[23] Propositions involving relations of ideas are *necessary*. In contrast to relations of ideas, one must make appeal to something beyond mere concepts when reasoning about matters of fact. Propositions dealing with matters of fact require experience *a posteriori* (and for Hume the repeated experience of resembling instances). Even so, these propositions are consistently deniable and so *contingent* (the course of experience might very well change and there is no guarantee that the future will resemble the past).

For example, take the proposition that "Either you will receive an 'A' on your paper or you will not receive an 'A' on your paper." This exclusive disjunction is based on a relation of ideas. All you need to know are the relevant concepts involved in the proposition (what it means to "receive an A," what a "paper" is, etc.) in order to relate the concepts in a proposition. Regardless of the grade you get on your paper, e.g., an "A" or an "F," the proposition is still true. Consequently, this proposition is analytic *a priori* based simply on a relation of ideas. It is also not very informative. Although it is true that either you will get an "A" on your paper or you will not, the proposition really does not tell you anything at all about the grade you will get. In contrast, the proposition that "You will receive an 'A' on your paper" is synthetic *a posteriori*. It is important to note that unlike the previous proposition, this proposition is highly informative (and most welcome when uttered by your instructor).[24] Even so, there is nothing in the concept of "receiving an A" that insures that your paper will receive one, nor is there anything in the concept of "your paper" that insures that your paper will receive an "A."[25] For Hume, an appeal to experience is necessary and regardless of how many "A's" your papers might have received in the past, there is no guarantee that your next paper will receive an "A" as well. Although you might be habituated to believe that by writing the paper you will receive an "A" on it, there is nothing that necessitates it. According to Hume, *experience* is the "something" necessary to relate the concepts in a synthetic *a posteriori* proposition.

If you have read Hume, you know that he is making a point about causation generally which he believes is the only way we can reason about matters of fact.[26] For Hume, causal claims are not necessary (in the way the claims concerning relations of ideas are), but are rather just the product of custom or habit. At most, they possess a certain kind of psychological necessity, though there is no reason to think that the world beyond our minds actually exhibits these kinds of causal relations.[27] Kant saw Hume's skepticism with regard to causation as posing a threat not only to traditional metaphysics which makes causal claims beyond the bounds of sense (e.g., Descartes' claim that God conserves the world in Meditation Three), but also natural science itself which makes causal claims within the bounds of sense (e.g., causal claims grounded on Isaac Newton's laws of motion). Kant took Hume's skepticism as an existential threat to natural science and argued that there was a third relationship between the epistemic and the judgmental that could safeguard the necessity of causal claims in natural science, viz., synthetic *a priori* judgments.[28]

Assuming that objects must conform to the way we cognize them, it seems as if we can learn certain things about these objects simply by examining our own faculty of cognition. What we learn will be logically independent of the experience of these objects (*a priori*) but at the same time will tell us something informative about the nature of these objects (a feature of "synthetic" propositions). Establishing the possibility of synthetic *a priori* cognition is one of the central functions of *CPR*. This kind of cognition is not available to either rationalists or empiricists since they labor under the shared assumption that cognition must conform to its object. Under this assumption, it is impossible to cognize *a priori* anything informative about the nature of the object in question.[29] Although rationalists are committed to synthetic *a priori* propositions that inform us about the existence and nature of things beyond the bounds of sense, Kant will argue these claims are illegitimate since they transcend the bounds of sense.[30]

As synthetic, judgment must rely on something beyond concepts alone in order to formulate the propositions. Consequently, these propositions will be informative in a way that mere analytic propositions are not (remember how uninformative the exclusive disjunction above is). As *a priori*, the judgments that generate these propositions will not require appeal to experience *a posteriori* and will carry a kind of necessity (though different from the logical necessity of analytic propositions).[31] An empiricist like Hume rejects synthetic *a priori* propositions since he views them as using relations of ideas to make claims about matters of fact. Although Kant would reject the idea that synthetic *a priori* propositions can inform us about a world beyond the bounds of sense, he thinks they can inform us about objects within the bounds of sense. He would criticize the empiricist for thinking that just because a proposition is *a priori* it must be based on relations of ideas (or be "analytic" in Kant's language). At the same time, he would likely agree with the empiricist that a mere relation of ideas cannot inform us about matters of fact (whether within or beyond the bounds of sense). Since concepts alone are insufficient to formulate synthetic proposition, judgment must appeal to *something* beyond concepts. Although Hume thought the only possible candidate for this something was experience *a posteriori*, this option will not work for Kant since the proposition is supposed to be synthetic *a priori*. One of Kant's goals in *CPR* is to discover what this something, or as he calls it "unknown = X," might be and how it will allow him to safeguard the necessity of synthetic *a priori* propositions, including those that are the result of causal judgments.[32] Kant's solution will be a central theme of the next part of this book. Before we get there, however, it is important to deal with one famous criticism of Kant's analytic/synthetic distinction.

If you have already started reading *CPR*, you might have noticed that the way in which we draw the analytic/synthetic distinction is somewhat different from the way in which Kant himself draws it. Kant says that a proposition is analytic if (1) its predicate-concept is "contained in" its subject-concept or (2) its denial entails a conceptual or logical contradiction.[33] W.V. Quine, in his seminal paper, "Two Dogmas of Empiricism," raises some worries for Kant's stated criteria: (1) the idea of conceptual containment is too "metaphorical," (2) even assuming Kant's idea of conceptual containment, his distinction is limited to judgments of subject/predicate form, and (3) the notion of self-contradictoriness is in just as much need of definition as the notion of analyticity itself.[34]

After dismissing Kant's view on the analytic/synthetic distinction, Quine goes on to criticize more contemporary formulations of the distinction. Notwithstanding these other criticisms, it is important to note that his general skepticism concerning the analytic/synthetic distinction poses problems not only for Kant but for all other modern philosophers who subscribe to some version of the distinction (e.g., Locke, Leibniz, and Hume). Although there is much more to be said in favor of Kant's position than what Quine affords it and it is unclear whether Quine's criticisms actually apply to Kant's position, our goal is to challenge neither Quine's reading of Kant nor his objections to other interpretations of analyticity.[35] This has already been done at length elsewhere.[36] As we hope to show in the first part of this book, however, once one identifies the unknown = X that is required to make synthetic *a priori* judgments, this will open a way of drawing the analytic/synthetic distinction that avoids Quine's criticisms. Put briefly, *intuition*, or the way in which objects are *given* to us in sensibility, is what judgment appeals to when generating synthetic propositions. Whereas a proposition is analytic when the judgment generating it relates, at most, accidentally to intuition, a proposition is synthetic when the judgment generating it relates essentially to intuition. In other words, a proposition can still be analytic even if the constitutive concepts and/or judgments are empirical as long as the judgment itself does not require appeal to intuition in order to combine the constitutive concepts and/or judgments. A synthetic proposition, in contrast, will always require appeal to intuition in order to combine the constitutive concepts and/or judgments. Although Kant makes this general point in the Introduction to *CPR*, it is not until the Transcendental Aesthetic that he distinguishes the formation of synthetic *a priori* propositions from the formation of synthetic *a posteriori* propositions. In the case of synthetic *a priori* propositions, judgment must make appeal to the *pure* (rather than empirical) intuitions of space and time *a priori* which will likewise safeguard the necessity of these propositions. Pure intuition *a priori* is the "unknown = X" Kant mentions in the Introduction to *CPR*. In contrast, judgment must appeal to empirical intuition *a posteriori* when formulating synthetic *a posteriori* propositions.

This book is broken into three parts, corresponding to the three main sections of the Transcendental Doctrine of Elements from *CPR*. The Transcendental Doctrine of Elements is broken into two parts: the Transcendental Aesthetic and the Transcendental Logic. The Transcendental Logic is itself divided into two sections: the Transcendental Analytic and the Transcendental Dialectic. Since most courses on *CPR* deal almost exclusively with the Transcendental Doctrine of Elements, our discussion will largely be limited to it.[37]

The first part of this book reconstructs Kant's arguments from the Transcendental Aesthetic where he argues that space and time are *a priori* forms of intuition. Sensibility is the faculty of intuition and Kant distinguishes between two kinds of intuition: pure intuition and empirical intuition. Whereas the former is the representation of space and time *a priori*, the latter is the representation of objects *a posteriori* in space and time through our five senses. Although the *matter* of appearance is given *a posteriori* in empirical intuition, its spatiotemporal *form* is *a priori*. The Transcendental Aesthetic is contrary to rationalism insofar as it demonstrates that there are things we can cognize about objects *a priori* (viz., their spatiotemporal character) independently of the way we think about objects through concepts.[38]

The second part of this book reconstructs Kant's arguments from the Transcendental Analytic where he attempts to deduce *a priori* the categories of pure understanding or the way in which objects are *thought* by the understanding *a priori* through concepts. He goes on to show *that* the categories are necessary conditions for the possibility of objects of experience, explain *how* the categories apply to objects of experience, as well as justify certain synthetic *a priori* propositions concerning the objects of possible experience. One of the most important synthetic *a priori* propositions that Kant will aim to justify is the causal principle of the Second Analogy (see chapter eleven). If his argument for the truth of this proposition is sound, he will have provided a response to Hume's skepticism and so safeguarded the necessity of causal claims in natural science. The Transcendental Analytic is contrary to empiricism insofar as it demonstrates that the way we think about objects through concepts *a priori* (*viz.* the categories) can offer cognition of the world.[39] Furthermore, all of the empirical concepts that we possess through experience must be in accordance with these *a priori* concepts.

The final part of this book deals with the Transcendental Dialectic where Kant examines a number of arguments that exemplify the kind of "transcendental illusion" reason is subject to once it uses the pure concepts of the understanding (categories) beyond the bounds of sense.[40] When used beyond the bounds of sense, the categories are transformed into mere "transcendental ideas." Kant believes that although reason naturally falls into transcendental illusion, it is important to recognize it so we can guard ourselves from being deceived by it. Below is a diagram that sketches Kant's theory of cognition in light of the three parts of Kant's project.

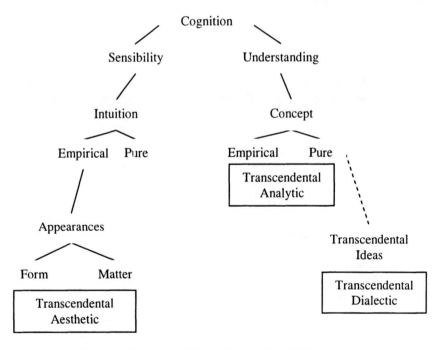

Figure 2: Structure of Cognition and the *Critique*

Returning to the opening metaphor, whereas the Transcendental Aesthetic and Transcendental Analytic delimit the realm within which reason can have a necessary and indispensible role (positive comments), the Transcendental Dialectic explains the errors and falsehoods that reason is subject to once it goes beyond this realm (negative comments). Here, it is important to distinguish between two conceptions of "reason." Reason in the broad sense supplies the principles of cognition *a priori*, both of sensibility and understanding. The task of the Transcendental Aesthetic (sensibility) and Transcendental Analytic (understanding) is to enumerate these principles and to show how they are conditions for cognition within the bounds of sense.[41] In the narrow sense, however, reason is considered as a separate faculty that misapplies many of these same principles by feigning cognition beyond the bounds of sense.[42] The Transcendental Dialectic explains the kind of illusion to which reason is subject once it transcends these bounds. Consequently, the three parts constitute Kant's complete *critique* of pure reason. Each part of this book will begin with a general introduction and end with an overall summary that explains how the arguments discussed fit together to support the main conclusions of that part as well as Kant's general theory of transcendental idealism.

Notes

1. For a similar point using the example of a movie critic, see Douglas Burnham and Harvey Young, *Kant's Critique of Pure Reason* (Bloomington, IN: Indiana University Press, 2001), 9.

2. Although we are focusing on how Kant relates to familiar figures in the history of Modern philosophy, it is important to note that several lesser-known German philosophers were equally influential on Kant and were certainly his primary audience. For more on these figures as well as for selections of their writings, see Eric Watkins, *Kant's Critique of Pure Reason: Background Source Materials* (Cambridge: Cambridge University Press, 2009).

3. Immanuel Kant. *Critique of Pure Reason*, trans. Paul Guyer and Allen Wood (Cambridge: Cambridge University Press, 1999), originally published 1781 (revised 1787), Bxxiv. Abbreviated *CPR*. Citations to *CPR* use the standard A/B notation. Citations to Kant's other works refer to the *Akadamie* edition.

4. *CPR* Bxvi.

5. As Descartes makes clear in the Meditation Two wax example, what we clearly and distinctly perceive in the wax (or any other purportedly external object) is not delivered by sensation or imagination but rather by reason. René Descartes, *Meditations on First Philosophy*, 2: 1-62 in *The Philosophical Writings of Descartes*, 3 vols., trans. John Cottingham, Robert Stoothoff, and Dugald Murdoch (Cambridge: Cambridge University Press, 1988), originally published 1641, 2: 16-23.

6. Gottfried Leibniz, *New Essays on Human Understanding*, trans. Peter Remnant and Jonathan Bennett (Cambridge: Cambridge University Press, 1981), originally published 1765, 81.

7. John Locke, *An Essay Concerning Human Understanding*, ed. P.H. Nidditch. (Oxford: Oxford University Press, 1975), originally published 1690, II.8.15.

8. George Berkeley, *Of the Principles of Human Knowledge*, 2: 41-113 in *The Works of George Berkeley, Bishop of Cloyne*, 9 vols., ed. A.A. Luce and T.E. Jessop (London: Thomas Nelson and Sons, 1948-1954), originally published 1710, I §8.

9. See Berkeley, *Principles*, I §29-33.

10. See Berkeley, *Principles*, I §19 and 50. Descartes recognizes that this is a problem for substance dualism and in an attempt to overcome it he makes an infamous appeal, in Meditation Six, to the 'common sense' or pineal gland which is supposed to serve as the nexus for mind/body interaction. This solution is less illuminating than it is perplexing, of course, since the pineal gland is still a material thing. See Descartes, *Meditations*, 2: 59.

11. For Berkeley, external objects are just collections of sensible qualities which are themselves sensible ideas. Consequently, that some external object might exist in itself unperceived (i.e., an unperceived collection of sensible ideas) simply makes no sense to Berkeley. See Berkeley, *Principles*, I §3. Although Berkeley admits we do not have sensible ideas of the soul or God, he believed we have 'notions' of these substances. See Berkeley, *Principles*, I §27. For Hume's skepticism concerning our idea of the soul as a simple substance, see David Hume, *A Treatise of Human Nature*, ed. L. A. Selby-Bigge, 2nd ed. revised by P.H. Nidditch (Oxford: Oxford University Press, 1975), originally published 1739, 1.4.6. For his skepticism concerning our idea of God as a true cause, see David Hume, *An Enquiry Concerning Human Understanding*, 5-149 in *Enquiries concerning Human Understanding and concerning the Principles of Morals*, ed. L. A. Selby-Bigge, 3rd ed. revised by P. H. Nidditch (Oxford: Oxford University Press, 1975), originally published 1748, 7.57.

12. *CPR* Bxvi and Bxxii.

13. It is important to note, however, that Kant already held similar views on space and time in his *Innaugural Dissertation* (1770) written more than ten years prior to the A edition of *CPR* (1781).

14. Immanuel Kant, *Prolegomena to Any Future Metaphysics*, trans. James Ellington (Indianapolis, IN: Hackett Publishing, 2001), originally published 1783, 4: 260.

15. *CPR* A407/B434.

16. For more on this point, see Anthony Savile, *Kant's Critique of Pure Reason: An Orientation to the Central Theme* (Oxford, Blackwell Publishing, 2005), 11

17. For a nice diagram illustrating these different points, see Georges Dicker, *Kant's Theory of Knowledge: An Analytical Introduction* (New York: Oxford University Press, 2004), 5. For a more detailed discussion of Kant's continuity as well as his break with rationalism, see Desmond Hogan, "Kant's Copernican Turn," in *The Cambridge Companion to Kant's Critique of Pure Reason*, ed. Paul Guyer (Cambridge: Cambridge University Press, 2010), 21-40. For the same with regard to empiricism, see Kenneth Winkler, "Kant, the Empiricists, and the Enterprise of Deduction," in *The Cambridge Companion to Kant's Critique of Pure Reason*, 41-72.

18. *CPR* B1-6, A3-10/B6-14, and B14-24. For a more detailed discussion of the *a priori/a posteriori* and analytic/synthetic distinctions, see R. Lanier Anderson, "The Introduction to the Critique: Framing the Question," in *The Cambridge Companion to Kant's Critique of Pure Reason*, 75-92.

19. There is Locke's distinction between 'trifling' and 'instructive' propositions, Leibniz' distinction between 'truths of reason' and 'truths of fact,' as well as Hume's

distinction between 'relations of ideas' and 'matters of fact.' We will return to Hume's distinction again below.

20. It is important to note that Kant does not preclude experience from playing some role in *a priori* cognition and draws a distinction between pure and impure *a priori* cognition. Whereas the former contains *no* empirical content whatsoever, the latter might involve empirical concepts though the connection between the concepts will still be made *a priori*. Many of the most important synthetic *a priori* propositions Kant's defends (e.g., his causal principle) will be examples of impure *a priori* cognition. See *CPR* B2-3.

21. *CPR* A6-A10/B10-14.

22. See Hume, *Enquiry*, 4.20-21.

23. Dicker makes this point. See Dicker, *Kant's Theory of Knowledge*, 7-8.

24. See also Kant's distinction between analytic propositions which merely *clarify* the subject concept and synthetic propositions that *amplify* the subject concept. *CPR* A7/B11.

25. See also Dicker's example of the proposition 'P' which describes the entire nature of the world. The proposition that 'P or not P' is clearly true regardless of the way the world turns out and is analytic *a priori*. The proposition 'P,' however, might well be false if the world turns out to be 'not-P' and so is synthetic *a posteriori*. Dicker, *Kant's Theory of Knowledge*, 13.

26. Hume, *Enquiry*, 4.20-21.

27. Hume, *Enquiry*, 7.59.

28. *CPR* B19-24. Both Kant and Hume would agree that there are no analytic *a posteriori* propositions. As analytic, one can judge that the concepts are connected without appeal to anything beyond the concepts themselves. See *CPR* A7/B11. Beyond the experience that might be necessary to acquire the concepts in question, no appeal to experience is necessary when making the judgment itself. For more on why there are no analytic *a posteriori* propositions see Jill Vance Buroker, *Kant's Critique of Pure Reason: An Introduction* (Cambridge: Cambridge University Press, 2005), 31 and Matthew Altman, *A Companion to Kant's Critique of Pure Reason* (Boulder, CO: Westview Press, 2007), 43. In contrast to the received view, Burnham and Young argue that there are analytic *a posteriori* propositions can exist in some limited cognitive settings, e.g., in taxonomy, though they cannot exist in *every* cognitive setting. See Burnham and Young, *Kant's Critique*, 29-30.

29. *CPR* Bxvii.

30. In Kant's pre-Critical phase, he was also committed to synthetic *a priori* propositions that inform us about the existence and nature of things beyond the bounds of sense. See Dicker, *Kant's Theory of Knowledge*, 23.

31. Buroker notes that since causal claims are not logically necessary (something recognized by Hume), there must be a form of non-logical necessity if causal claims are to be necessary at all. Synthetic *a priori* propositions seem to carry the exact kind of necessity that causal claims require. They are consistently deniable (unlike analytic propositions) while at the same time being necessary relative to our forms of experience. This point will be discussed at greater length in the next section. Buroker, *Kant's Critique*, 31-32.

32. See *CPR* A9-10/B13-14.

33. See *CPR*, A6-10/B10-14, A151/B190. Concept X is contained in concept Y just in case Y is part of the semantic content (or intension) of X. In other words, when analyz-

ing concept X, you discover concept Y. For example, in the concept 'bachelor' one discovers (at least) the concepts of 'unmarried,' 'adult,' and 'male.'

34. W.V. Quine, "Two Dogmas of Empiricism," *Philosophical Review* 60, no. 1 (January, 1951): 20-43, especially 21. Criticisms of the conceptual containment criterion, however, can be traced back to Kant's own day. See J.G. Maaß, "Über den höchsten Grundsatz der synthetischen Urtheile; in Beziehung auf die Theorie von der mathematischen Gewissheit," *Philosophische Magazin* 2, no. 2, (1789-1790): 186-231.

35. To take just one example, however, when it comes to Quine's second criticism, although the containment criterion is limited to sentences of categorical form, it is only a *sufficient* condition for analyticity. Sentences can have other forms, however, and still be analytic via Kant's other criterion. For a more detailed discussion of how I believe Kant can respond to Quine see Bryan Hall, "Kant and Quine on the Two Dogmas of Empiricism," *Proceedings of the 11th International Kant Congress* (forthcoming).

36. For example, see H.P. Grice and P.F. Strawson, "In Defense of a Dogma," *Philosophical Review* 65, no. 2 (April, 1956): 141-158, Jerrold Katz, *Cogitations A Study of the Cogito in Relation to the Philosophy of Logic and Language and a Study of Them in Relation to the Cogito* (Cambridge: Cambridge University Press, 1988), chapter six, and Robert Hanna, *Kant and the Foundations of Analytic Philosophy* (Oxford: Oxford University Press, 2001), chapter three.

37. Kant himself previews the structure of his book at the end of the Introduction. See *CPR* A15-16/B29-30. Although Kant mentions both the Transcendental Doctrine of Elements as well as the Transcendental Doctrine of Method that follows it, the Transcendental Doctrine of Method is usually not covered in a course on Kant. Even so, it contains many interesting reflections on the differences between philosophy and other areas of human inquiry, e.g., mathematics and natural science, as well as the differences between Kant's Critical philosophy and other philosophical approaches. One of its chapters, 'The Canon of Pure Reason,' outlines Kant's Critical moral theory which he later expands upon in works like the *Groundwork of the Metaphysics of Morals* (1785), the *Critique of Practical Reason* (1788), and the *Metaphysics of Morals* (1797). For a good summary of the Transcendental Doctrine of Method see Burnham and Young, *Kant's Critique*, 169-179. We will have occasion to return to the Canon of Pure Reason in the final chapter of this book.

38. See Altman, *A Companion to Kant's Critique*, 53.

39. See Altman, *A Companion to Kant's Critique*, 54.

40. *CPR* A295/B352.

41. Kant makes clear, however, that *CPR* is not a complete enumeration (or 'organon') of such principles though he does aim to enumerate the 'principles of *a priori* synthesis.' See *CPR* A11-12/B24-25. In the Introduction to *CPR*, Kant describes the positive role of his critique differently as maintaining a separate domain for practical (moral) reason. We will discuss the latter at greater length at the end of Part Three. See *CPR* Bxxiv-xxv.

42. Norman Kemp Smith distinguishes between three senses of 'reason' in *CPR*. In addition to the two senses mentioned above, he also identifies an intermediary view of reason where it is identified with the understanding. See Norman Kemp Smith, *A Commentary to Kant's Critique of Pure Reason* (New York: Humanities Press, 1962), originally published 1918, 2.

Part One

The Transcendental Aesthetic

Chapter One
Introduction to the Transcendental Aesthetic

Once one understands the meaning of "transcendental" and "aesthetic," Kant's project in the Transcendental Aesthetic becomes pretty clear. A "transcendental" examination is one that aims to discover the conditions for the possibility of cognizing objects *a priori*.[1] By "aesthetic," Kant is not referring to artistic beauty, but rather to the Greek word "aesthesis" which means "sensation" or "perception."[2] Put simply, Kant's project in the Transcendental Aesthetic is to discover the *a priori* conditions for the possibility of sensibility, or that faculty through which objects are *given* to us. Kant first isolates sensibility from the understanding, or the way in which objects are *thought* (we will discuss the latter in Part Two). Secondly, he separates out what is given by sensation *a posteriori*. This leaves him with only sensibility to consider *a priori*.[3] By limiting his scope to an *a priori* examination of sensibility itself, Kant hopes to discover the *a priori* principles of sensibility, i.e., the *a priori* conditions for the possibility of objects being given to us.

Sensibility is a completely passive faculty in that it is merely the capacity to be affected by objects. Sensibility relates to objects through intuition and the appearances that result from affection are the "undetermined" objects of empirical intuition.[4] In other words, intuition is the means by which objects are given to us in sensibility; objects appear to subjects via intuition. Intuitions come prior to thought and for creatures like us are always sensible. Even so, what appears in intuition is undetermined unless it is subsumed under our concepts of an object, i.e., how we think about objects. As mentioned above, Kant will argue that appearances have a *matter* that is given *a posteriori* but a *form* that is given *a priori* by the subject.[5] Whereas sensation is the matter of appearance, he argues that

17

space and time are the *a priori* forms of appearance. In other words, space and time are the ways in which objects appear to subjects in empirical intuition. Although Kant will argue that these forms are not conceptual (since they are prior to thought), without them nothing could appear to us at all.[6] Space and time are the two main *a priori* principles of sensibility that Kant hopes to establish in the Transcendental Aesthetic.

Kant talks about space before he talks about time, but in both cases he first offers a "Metaphysical Exposition" of space and time. The exposition is "metaphysical" since it aims to reveal the *nature* of space and time. Kant deploys two sets of arguments, one set concerning space and a parallel set concerning time, in order to establish that space and time are (1) *a priori* rather than *a posteriori* representations and (2) intuitions rather than concepts.[7] When it comes to the contrast between intuitions and concepts, the idea is that whereas intuitions are singular and immediate, concepts are general and mediate. For example, the concept of a textbook contains the *general* features of textbooks (has pages, deals with some academic subject, is soporific, etc.), but these do not fully determine any *singular* or particular textbook.[8] The concept "textbook" does not tell you what the subject of any particular textbook will be and any number of different textbooks could instantiate the concept. Concepts are *mediate* representations since we can think of things not present (e.g., one's dream car) or even non-existent (e.g., a unicorn) though the object of thought of is not given *immediately* through this representation (wishing, unfortunately, does not make it so).[9] The first and second Metaphysical Expositions of space and time go to establish the *a priority* of our representations of space and time, whereas the third and fourth Metaphysical Expositions of space and time go to establish that space and time are intuitions rather than concepts.

In addition to Metaphysical Expositions of space and time, Kant offers Transcendental Expositions of space and time. These expositions are "transcendental" since they are concerned with uncovering the conditions for the possibility of cognizing objects *a priori*, i.e., uncovering the conditions for synthetic *a priori* propositions. These are regressive arguments which begin by assuming that there are synthetic *a priori* propositions and then inquire into the conditions of their possibility.[10] They argue that synthetic *a priori* propositions are possible only if space and time are *a priori* intuitions. For example, Kant argues that judgment can only form the synthetic *a priori* proposition that "The straight line between two points is the shortest" by appealing to the pure intuition of space *a priori* (the same goes for mathematical propositions and time). Pure intuition is the solution to the "unknown = X" that Kant mentions in the Introduction to *CPR*.[11] Pure intuition allows judgment to connect concepts with one another (e.g., "the straight line" and "the shortest line") without appeal to empirical intuition *a posteriori* since the latter would undermine the *a priori* status of synthetic *a priori* propositions. If synthetic *a priori* propositions exist and Kant's arguments in the Transcendental Expositions are sound, then he has given another set of arguments for space and time as *a priori* intuitions independent from his arguments in the Metaphysical Expositions of space and time. We will deal with Kant's arguments with regard to space in the next chapter and with regard to time in chapter three.

After the Metaphysical Expositions and Transcendental Expositions of space and time, Kant draws a number of conclusions from the preceding discussion. For example, a distinction must be drawn between space and time as *pure* intuitions *a priori* and as the *a priori* forms of *empirical* intuition where the content of empirical intuition (matter of appearance) is given *a posteriori*. Space and time as pure intuitions *a priori* are required for the formation of synthetic *a priori* propositions (like the one mentioned above). In reference to empirical intuition, however, space and time provide the form of appearance *a priori* where the matter of appearance is provided by affection *a posteriori*.[12] Space is the *a priori* form of outer sense within which external objects exist simultaneously, whereas time is the *a priori* form of inner sense within which representations exist successively. Since everything the subject perceives is incorporated into the stream of consciousness in inner sense, however, time is the form of *all* appearances whatsoever.[13] The spatiotemporal character of objects is not *derived* from our perceptions of these objects but is rather *presupposed* for the possibility of these perceptions. It is not a matter of how the object is constituted, but rather how the subject is constituted so as to perceive these objects spatiotemporally. As forms of intuition, space and time are the manners of disposition or orders of presentation of appearances. They are how appearances are displayed in empirical intuition *a posteriori*.[14] For example, if you have ever had the need to use a typewriter (thankfully a need that is increasingly rare), you might have noticed that no two keys can be struck *simultaneously*. Whereas the single keys provide the *matter* for what is typed on the page, *succession* is the *form* of the typing. In the same way, given the nature of time as the form of inner sense, no two moments can be simultaneous, but can only be successive (see the temporal axiom established in the Transcendental Exposition of time below).[15]

Kant also notes that his arguments, if sound, undermine two received views on space and time, one of which characterizes space and time as things-in-themselves (Newton), the other which characterizes space and time as relations between things-in-themselves (Leibniz). Newton thinks that space and time are *real* in themselves. They are absolute containers for external objects existing independently of the cognitive subject.[16] Leibniz thinks space and time are constructed from the *ideal* (perceptual) relations monads bear to one another. These monads (simple substances with perceptual powers), for Leibniz, are *real* in themselves though they do not exist in space and time and do not have any real (e.g., causal) relations to one another (monads "have no windows"). Leibniz suggests that space is constructed from the *simultaneity* of perceptions while time is constructed from the *succession* of perceptions.[17]

Since Kant believes that space and time are *a priori* intuitions, he both agrees and disagrees with Newton and Leibniz. Whereas he agrees with Newton that space and time are *absolute*, he disagrees that space and time are *real* in themselves. Whereas he agrees with Leibniz that space and time are *ideal*, he disagrees that space and time are constructed from *relations*. In addition to the arguments in the Transcendental Aesthetic, we will also discuss an argument outside of *CPR* that is directed specifically at Leibniz, viz., Kant's incongruent counterparts argument from the *Prolegomena to Any Future Metaphysics* (chapter two). If one accepts Kant's arguments, then space and time do not exist independently of the subject and her cognitive constitution as things-in-themselves or relations between them. To the contrary, space and time are essential cognitive contributions of the subject to her own experience. This conclusion is a central component in Kant's doctrine of transcendental idealism. If space and time are *a priori* forms of intuition, then subjects can come to know objects only insofar as they appear in space and time and not as they might be in themselves independently of the subject and her cognitive constitution.[18]

Notes

1. *CPR* A11/B25.
2. See Savile, *Kant's Critique*, 14.
3. *CPR* A22/B36.
4. *CPR* A20/B34.
5. When Kant uses the term "appearance" (*Erscheinung*), he does not mean "illusion" (*Schein*). For Kant, one distinguishes between reality and illusion within the world of appearances. See Savile, *Kant's Critique*, 22 and Jay Rosenberg, *Accessing Kant: A Relaxed Introduction to the Critique of Pure Reason* (Oxford: Oxford University Press, 2005), 78.
6. As Burnham and Young note, Kant's distinction between form and matter is ultimately Aristotelian, where form is the means by which matter comes to have order. See Burnham and Young, *Kant's Critique*, 41. As Gardner argues, Kant does not allow for sensation without form. This would be a mere "buzzing confusion" of which we could not be conscious. See Sebastian Gardner, *Routledge Philosophy Guidebook to Kant and the Critique of Pure Reason* (London: Routledge, 1999) 72.
7. As Savile and Rosenberg note, in this respect, Kant parts company with philosophers like Locke and Hume who believe that space and time are *a posteriori* concepts. See Savile, *Kant's Critique*, 16 and Rosenberg, *Accessing Kant*, 62. As Winkler notes, however, there is a continuity with Locke insofar as what Kant means by "representation" [*Vorstellung*] is the same as what Locke meant by "idea." See Winkler, "The Enterprise of Deduction," 46 and Locke, *Essay*, IV.21.4.
8. Burnham and Young approach the distinction in a similar way using the example of a teakettle. See Burnham and Young, *Kant's Critique*, 46-47.
9. See also Buroker, *Kant's Critique*, 38. For Kant, divine intuition and intellectual intuition stand in contrast to our own. Given his omnipotence, God's intuition is *productive* where wishing really does make it so. See *CPR* B145. Intellectual intuition is the kind of intuition that rationalists think we possess. It is cognition through reason alone. Although the rationalist cannot wish things into existence, reason alone is supposed to provide the immediate representation of an individual through concepts. See *CPR* B307. Admittedly, Kant sometimes conflates the two. See *CPR* B72.

10. The Transcendental Analytic uses a "synthetical method" which deploys "progressive arguments" that assume only premises that a skeptic would have to accept in order to infer certain synthetic *a priori* truths. This stands in contrast to the "analytical method" of the Transcendental Aesthetic and the *Prolegomena* which deploy "regressive arguments" that assume the truth of certain synthetic *a priori* propositions and then infer their necessary conditions. See Kant, *Prolegomena*, 4:277. As Dicker notes, however, Kant does not always keep the methods distinct. See Dicker, *Kant's Theory of Knowledge*, 24-25.

11. See *CPR* A9/B13 as well as the discussion in the introduction to this book.

12. *CPR* A27/B43.

13. *CPR* A34/B50-51.

14. See Lorne Falkenstein, "Was Kant a Nativist?," in *Kant's Critique of Pure Reason: Critical Essays*, ed. Patricia Kitcher (Lanham, MD: Rowman & Littlefield, 1998), 34. Falkenstein is skeptical, however, of the status of space and time as pure intuitions.

15. Falkenstein offers this example. See Falkenstein, "Was Kant a Nativist?," 40.

16. Isaac Newton, *Mathematical Principles of Natural Philosophy*, trans. Andrew Motte, revised by Florian Cajori (Berkeley: University of California Press, 1934), originally published 1687, Bk. 1, Scholium to the Definitions, 6-12.

17. Gottfried Leibniz, *G.W. Leibniz and Samuel Clarke: Correspondence*, trans. Roger Ariew (Indianapolis, IN: Hackett Publishing, 2000), especially the third paper §4 and the fifth paper. Since Kant would reject any view that holds space and time are constructed from the relations between things, he would reject Berkeley's view as well. See Berkeley, *Principles*, I §110-17. In addition to pointing out that both Berkeley and Leibniz believe space and time are constructed from the relations between things, Buroker notes that they agree with Kant that space and time are ideal and subjective. See Buroker, *Kant's Critique*, 45.

18. As Buroker notes, this is another similarity between Kant and Leibniz. Both would agree, contra Newton, that things-in-themselves (for Leibniz, monads) do not exist in space and time. See Buroker, *Kant's Critique*, 46.

Chapter Two
Space

First Metaphysical Exposition of Space

Quote

> Space is not an empirical concept that has been drawn from outer experiences. For in order for certain sensations to be related to something outside me (i.e., to something in another place in space from that in which I find myself), thus in order for me to represent them as outside and next to one another, thus not merely as different but as in different places, the representation of space must already be their ground. Thus the representation of space cannot be obtained from the relations of outer appearance through experience, but this outer experience is itself first possible only through this representation. [A23/B38]

Synopsis

Of the two positions on space that Kant hopes to refute (Newton and Leibniz), the first Metaphysical Exposition of space is primarily directed against Leibniz's view that the representation of space is constructed from ideal relations between monadic perceptions, but would likewise run contrary to any view that attempts to construct the representation of space from the relations between things. Reconstructing Kant's argument, however, is no easy task. He seems to be saying that we cannot represent things in space unless we possess the representation of space, but this is little more than a tautology.[1] In addition, since Kant's ultimate goal is to show that the representation of space is *a priori*, the argument would prove too much. Any empirical concept would turn out to be *a priori* using the same form of argumentation. For example, since any experience of something as a textbook requires the concept of a textbook, this concept (like the representation of space) would need to be *a priori*.

The solution to these problems lies in finding a way of distinguishing what needs to be explained from its explanation. What needs to be explained is our representation of things as *related* in space. Kant's explanation is that the representation of *space* is necessary for the representation of things as related in space. The constructivist about space reverses this order holding that the representation of things as *related* in space is necessary for the representation of *space* itself. How could we ever represent the spatial *relations* between things, however, without already possessing the representation of *space* within which these things are related?[2] The crux of Kant's argument comes in the third premise below where he observes that in order to represent objects as related in space the representation of space is assumed, i.e., it "must already be their ground" as he puts it in the above quote. Kant's point is no longer a tautology since "spatial relation" is not equivalent to "space." Likewise, the argument would not prove too much since one could not indifferently substitute a term like "textbook" for "spatial relation" as well as for "space."

If Kant is right, then Leibniz' theory cannot explain the origin of our representation of space unless it is supplemented by a contradictory theory (e.g., space as an original *a priori* representation).[3] As mentioned in the previous chapter, Leibniz thinks that the representation of space is constructed from the simultaneity of monadic perceptions. As Kant will argue in the next chapter, however, simultaneity is itself a temporal relation which will assume the representation of time *a priori*. To perceive two things at the same time, furthermore, seems to assume a spatial relationship between them such that they can be perceived simultaneously.[4] If the representation of space is assumed for the representation of spatial relations between monadic perceptions, however, then the representation of space clearly cannot be grounded on the representation of these relations. As a mundane example, in order to represent one textbook to the left of another (i.e., as spatially related), one must assume the representation of space within which the two textbooks could coexist and have this spatial relation. Without the representation of space, one could neither comprehend the relationship "to the left of" nor could one represent these objects as coexistent (time without space seems insufficient to represent *two* objects at *one* time). Since the representation of space is a necessary condition for the representation of spatial relations, Kant concludes that the representation of space cannot be an empirical concept derived from the *a posteriori* experience of these spatially related objects. Leibniz might respond by saying that the relations between monadic perceptions are not spatial but rather conceptual. If this were true, however, then it is unclear how the representation of space could be constructed from relationships that are not themselves spatial. In any case, Kant's argument from incongruent counterparts is squarely aimed at refuting this option.

Although the first Metaphysical Exposition of space gives one reason to believe that the representation of space is a necessary condition for the *a posteriori* representation of spatially related objects, he leaves open the possibility that the representation of spatially related objects is itself necessary for the representation of space (perhaps they are mutually conditioning representations).[5] This alternative, if not ruled out, could very well render the second premise of the first Metaphysical Exposition of space false and the argument as a whole unsound. Precluding this alternative will be the task of the second Metaphysical Exposition of space and will insure that the representation of space does not at all require the representation of spatially related objects, i.e., that the representation of space is *a priori*.

Reconstruction

1) If space is an empirical concept derived from outer experience, then the representation of space is derived from the representation of spatially related objects.
2) If the representation of spatially related objects assumes the representation of space, then the representation of space is not derived from the representation of spatially related objects.
3) The representation of spatially related objects assumes the representation of space.
4) From (2) and (3), the representation of space is not derived from the representation of spatially related objects (modus ponens).
5) From (1) and (4), space is not an empirical concept derived from outer experience (modus tollens).

Second Metaphysical Exposition of Space

Quote

Space is a necessary representation, *a priori*, that is the ground of all outer intuitions. One can never represent that there is no space, though one can very well think that there are no objects to be encountered in it. It is therefore to be regarded as the condition of the possibility of appearances, not as a determination dependent on them, and is an *a priori* representation that necessarily grounds outer appearances. [A24/B38-39]

Synopsis

As mentioned above, if the *a posteriori* representation of spatially related objects is assumed (necessary condition) for the representation of space, then this would seem to preclude the representation of space from being *a priori*. Even if the representation of space is assumed (necessary condition) for the *a posteriori* representation of spatially related objects, the representation of space would not be prior to the *a posteriori* representation of spatially related objects much as the *a posteriori* representation of externally related objects would not be prior to the representation of space. Instead, both representations would be mutually necessary. Kant must, therefore, rule out this alternative left open by the first Metaphysical Exposition of space to secure the *a priority* of the representation of space. The key to Kant's argument lies in the second premise below. If we can represent space without the *a posteriori* representation of externally related objects, then the representation of space does not assume the *a posteriori* representation of spatially related objects. This representation of space would be *a priori*.

It seems as if we can form the representation of a universal space *a priori* without objects. Such a representation is necessary for the construction of pure geometrical objects (e.g., drawing lines or triangles in thought) and will also be required for the construction of geometrical propositions (see the Transcendental Exposition below). Once one adds in the fourth premise (from the first Metaphysical Exposition of space), then one can establish that the representation of space is not only *a priori* but also *necessary* for the *a posteriori* representation of these spatially related objects (since their relations cannot be represented without the representation of space). Notice that the reverse is not true. Although the representation of spatially related objects assumes the representation of space, the representation of space does not assume the representation of spatially related objects.[6]

One might object to the second Metaphysical Exposition of space by claiming that it is merely a psychological thesis about what creatures like us can imagine, but this should have no impact on the epistemic or logical status of the representation of space. It is important to note, however, that *any* representation of spatial relation requires the representation of a universal space within which those relations obtain. Without this representation, we simply could not represent external existence at all. The representation of things as spatially distinct from one another or oneself, after all, is the representation of spatial relation which depends upon the representation of space. Consequently, the point is not merely psychological, but fundamental to our spatial cognition.[7]

The first and second Metaphysical Expositions of space serve to refute Leibniz' theory of space in particular and constructivist theories of space more generally. If Kant's arguments are sound, not only are the representations of the relations of things in space (between perceptions, material objects, etc.) not necessary for the representation of space, but the representation of space is itself necessary for the representation of these relations. Consequently, the representation of space cannot be constructed from these relations. In the final two Metaphysical Expositions, Kant will argue that space is not a concept but is rather an intuition. The four Metaphysical Expositions together, we will argue, are sufficient to undermine Newton's position on space.[8]

Reconstruction

1) One can represent space without representing spatially related objects.
2) If one can represent space without representing spatially related objects, then the representation of space does not assume the representation of spatially related objects.
3) From (1) and (2), the representation of space does not assume the representation of spatially related objects (modus ponens).
4) The representation of spatially related objects assumes the representation of space.
5) If the representation of space does not assume the representation of externally related objects but the representation of spatially related objects assumes the representation of space, then the representation of space is *a priori* and a necessary condition for the possibility of outer experience.
6) From (3), (4), and (5), the representation of space is *a priori* and a necessary condition for the possibility of outer experience (modus ponens).

Third Metaphysical Exposition of Space

Quote

> Space is not a discursive or, as is said, general concept of relations of things in general, but a pure intuition. For, first, one can only represent a single space, and if one speaks of many spaces, one understands by that only parts of one and the same unique space. And these parts cannot as it were precede the single all-encompassing space as its components (from which its composition would be possible), but rather are only thought in it. It is essentially single; the manifold *in it*, thus also the general concept of spaces in general, rests merely on limitations. From this it follows that in respect to it an *a priori* intuition (which is not empirical) grounds all concepts of it. [A24-25/B39]

Synopsis

Now that Kant has shown that the representation of space is *a priori*, he must demonstrate that space is not a concept but rather an intuition. One of the features that distinguish concepts from intuitions is that concepts are general and intuitions are singular representations. As mentioned in the previous chapter, for example, the concept of a textbook contains the *general* features of textbooks, but these do not fully determine any *singular* or particular textbook. The concept "textbook" does not tell you what the subject of any particular textbook will be and any number of different textbooks could instantiate the concept. In order to undermine Newton's position, Kant must show not only that the representation of space is *a priori* but also that it is an intuition rather than a concept. If New-

ton is right, then our representation of space is merely the concept of something
that exists in itself independently of the subject. Kant will argue that if space is
an intuition, then it is a feature of the subject's sensibility that cannot exist in
itself independently of the subject.

The crux of Kant's argument comes in the fourth premise below where he
claims that different parts of space are all parts of one unique space. In other
words, the parts are found *within* the whole where the whole is itself a single
thing. For example, whether a textbook is in front of you, behind you, or beside
you, you and the textbook occupy parts of a *single* space (otherwise you could
not be spatially related to one another). Unlike space, concepts are not singular
representations. Returning to the concept of a textbook, it contains a number of
partial representations like "is a book," "deals with an academic subject," "is
soporific," which are the "common marks" that make up our concept of a textbook.[9] This concept is not a *complete* representation, however, and so does not
pick out any *single* textbook. Since the concept of a textbook is a general representation, it can refer to any textbook whatsoever (e.g., one on Philosophy, or
Biology, etc.), but since it is not a singular representation, it does not pick out
any individual one. In other words, any number of different textbooks could
serve as instances of the concept. If the concept were identical with any one of
these instances (e.g., the exact book you have in your hands), then it could no
longer serve as a *general* representation which could pick out any of them.

Once one imports the conclusion of the second Metaphysical Exposition into the third and fourth Metaphysical Expositions (latter discussed below), one
can claim not only that space is an intuition, but an *a priori* intuition. As Kant
says immediately after the above quote, the status of space as an *a priori* intuition will be vital to geometry. This is something he will discuss at greater length
in the Transcendental Exposition of space (see below). On a related point, Kant
makes clear in the above quote that the status of space as an *a priori* intuition is
not meant to deny that we possess concepts of space (e.g., those involved in geometry). Returning again to the textbook example, although the textbook in your
hands as well as the space it occupies are not concepts, you nevertheless possess
a concept of a textbook as well as concepts of space.[10] In fact, the intuition of
space grounds all of our spatial concepts since without the intuition of space we
could never construct these concepts. A concept of space (e.g., measurement or
figure), as a general representation applicable to many things (e.g., different
things in space), must originally derive its content (partial representation) from
the singular representation of space (complete representation). The same is also
true, of course, when it comes to our empirical concept of a textbook. We first
must experience many individual textbooks (complete representations) in order
to determine what features are common among them. These common features
form the content of the concept of a textbook (partial representation). Since the
concept is general rather than singular, it can pick out any number of different
textbooks including the one in your hands.

Reconstruction

1) The representation of space is either general or it is singular.
2) If the representation of space is general, then the representation of space is a concept.
3) If the representation of space is a concept, then different spaces are instances of space but not parts of one unique space.
4) Different spaces are parts of one unique space.
5) From (3) and (4), the representation of space is not a concept (modus tollens).
6) From (2) and (5), the representation of space is not general (modus tollens).
7) From (1) and (6), the representation of space is singular (disjunctive syllogism).
8) If the representation of space is singular, then the representation of space is an intuition.
9) From (7) and (8), the representation of space is an intuition (modus ponens).
10) From (9) and the second Metaphysical Exposition, the representation of space is an *a priori* intuition (modus ponens).

Fourth Metaphysical Exposition of Space

Quote

> Space is represented as an infinite *given* magnitude. Now one must, to be sure, think of every concept as a representation that is contained in an infinite set of different possible representations (as their common mark), which thus contains these *under itself*; but no concept, as such, can be thought as if it contained an infinite set of representations *within itself*. Nevertheless space is so thought (for all the parts of space, even to infinity, are simultaneous). Therefore the original representation of space is an *a priori intuition*, not *a concept*. [A25/B39-40]

Synopsis

Besides singularity, the other feature that distinguishes an intuition from a concept is that the former is an immediate representation whereas the latter is a mediate representation. A representation is immediate just in case it yields information on an existing state of affairs. There is a direct relationship between the subject and the state of affairs represented. This fits with Kant's characterization of intuition as being the cognitive faculty through which objects are *given* to us. Mediate representations, in contrast, allow us to *think* about things not given presently or that are even non-existent. Concepts are inherently mediate representations. As explained above, an empirical concept is acquired by comparing representations of particular things with one another to determine what is common to them. Once we have picked out the "common marks," this allows us to think about these things even when they are not present (e.g., thinking about the textbook that you are not reading during spring break). We can combine this concept (e.g., a horse) with other concepts (e.g., horned, immortal, magical, etc.) to think of things that do not exist at all (a unicorn). What's important is that the content of the concept mediates between the subject representing the object and the object that instantiates this concept. A concept allows us to *think* of all the possible instances that might fall under the concept and to recognize them when they are *given* in intuition.

In the fourth Metaphysical Exposition of space, Kant argues that space is an immediate representation. As in the third Metaphysical Exposition, the parts of space are not instances of a concept but are rather parts of one unique space. What Kant adds in the fourth Metaphysical Exposition, is that all these parts are *given* (immediate representation) in one infinite whole of space. This whole is infinitely complex since the pure intuition of space is both unbounded and infinitely divisible (think again here of the space of pure geometry). This is the key to Kant's argument which again comes in the fourth premise below. If these parts formed the content of a concept, however, then the concept would be infinitely complex and so incomprehensible. As Kant says in the above quote, "no concept, as such, can be thought as if it contained an infinite set of representations *within itself*." For example, if the content of the concept "textbook" were infinitely complex, and this complexity had to be comprehended to identify any instances of the concept, then we could never recognize something as a textbook. Although a concept might have an infinite extension (i.e., things that instantiate the concept), a concept cannot have an infinite intension (i.e., an infinitely complex meaning).[11] If *all* the parts of space were somehow contained in the concept of space, furthermore, the concept would be a *complete* representation and so could not serve its function as a *partial* representation. It could not pick out individual spaces as instances of the concept, since the concept would contain *all* the features those different spaces possess not only those that they share in *common*. For example, if your concept of a textbook contained *all* the features that textbooks possess including those that are unrelated (e.g., one deals with Calculus another deals with Art History) and even mutually exclusive (e.g., one is 200 pages another is 700 pages), your concept could never pick out any individual textbook.

Again, just as in the third Metaphysical Exposition, this should not be taken to imply that we do not possess concepts of space. We do possess these concepts and they allow us to *think* about space (mediate representation), but they are derived from the intuition of space which is itself *given* (immediate representation). A final similarity to the third Metaphysical Exposition shows up in the conclusion of the argument. Once the conclusion of the second Metaphysical Exposition is conjoined to the preliminary conclusion of the fourth Metaphysical Exposition in premise nine, Kant can conclude not only that the representation of space is an intuition but also that this intuition is *a priori*.

Kant takes the four Metaphysical Expositions of space collectively to undermine Newton's position on space. If the representation of space is an *a priori* intuition, it would seem to be an essential feature of the subject's sensibility and so could not be a thing-in-itself existing independently of sensibility. We will have occasion to revisit this inference, however, in the final chapter of Part One.

Reconstruction

1) The representation of space is either mediate or immediate.
2) If the representation of space is mediate, then the representation of space is a concept.
3) If the representation of space is a concept, then its content cannot be infinitely complex.
4) Space is an infinitely complex given whole.
5) From (3) and (4), the representation of space is not a concept (modus tollens).
6) From (2) and (5), the representation of space is not mediate (modus tollens).
7) From (1) and (6), the representation of space is immediate (disjunctive syllogism).
8) If the representation of space is immediate, then the representation of space is an intuition.
9) From (7) and (8), the representation of space is an intuition (modus ponens).
10) From (9) and the second Metaphysical Exposition, the representation of space is an *a priori* intuition (conjunction introduction).

Transcendental Exposition of the Concept of Space

Quote

Geometry is a science that determines the properties of space synthetically and yet *a priori*. What then must the representation of space be for such a cognition of it to be possible? It must originally be intuition; for from a mere concept no propositions can be drawn that go beyond the concept, which, however, happens in geometry (Introduction V). But this intuition must be encountered in us *a priori*, i.e., prior to all perception of an object, thus it must be pure, not empirical intuition. For geometrical propositions are all apodictic, i.e., combined with consciousness of their necessity, e.g., space has only three dimensions; but such propositions cannot be empirical or judgments of experience, nor inferred from them (Introduction II).

Now how can an outer intuition inhabit the mind that precedes the objects themselves, and in which the concept of the latter can be determined *a priori*? Obviously not otherwise than insofar as it has its seat merely in the subject, as its formal constitution for being affected by objects and thereby acquiring *immediate representation*, i.e., *intuition*, of them, thus only as the form of outer *sense* in general.

Thus our explanation alone makes the *possibility* of geometry as a synthetic *a priori* cognition comprehensible. Any kind of explanation that does not accomplish this, even if it appears to have some similarity with it, can most surely be distinguished from it by means of this characteristic. [B40-41]

Synopsis

In the Transcendental Exposition of space, Kant argues that the claims of geometry are synthetic *a priori* only on the assumption that space is a pure *a priori* intuition. It has the form of a regressive argument. Assuming that there are synthetic *a priori* propositions in geometry, the Transcendental Exposition of space aims to uncover the necessary conditions for the possibility of these propositions. As you might recall from the Introduction to *CPR*, Kant took explaining how synthetic *a priori* propositions are possible to be his book's central task.[12] For a proposition to be synthetic *a priori* means that the predicate concept is not contained in the subject concept (synthetic) and its truth or falsity can be known without an appeal to experience or the world around us (*a priori*). Since the predicate concept lies outside the subject concept, judgment must find a way of connecting these concepts that does not rely on conceptual analysis. Since the proposition is *a priori*, judgment cannot appeal to experience *a posteriori* to connect these concepts. It is here in the Transcendental Exposition of space, that Kant provides an account of that "unknown = X" that allows judgment to connect the concepts in a synthetic *a priori* proposition.

As mentioned in the last chapter, an example Kant gives of a synthetic *a priori* proposition is "The straight line between two points is the shortest."[13] In this case, it is synthetic since the concept of the shortest is not contained within the concept of the straight. That is to say, if we analyze the concept of the straight, which is a *quality* of something, we will not discover the shortest, which is a *quantity*. Additionally, the proposition is said to be known *a priori* since it is necessary, i.e., it is impossible that something other than a straight line could be the shortest distance between two points, and we do not need to have experiences of particular straight lines to know that it is true.

So, according to Kant, geometrical propositions are synthetic and *a priori*. However, the main question Kant wants to answer is, since these propositions are synthetic *a priori*, and spatial concepts are used in geometry, what must our representation of space be to have cognition of such geometrical propositions? First, he says that our spatial representation must be an intuition rather than a concept. Since geometrical propositions are synthetic, forming those propositions requires going beyond the concepts used in the propositions, just as forming the proposition that "The straight line between two points is the shortest" requires going beyond the concept of "the straight line" to make the connection with "the shortest line." Since the concepts alone will not give us the connection, it must be intuition. Secondly, Kant says that our representation of space must be *a priori* rather than *a posteriori*. Because geometrical propositions are necessary or "apodictic," judgment cannot base them on *a posteriori* experience of the world since the world could have always turned out otherwise. True geometrical propositions, on the other hand, must necessarily be the case, and therefore be based on an *a priori* representation of space. To summarize Kant's argument: if geometrical propositions are synthetic *a priori*, then the representation of space must be an *a priori* intuition. Geometrical propositions are synthetic *a priori*. Therefore, the representation of space is an *a priori* intuition. In this respect, one can see how the Transcendental Exposition of space complements the Metaphysical Expositions of space. Synthetic *a priori* propositions concerning space are possible only if the representation of space is an *a priori* (first two Metaphysical Expositions) intuition (second two Metaphysical Expositions).

Propositions, like the one mentioned above, are synthetic since they tell us something about the form of our experience which could not be revealed through concepts alone. They are *a priori* insofar as what we learn is determined by our own cognitive natures.[14] These kinds of propositions would be impossible without Kant's Copernican turn. In this respect, the Transcendental Exposition of space illustrates the advantage that Kant's view possesses over Newton's and Leibniz's views. Insofar as geometrical propositions are informative about the world beyond our concepts and necessary, Newton and Leibniz simply cannot account for them. Since geometrical propositions tell us about the world beyond our concepts, they are synthetic and not analytic. If space is a mind-independent thing-in-itself experienced only *a posteriori* (Newton) or if space is constituted by the relationships among things that exist in themselves where these relationships are experienced *a posteriori* (Leibniz), however, then geometrical propositions, which rely on the representation of space for their formation, could not be necessary since they would not be formed *a priori*.[15] Consequently, even if Kant's arguments against Newton and Leibniz in the Metaphysical Expositions of space fail, the Transcendental Exposition of space offers good reason to reject their views.

Reconstruction

1) If geometrical propositions (e.g., that the straight line between two points is the shortest) cannot be formed simply by analyzing the concepts used in the propositions, then geometrical propositions are synthetic.
2) Geometrical propositions cannot be formed simply by analyzing the concepts used in the propositions (e.g., "the straight" says nothing about quantity, "the shortest" says nothing about quality).
3) From (1) and (2), geometrical propositions are synthetic (modus ponens).
4) If geometrical propositions are synthetic, then they are formed either via the *a posteriori* intuition of space or the *a priori* intuition of space.
5) From (3) and (4), geometrical propositions are formed either via the *a posteriori* intuition of space or the *a priori* intuition of space (modus ponens).

6) If geometrical propositions are formed via the *a posteriori* intuition of space, then geometrical propositions are contingent.

7) Geometrical propositions are necessary (e.g., a straight line between any two points *must* be the shortest line between those points).

8) From (6) and (7), geometrical propositions are not formed via the *a posteriori* intuition of space (modus tollens).

9) From (5) and (8), geometrical propositions are formed via the *a priori* intuition of space (disjunctive syllogism).

Argument from Incongruent Counterparts

Quote

If two things are quite equal in all respects as much as can be ascertained by all means possible, quantitatively and qualitatively, it must follow that the one can in all cases and under all circumstances replace the other, and this substitution would not occasion the least recognizable difference. This is in fact true of plane figures in geometry; but some spherical figures exhibit, notwithstanding a complete internal agreement, such a difference in their external relation that the one figure cannot possibly be put in place of the other. For instance, two spherical triangles on opposite hemispheres which have an arc of the equator as their common base may be quite equal, both as regards sides and angles, so that nothing is to be found in either, if it be described for itself alone and completed, that would not equally be applicable to both; and yet the one cannot be put in the place of the other (on the opposite hemisphere). Here, then, is an internal difference between the two triangles; this difference our understanding cannot show to be internal but only manifests itself by external relations in space. But I shall adduce examples, taken from common life, that are more obvious still.

What can be more similar in every respect and in every part more alike to my hand and to my ear than their images in a mirror? And yet I cannot put such a hand as is seen in the mirror in the place of its original; for if this is a right hand, that in the mirror is a left one, and the image or reflection of the right ear is a left one, which never can serve as a substitute for the other. There are in this case no internal differences which our understanding could determine by thinking alone. Yet the differences are internal as the senses teach, for, notwithstanding their complete equality and similarity, the left hand cannot be enclosed in the same bounds as the right one (they are not congruent); the glove of one hand cannot be used for the other. What is the solution? These objects are not representations of things as they are in themselves, and as some pure understanding would cognize them, but sensuous intuitions, that is, appearances, whose possibility rests upon the relation of certain things unknown in themselves to something else, viz., to our sensibility. Space is the form of the external intuition of this sensibility, and the internal determination of any space is possible only by the determination of its external relation to the whole of space, of which it is a part (in other words, by its relation to external sense). That is to say, the part is possible only through the whole, which is never the case with things in themselves as objects of the mere understanding, but can well be the case with mere appearances. Hence the difference between similar and equal things which are not congruent (for instances, helices winding in opposite ways) cannot be made intelligible by any concept, but only by the relation to the right and the left hands, which immediately refers to intuition. [*Prolegomena* 285-86]

Synopsis

Incongruent counterparts are objects that are internally identical to one another (every intrinsic property had by one is had by the other) yet they can still be distinguished from one another. An example Kant gives is a pair of hands. The complete concept of each hand is the same in every respect, yet the hands are different since they cannot be substituted for one another, i.e., they cannot enclose the same space since one is a left hand and one is a right hand. The question, then, is how do we account for this difference in the counterparts? The above argument from the *Prolegomena to Any Future Metaphysics* attempts to show that the difference between incongruent counterparts can only be accounted for through the objects' external spatial relations. Any attempt to differentiate between them based solely on the objects themselves will fail to explain their incongruency.

Kant's target is Leibniz who holds that the understanding alone, by examining the complete concepts of the objects, can cognize the objects as they are in themselves. For Kant, in the above quote, "as some pure understanding would cognize them." According to Leibniz, if two objects are counterparts, then their complete concepts are identical. We already know, however, that some counterparts are incongruent. If Leibniz is correct, then the incongruency of objects must be explained by a difference in the complete concepts of the objects (i.e., a disagreement between the concepts of these objects). This is where Leibniz has a problem, since when we analyze the complete concepts of the hands "there are…no internal differences which our understanding could determine by thinking alone." The third premise below reflects this crucial idea and it follows from it that the objects themselves cannot account for their incongruency. Leibniz' position simply cannot explain it.

Kant, on the other hand, holds that objects are represented through intuition, as mere appearances, i.e., not as things-in-themselves. Intuition in turn assumes space as an *a priori* form of appearance. Given that space is distinct from the objects as appearances, it then becomes the ideal means by which counterparts can be distinguished, viz., through their external relations in space. Therefore, on Kant's position one could say that a left and right hand are internally identical (counterparts) and yet distinguish between them (incongruent) based on left and right handedness being spatial characteristics irreducible to the content of these appearances.

The argument from incongruent counterparts completes Kant's case against Leibniz and constructivist positions more generally. The constructivist seems to be faced with a dilemma. Either the relations between things are spatial or they are not spatial. If they are spatial, then the constructivist seems to be begging the question. If they are not spatial, then how do we construct the representation of space from representations that are not spatial?[16] Whereas the first two Metaphysical Expositions of space expose the first horn of this dilemma, the incongruent counterpart argument exposes the second by showing that the representation of space cannot be derived from the non-spatial relations of things-in-themselves (i.e., differences between the concepts of these things-in-themselves). This way of explaining space (and by extension time) offers no way to account for our experience of incongruent counterparts. Consequently, Kant thinks it should be rejected in favor of his view which is able to explain our experience of incongruent counterparts.

Reconstruction

1) The representation of incongruent counterparts is either the representation of these counterparts as they are in themselves or as they appear in empirical intuition.

2) If the representation of incongruent counterparts is the representation of these counterparts as they are in themselves, then there must be some difference between the complete concepts of the counterparts to account for the representation of the incongruence.

3) There is no difference between the complete concepts of counterparts that could account for the representation of their incongruence.

4) From (2) and (3), the representation of incongruent counterparts is not the representation of these counterparts as they are in themselves (modus tollens).

5) From (1) and (4), the representation of incongruent counterparts is the representation of these counterparts as they appear in empirical intuition (disjunctive syllogism).

6) If the representation of incongruent counterparts is the representation of these counterparts as they appear in empirical intuition, then the representation of incongruent counterparts presupposes space since space is an *a priori* form of empirical intuition.

7) From (5) and (6), the representation of incongruent counterparts presupposes space since space is as an *a priori* form of empirical intuition (modus ponens).

8) If the representation of incongruent counterparts presupposes space as an *a priori* form of empirical intuition, then the difference in the external relations of these counterparts within space accounts for the representation of their incongruence.

9) From (7) and (8), the difference in the external relations of these counterparts within space accounts for the representation of their incongruence (modus ponens).

Notes

1. Allison makes this point. See Henry Allison, *Kant's Transcendental Idealism*, 2nd ed. (New Haven, CT: Yale University Press, 2004), 100. Put slightly differently, this proposition is equivalent to the claim that if I do not possess the representation of space, then I cannot represent anything in space. Of course, the same is true of some made-up concept like "borogove." If I do not possess the concept of a borogove, I cannot represent something as a borogove. Neither claim tells us much about the nature of space or of borogoves.

2. Allison discusses both of the above problems as well as this solution. Whereas some philosophers hold that Kant's argument turns on the idea that the representation of space is required for the representation of objects as *numerically* distinct from one another, this simply is not true. As long as two things are qualitatively different, one can represent their numerical distinctness without the representation of space. See Allison, *Kant's Transcendental Idealism*, 101-4.

3. Altman makes this point. See Altman, *A Companion to Kant's Critique*, 60.

4. We will touch on this idea again in the Third Analogy (see chapter eleven).

5. This objection can be traced back to J.G. Maaß in 1789. See Henry Allison, *The Kant-Eberhard Controversy* (Baltimore: Johns Hopkins University Press, 1973), 35-36.

6. This also provides a response to the objection that the representation of space and the representation of spatially related objects might be contemporaneous, with neither representation assuming the other. Even if the representations are *temporally* contemporaneous, this does not change the order of *logical* priority. If the first and second Metaphysical Expositions are sound, the representation of space is a necessary condition for the representation of spatially related objects. The reverse is not true. Gardner also makes the point that if one holds that the two representations are contemporaneous and unconnected, this makes their agreement a complete accident and so does not explain how objects are possible for us. See Gardner, *Kant and the Critique*, 83.

7. Altman makes a similar point. See Altman, *A Companion to Kant's Critique*, 62.

8. This is the way that Altman explains the focus of the different Metaphysical Expositions. See Altman, *A Companion to Kant's Critique*, 66. Rosenberg argues, however, that the second Metaphysical Exposition, if sound, is sufficient to undermine Newton's position. Insofar as Newton must hold that space could only be given to us in experience as a sensory content (given its status as a quasi-substance) and the second Metaphysical Exposition of space eliminates all such content from the representation of space, the second Metaphysical Exposition of space is incompatible with Newton's position. See Rosenberg, *Accessing Kant*, 68.

9. *CPR* A25/B40.

10. Dicker uses the example of a kettle. See Dicker, *Kant's Theory of Knowledge*, 37.

11. Buroker makes this point. See Buroker, *Kant's Critique*, 55.

12. *CPR* B19.

13. *CPR* B16.

14. Savile makes a similar point. See Savile, *Kant's Critique*, 30.

15. *CPR* A39-40/B56-57. Although Kant's objection in the text seems directed toward Leibniz, Altman extends the objection to Newton as well. He also notes that Descartes' view on geometry faces a problem since the latter holds that our cognition must conform to external objects existing as things-in-themselves. Unless one assumes that

objects conform to our cognition of them (i.e., accepts the Copernican turn), however, there is no guarantee whatsoever that *a priori* geometrical principles are true of them. See Altman, *A Companion to Kant's Critique*, 67-72.

16. Buroker points out this dilemma for constructivist views. See Buroker, *Kant's Critique*, 48-49. Arguably, in addition to posing a problem for Leibniz' view, Kant's arguments pose problems for all of the empiricist views of the origin of our representation of space (Locke, Berkeley, Hume).

Chapter Three
Time

First Metaphysical Exposition of Time

Quote

> Time is not an empirical concept that is somehow drawn from an experience. For simultaneity or succession would not themselves come into perception if the representation of time did not ground them *a priori*. Only under its presupposition can one represent that several things exist at one and the same time (simultaneously) or in different times (successively). [A30/B46]

Synopsis

Since Kant's Metaphysical Expositions of time largely mirror his Metaphysical Expositions of space, objections to the latter will likewise be objections to the former. We will not take the time to repeat those objections here. If the responses offered in the previous chapter to these objections are successful, however, we believe they will likewise be successful in this one. We will leave it up to the reader to apply these objections within the context of time and to evaluate the success of the responses offered in the previous chapter. In this chapter, we will only aim to explain the arguments and their relationships to one another.

Just like the first Metaphysical Exposition of space, the first Metaphysical Exposition of time attempts to establish that time is not an empirical concept derived from experience. Likewise, it is directed against philosophers like Leibniz who hold that the representation of time is somehow constructed from the representation of relations between things (e.g., monadic perceptions). Just as the representation of spatial *relations* assumes the representation of *space*, so too does Kant claim that the representation of *temporal* relations assumes the representation of *time*. Again, the crucial step in Kant's argument is the third premise below where he observes that the representation of simultaneous and successive appearances assumes the representation of time. Consider the experience of the sun rising in the morning and then setting in the evening. This particular sunset came before or was successive to the sunrise. Now consider having this experience without the representation of time. Representing something as happening *before* something else or *after* another thing would itself be impossible without the representation of time through which we order these representations as successive to one another. In the same way, the experience of the cock crowing as simultaneous with the sun rising would not be possible without the representation of time within which we identify these two events as occurring at the same time. It follows that the representation of appearances as simultaneous or successive assumes the representation of time, i.e., the representation of time is a necessary condition for the representation of temporal relations. Kant concludes from this that the representation of time is not an empirical concept derived from our *a posteriori* experience of temporal relations.

Just as the first Metaphysical Exposition of space leaves open the possibility that the representation of spatially related objects is itself necessary for the representation of space, however, the first Metaphysical Exposition of time leaves open the possibility that the representation of temporally related appearances is itself necessary for the representation of time. As before, this could very well render the second premise of the first Metaphysical Exposition of time false and the argument as a whole unsound. The purpose of the second Metaphysical Exposition of time will be to preclude this possibility and so insure that the representation of time is *a priori*.

Reconstruction

1) If time is an empirical concept derived from experience, then the representation of time is derived from the representation of simultaneous and successive appearances.
2) If the representation of simultaneous and successive appearances assumes the representation of time, then the representation of time is not derived from the representation of simultaneous and successive appearances.
3) The representation of simultaneous and successive appearances assumes the representation of time.
4) From (2) and (3), the representation of time is not derived from the representation of simultaneous and successive appearances (modus ponens).
5) From (1) and (4), time is not an empirical concept derived from experience (modus tollens).

Second Metaphysical Exposition of Time

Quote

> Time is a necessary representation that grounds all intuitions. In regard to appearances in general one cannot remove time, though one can very well take the appearances away from time. Time is therefore given *a priori*. In it alone is all actuality of appearances possible. The latter could all disappear, but time itself (as the universal condition of their possibility) cannot be removed. [A31/B46]

Synopsis

Just as the second Metaphysical Exposition of space aims to show that the representation of space does not assume (necessary condition) the representation of spatially related objects, so too does the second Metaphysical Exposition of time aim to show that the representation of time does not assume (necessary condition) the representation of temporally related appearances. If Kant's argument is successful, then he will have proven that the representation of time is not at all derived from appearances *a posteriori* and so is an *a priori* representation. Again, the crux of Kant's argument lies in the second premise below. If we can represent time without representing appearances *a posteriori*, then the representation of time does not assume the representation of these appearances. This representation of time would be *a priori*.

It seems as if we can represent time *a priori* without appearances. For example, take a certain date, e.g., April 6, 1977. If you are told that there is a *different* date in the endnote attached to this sentence, you can be certain that it is either going to be after or before the date mentioned in the previous one based simply on your *a priori* representation of time.[1] You do not need to know *what* the date is *a posteriori* to know *that* it comes before or after the other date *a priori*. Just as in the case of space, Kant later claims in the Transcendental Exposition of time (discussed below) that the *a priori* representation of time is required to insure the necessary truth of temporal axioms (e.g., that different times are not simultaneous but successive). Once one adds in the fourth premise (from the first Metaphysical Exposition of time), one can establish that the representation of time is not only *a priori* but also *necessary* for the *a posteriori* representation of these temporally related appearances (since simultaneity and succession cannot be represented without the representation of time), though just as in the case of space, the reverse is not true.

If Kant's first two Metaphysical Expositions of time succeed in demonstrating that the representation of time is *a priori*, then Leibniz must be wrong and our representation of time is not at all derived from our representations of temporal relations *a posteriori*. Even if Leibniz were to claim that the representation of time is constructed from conceptual relationships that are non-temporal, it is unclear how this could account for our representation of time. Appealing to the succession of perceptions does not help, since succession is itself a temporal relation. If Kant can establish that the representation of time is not only *a priori* but also an intuition, then it seems he will undermine Newton's position on time as well. This is the task of the fourth and fifth Metaphysical Expositions of time.

Reconstruction

1) One can represent time without representing appearances in time.
2) If one can represent time without representing appearances in time, then the representation of time does not assume the representation of appearances in time.
3) From (1) and (2), the representation of time does not assume the representation of appearances in time (modus ponens).
4) The representation of appearances in time assumes the representation of time.
5) If the representation of time does not assume the representation of appearances in time but the representation of appearances in time assumes the representation of time, then the representation of time is *a priori* and a necessary condition for the possibility of experience.
6) From (3), (4), and (5), the representation of time is *a priori* and a necessary condition for the possibility of temporal experience (modus ponens).

Fourth Metaphysical Exposition of Time

Quote

> Time is no discursive or, as one calls it, general concept, but a pure form of sensible intuition. Different times are only parts of one and the same time. That representation, however, which can only be given through a single object, is an intuition. [A31-32/B47]

Synopsis

This is where the order of the Metaphysical Expositions of time differs from the Metaphysical Expositions of space. Whereas Kant gives his Transcendental Exposition of time partially in the third Metaphysical Exposition of time, the fourth Metaphysical Exposition of time corresponds to the third Metaphysical Exposition of space. To maintain the parallel structure with Kant's arguments concerning space, we will first deal with the fourth Metaphysical Exposition of time.

In this argument, Kant uses the singularity of time to show that the representation of time is an intuition and not a concept. Just as with space, the key to Kant's argument comes in the fourth premise below where he claims that different times are part of one single time. For time to be singular means that it is represented as one *unitary* time as opposed to *multiple* times. Multiple times are not the same as *different* times which we obviously can and do represent. Multiple times are times that cannot be connected to one another on a single timeline, whereas different times all occupy places on a single timeline. Our experience of time represents the latter but not the former. Whenever someone asks you "When did X happen?" where X is some event like Caesar crossing the Rubicon, Napoleon's defeat at Waterloo, or your first kiss (all equally momentous), the answer will always be some time that you can connect with the others on a single timeline. Whereas these different times are all part of the *singular* representation of time, concepts are *general* representations that apply to many *singular* instances of the concept (e.g., the concept of a textbook applying to what you hold in your hands) but are not themselves singular representations on pain of no longer being able to serve this general function.

Just as with the arguments dealing with space, once one imports the conclusion of the second Metaphysical Exposition of time into the fourth and fifth Metaphysical Expositions (latter discussed below), one can claim that the representation of time is not only an intuition but is also a pure intuition *a priori*. Likewise, the status of time as a pure intuition will be relevant to the justification of synthetic *a priori* propositions in the Transcendental Exposition of time. In fact, Kant makes this very point immediately after the quote given above. Finally, just as there are concepts of space there are also concepts of time (e.g., simultaneity, succession, etc.). These concepts, however, much as the propositions they go to constitute, are grounded in the intuition of time.

Reconstruction

1) The representation of time is either general or it is singular.
2) If the representation of time is general, then the representation of time is a concept.
3) If the representation of time is a concept, then different times are instances of time but not parts of one and the same time.
4) Different times are parts of one single time.
5) From (3) and (4), the representation of time is not a concept (modus tollens).
6) From (2) and (5), the representation of time is not general (modus tollens).
7) From (1) and (6), the representation of time is singular (disjunctive syllogism).
8) If the representation of time is singular, then the representation of time is an intuition.
9) From (7) and (8), the representation of time is an intuition (modus ponens).
10) From (9) and the second Metaphysical Exposition, the representation of time is an *a priori* intuition (conjunction introduction).

Fifth Metaphysical Exposition of Time

Quote

> The infinitude of time signifies nothing more than that every determinate magnitude
> of time is only possible through limitations of a single time grounding it. The origi-
> nal representation *time* must therefore be given as unlimited. But where the parts
> themselves and every magnitude of an object can be determinately represented only
> though limitation, there the entire representation cannot be given through concepts,
> (for they contain only partial representations), but immediate intuition must ground
> them. [A32/B47-48]

Synopsis

The purpose of this argument, which parallels the fourth Metaphysical Exposition of space, is to prove that time is an intuition by showing that time is an immediate representation. As mentioned above, whereas concepts are *mediate* representations that allow us to *think* of things regardless of whether they are
present or even exist, intuitions are *immediate* representations whereby existing
states of affairs are *given* to us. As the fourth Metaphysical Exposition of time
established, different times are not disconnected instances of a concept but are
rather parts of one single time. What Kant adds in the fifth Metaphysical Exposition, is that all these different times are *given* (immediate representation) in one
unlimited time. Different times are simply limitations of this single unlimited
time. For example, one can think about the time it takes to walk across the room
or to just take the first step. The latter is just a limitation of the former which
could itself be divided into an infinite number of intermediary moments.[2] The
time it takes to walk across the room is likewise a limitation of something that is
itself unlimited since one can always think of any number of moments preceding
the first step or any number of moments following the last one.

This is the crux of Kant's argument which again comes in premise four below. If these parts (moments) formed the content of a concept, however, then the
concept would be infinitely complex and so incomprehensible. If its content
were *unlimited*, furthermore, it would need to somehow contain *all* the moments
of time. The concept would then be a *complete* representation and so could not
serve its conceptual function as a *partial* representation. It would contain not
only the features that all these individual moments share in *common* but also
those that are unrelated or mutually exclusive. This would prevent the concept
from having any instances.

Although Kant does not explicitly conjoin the conclusion of the second Metaphysical Exposition of time with the preliminary conclusions of the fourth and
fifth Metaphysical Expositions of time as he does in the Metaphysical Expositions of space, we have done so to maintain parity. This allows Kant to conclude
not only that the representation of space is an intuition but also that this intuition

is *a priori*. Much as the Metaphysical Expositions of space seem to collectively undermine Newton's position on space, so too do the Metaphysical Expositions of time seem to collectively undermine Newton's position on time. If the representation of time is an *a priori* intuition, then it would seem to be a feature of the subject's sensibility and not a thing-in-itself existing independently of sensibility. As mentioned above, this is an inference we will return to in the final chapter of Part One.

Reconstruction

1) The representation of time is either mediate or immediate.
2) If the representation of time is mediate, then the representation of time is a concept.
3) If the representation of time is a concept, then its content cannot be unlimited.
4) Time is given as unlimited.
5) From (3) and (4), the representation of time is not a concept (modus tollens).
6) From (2) and (5), the representation of time is not mediate (modus tollens).
7) From (1) and (6), the representation of time is immediate (disjunctive syllogism).
8) If the representation of time is immediate, then the representation of time is an intuition.
9) From (7) and (8), the representation of time is an intuition (modus ponens).
10) From (9) and the second Metaphysical Exposition, the representation of space is an *a priori* intuition (conjunction introduction).

Transcendental Exposition of the Concept of Time

Quote

3) This *a priori* necessity also grounds the possibility of apodictic principles of relations of time, or *axioms* of time in general. It has only one dimension: different times are not simultaneous, but successive (just as different spaces are not successive, but simultaneous). These principles could not be drawn from experience, for this would yield neither strict universality nor apodictic certainty. We would only be able to say: This is what common perception teaches, but not: This is how matters must stand. These principles are valid as rules under which alone experiences are possible at all, and instruct us prior to them, not through it. . .

4) Further, the proposition that different times cannot be simultaneous cannot be derived from a general concept. The proposition is synthetic, and cannot arise from concepts alone. It is therefore immediately contained in the intuition and representation of time. . .

I can appeal to No. 3 where, in order to be brief, I have placed that which is properly transcendental under the heading of the metaphysical exposition. Here I add further that the concept of alteration and, with it, the concept of motion (as alteration of place), is only possible through and in the representation of time — that if this representation were not *a priori* (inner) intuition, then no concept, whatever it might be, could make comprehensible the possibility of an alteration, i.e., of a combination of contradictorily opposed predicates (e.g., a thing's being in a place and the not-being of the very same thing in the same place) in one and the same object. Only in time can both contradictorily opposed determinations in one thing be encountered, namely *successively*. Our concept of time therefore explains the possibility of as much synthetic *a priori* cognition as is presented by the general theory of motion, which is no less fruitful. [A31-32/B47-49]

Synopsis

Just as the Transcendental Exposition of space aims to uncover what makes synthetic *a priori* propositions that deal with space possible (e.g., geometrical propositions), the Transcendental Exposition of time aims to uncover what makes synthetic *a priori* propositions that deal with time possible (e.g., temporal axioms). Although Kant's explicit discussion of the Transcendental Exposition of time does not include an explanation of the synthetic *a priori* character of temporal axioms, this is something that he discusses in the Metaphysical Expositions of time. Furthermore, as can be seen from the first sentence of the Transcendental Exposition, he considers the third Metaphysical Exposition of time to really be a Transcendental Exposition. If the third Metaphysical Exposition of time is contrasted with the Transcendental Exposition of space, however, one will notice that in the former Kant only discusses the *a priori* character of temporal axioms but not their synthetic character. For that reason, the second half of the fourth Metaphysical Exposition of time needs to be brought in since there he makes clear that temporal axioms are also synthetic. Kant argues that if temporal axioms are synthetic *a priori*, then the representation of time must be an *a priori* intuition.

One axiom of time that Kant examines is that "Different times are not simultaneous but successive." This proposition is synthetic since the concept of difference has nothing to say about *succession* whereas the concept of succession has nothing to say about *difference*. Just because two things are different does not entail they are successive (e.g., two different textbooks sitting on a table simultaneously). Just because two things are successive does not mean they are different (e.g., the textbook right now and the same textbook a moment later). How can there be a necessary connection between the concepts in the case of *time*? Since the proposition is necessarily true and one need not appeal to any particular instances of time *a posteriori* in order to discover its truth, the proposition is *a priori*. Next, the representation of time must be an intuition in order to form the axiom since the connection between the concepts of difference and succession cannot be made by analyzing the concepts themselves. One must go beyond the concepts to make such a connection. Finally, this intuition must itself be *a priori* in order to safeguard the necessity of the proposition. Any judgment based on empirical intuition *a posteriori* would be contingent since the world could have always turned out otherwise. Since the axiom of time that Kant mentions is both synthetic and *a priori*, it must be formed via the pure intuition of time *a priori*. Again, the pure intuition *a priori* ends up being the "unknown = X" that judgment relies upon to connect concepts in synthetic *a priori* propositions. Insofar as Kant's position in the Transcendental Exposition of time is an improvement over both Leibniz' and Newton's views (which we have reason to believe given its advantages in the context of space), then this argument would again provide reason to reject their positions on time notwithstanding Kant's arguments in the Metaphysical Expositions.

Reconstruction

1) If temporal axioms (e.g., that different times are not simultaneous but successive) cannot be formed simply by analyzing the concepts used in the propositions, then temporal axioms are synthetic.
2) Temporal axioms cannot be formed simply by analyzing the concepts used in the judgments (e.g., "difference" says nothing about succession, "succession" says nothing about difference).
3) From (1) and (2), temporal axioms are synthetic (modus ponens).
4) If temporal axioms are synthetic, then they are formed either via the *a posteriori* intuition of time or the *a priori* intuition of time.
5) From (3) and (4), temporal axioms are formed either via the *a posteriori* intuition of time or the *a priori* intuition of time (modus ponens).
6) If temporal axioms are formed via the *a posteriori* intuition of time, then temporal axioms are contingent.
7) Temporal axioms are necessary (e.g., different times *must* be successive and *cannot* be simultaneous).
8) From (6) and (7), temporal axioms are not formed via *a posteriori* intuition (modus tollens).
9) From (5) and (8), temporal axioms are formed via *a priori* intuition (disjunctive syllogism).

Notes

1. Altman offers this example using a starting date of May 11, 1972. See Altman, *A Companion to Kant's Critique*, 74 and 84.
2. In this connection, one might think of Zeno's paradoxes concerning motion as described in the sixth book of Aristotle's *Physics*. See Aristotle, *Selections*, trans. Terence Irwin and Gail Fine (Indianapolis, IN: Hackett Publishing, 1995), 233a13-240a15.

Chapter Four
Conclusions from the Transcendental Aesthetic

There are several conclusions that Kant draws from the Metaphysical and Transcendental Expositions of space and time. Some of these were outlined above in chapter one, though they bear repeating here again. To begin, although the Metaphysical Expositions explicitly establish only that space and time are *pure* intuitions *a priori*, Kant thinks that space and time are also *a priori* forms of *empirical* intuition which is *a posteriori*.

This claim underpins one of the central views of *CPR*, viz., the twin theories of transcendental idealism and empirical realism.[1] According to Kant, since space and time are the forms of empirical intuition, they are going to be *objectively valid*. That space and time are objectively valid means that objects of experience are possible only through the representation of space and time.[2] Based on the objective validity of the forms of intuition, Kant says that space and time as well as objects in space and time are empirically real. Since space and time are the universal and necessary subjective conditions for intuition, they will be valid of anything that appears to us in empirical intuition, and so there is no reason to be skeptical of the reality of space and time or of the existence of objects in space and time.

This is not to say, however, that space and time are transcendently real, i.e., real notwithstanding our subjective forms of intuition.[3] On the contrary, space and time are transcendentally ideal, meaning that once the "human standpoint" is removed, space and time do not exist.[4] Space and time are contributions of the subject to her own experience and are nothing once one leaves aside the subjective conditions of possible experience.[5] Objects apart from our sensible intuition of them are things-in-themselves and are to be contrasted with these same objects as they appear. Since cognition of any object must include the subjective conditions of space and time, things as they might exist in themselves are nothing to us. Apart from our way of intuiting things, objects do not exist in space or time. They do not have extension or bear causal relations. They do not possess any qualities that we might cognize. Therefore, we cannot be concerned with things as they might be in themselves, but should rather focus our attention on what we can cognize, viz., empirically real objects.

Just because the latter depend on our cognitive constitution for their spatio-temporal form does not mean that we cannot talk about them independently of the way they appear to individual cognizers. To the contrary, like philosophers before him, Kant maintains a distinction between the primary and secondary qualities of objects. Whereas the secondary qualities of an object (e.g., color, taste, smell, etc.) might appear differently to individual cognizers, the primary qualities of an object (e.g., shape, size, motion/rest, etc.) belong to it as an empirically real thing. Kant uses the metaphor of a rainbow to illustrate his point.[6] Whereas the droplets of water are empirically real and intersubjective (primary qualities), the colors of the rainbow are not (secondary qualities). Depending on where you are and what the light is like, the colors will appear differently to you even though the size and spatial arrangement of the water droplets remains the same. Do not forget that the intersubjectivity of their size and spatial arrangement depends on our sharing the same cognitive constitution. Even so, the intersubjectivity of space and time should not be confused with the subjectivity of secondary qualities. Whereas the former are shared by all subjects cognitively constituted like we are, the latter vary between individual subjects.[7] Considered apart from our cognitive constitution, however, the droplets possess neither size nor spatial arrangement since space and time are features of our cognitive constitution and not things-in-themselves.

Is Kant too hasty in denying the alternative? In a famous criticism, Friedrich Adolf Trendelenburg suggests that space and time might both be things-in-themselves as well as subjective forms of intuition.[8] As mentioned in chapter one, another conclusion that Kant draws in the Transcendental Aesthetic is that space and time are neither things-in-themselves (Newton) nor relations between things-in-themselves (Leibniz). Although Leibniz thinks space and time are *ideal* relations (between perceptions), these ideal relations obtain between things that exist in themselves (monads). Newton certainly thinks that space and time are *real* in themselves independently of the subject. Does Kant really do enough to preclude these options?

Here it is important to distinguish between the *epistemology* of space and time and the *metaphysics* of space and time. The first two metaphysical expositions are arguably sufficient to undermine both Leibniz' as well as Newton's epistemologies of space and time. They undermine Leibniz' epistemology since they show that the representations of space and time cannot be originally constructed from our experience of spatial and temporal relations *a posteriori*.

Likewise, they undermine Newton's epistemology insofar as his view requires that space and time be given as things-in-themselves *a posteriori* in sensibility. When it comes to the metaphysics of space and time, however, the issue is different. Even if Newton's and Leibniz' epistemologies of space and time are incorrect, could their metaphysics of space and time still be right? Could space and time still be real in themselves or relations among things that are real in themselves even if we cannot cognize this fact?

When it comes to the former option, Newton's metaphysical view seems paradoxical to Kant, i.e., that there could be two self-subsistent (exist in themselves) non-entities (empty in themselves). This second characteristic seems to undermine the first since it suggests that nothing is capable of being something.[9] In addition, since Kant has established that space and time are essential features of sensible intuition, could they really exist independently of sensible intuition? When it comes to the latter of the above options, if what was said concerning incongruent counterparts in chapter two was correct, it does not seem like space could be generated from conceptual relations among things-in-themselves. Since the concepts of incongruent counterparts agree in every way, these conceptual relations could never reveal that their objects are incongruent. This difference is based on spatial relationships which are not themselves grounded in any conceptual difference.[10] Even if space (and by extension time) cannot be relations among the concepts of things-in-themselves, could there somehow still be spatial relations among things-in-themselves or could space and time somehow be things-in-themselves? Kant would likely see both positions as posing a single problem, viz., that space and time could somehow be "transcendentally real."

There are two ways that commentators typically deal with this problem. Either one can hold that Kant is entitled to *reject* the transcendental reality of space and time or one can hold that Kant is only entitled to be *agnostic* as to the transcendental reality of space and time.[11] In deciding which view to adopt, we should consider what we can really *think* about space and time. Whereas one should *reject* the idea that there are square circles since one possesses no coherent concept of a square circle, one might be merely *agnostic* about the existence of aliens since one does at least possess a coherent concept of an alien (life form of extraterrestrial origins) even if one has never seen an alien. The agnostic position seems to assume that we can coherently *think* of the transcendental reality of space and time. Kant himself admits that we can think whatever we like as long as we do not contradict ourselves.[12] In other words, as long as we possess a coherent concept of space and time existing as things-in-themselves or as relations among things-in-themselves we can entertain the neglected alternative. Since our concepts of space and time are themselves *grounded* in the representation of space and time as *a priori* intuitions, however, it is unclear whether we really possess such a concept. For example, the concept of a textbook is grounded on the representations of different books that one has experienced in space and time. Can one think of a textbook existing non-spatially (e.g., not occupying space) or non-temporally (not existing at a time)? Although there are electronic editions of textbooks (which exist in time even if they do not exist in space), can you form any coherent conception of what you are holding in your hands not existing spatiotemporally? It is likely that you cannot. Given the source of our concepts of space and time, Kant would likely say that we can form no coherent concept of the transcendental reality of space and time. If one cannot even entertain the idea, however, this provides some reason for thinking that they are not transcendentally real.

Even so, inconceivability is not necessarily a good guide to impossibility. Perhaps, the transcendental reality of space and time is only incoherent from the human standpoint, but is not from God's omniscient standpoint. Although we cannot conceptualize it, perhaps there is some *resemblance* between space and time as God understands them as they are in themselves and space and time as forms of human sensible intuition. There are two points to be made here. First, if the resemblance between God's concept of space and time and our concept is *perfect*, then they are *identical*. If they are identical, then God's concept would be equally incoherent (not even God can consistently conceptualize a square circle or bring about contradictions). If they are not perfectly identical but just resembling to some degree, then it would no longer seem as if we are talking about *space* and *time* existing as things-in-themselves or as relations between things-in-themselves but rather about something different (call them "shmace" and "shmime") with which our space and time are somehow related. At the end of the day, there seems no way to even entertain Trendelenberg's alternative from the human standpoint, which for Kant is the only standpoint that ultimately matters.

Even if Kant is able to preclude Trendelenberg's neglected alternative, however, what of Quine's objections to the analytic/synthetic distinction discussed in the Introduction to this book? The problem is how one might draw the analytic/synthetic distinction without appeal either to conceptual containment or self-contradictoriness, ideas that Quine finds problematic. In the Introduction to this book, we suggested that Kant offers a way, in the Transcendental Aesthetic, of overcoming these problems. What is it? The key is found in the Transcendental Expositions of space and time where Kant discusses the different ways in which judgment can relate to intuition though his solution is implicit in the Introduction to *CPR*.

When the content of a judgment relates, at most, accidentally to intuition (either pure or empirical), then the proposition generated is analytic *a priori* by virtue of essential relations between concepts. Although the concepts themselves can be acquired empirically, one need only possess the relevant concepts in order to relate through judgment, with a necessity that flows from the nature of the concepts themselves, the constituent concepts in a proposition. For example, in the Introduction to *CPR*, Kant holds that one need only possess the *concepts* of "body" and "extension" in order to *judge* that "All bodies are extended" *a priori*.[13] No appeal to intuition is required to make the judgment once one has acquired the appropriate concepts.

In contrast, when a judgment relates essentially to intuition (either pure or empirical), the proposition generated is synthetic. With synthetic propositions, intuition is always required to semantically ground the judgment.[14] When a judgment requires pure intuition, the proposition generated is synthetic *a priori*. For example, as mentioned above in the Transcendental Exposition of space, Kant notes when judging that "The straight line between two points is the shortest," the concept of "the straight" has nothing to do with quantity nor does the concept of "the shortest" have anything to do with quality. Even so, the two concepts can be connected necessarily through appeal to the pure (*a priori*) intuition of space.[15] Finally, when a judgment requires empirical (*a posteriori*) intuition, the proposition generated is synthetic *a posteriori*.

Notice that the above characterization of the analytic/synthetic distinction does not make appeal to the notions of conceptual containment or self-contradictoriness. What about propositions that do not possess subject-predicate form? Since this account does not make appeal to conceptual containment, does it allow for analytic propositions that do not have subject-predicate form? This final problem requires us to have a closer look at Kant's theory of judgment in the Transcendental Analytic, something we will do in the next part of this book.

Although the Transcendental Aesthetic goes some way toward establishing transcendental idealism, it does not provide a completed argument. As mentioned above, this central thesis of *CPR* holds that we cannot cognize objects as they might exist in themselves but only insofar as they appear to us spatiotemporally and in accordance with our concepts of them where not only these concepts but space and time themselves are contributions of the subject to her experience of these objects. If Kant's arguments in the Transcendental Aesthetic are sound, then he can claim that space and time are the *a priori* forms of empirical intuition. If this is true, then he can make two other claims directly relevant to the above definition of transcendental idealism. First, as forms of intuition, space and time are contributions of the subject to her experience of objects. Secondly, since we can cognize objects only as they are given to us in accordance with these forms, we cannot cognize objects as they might exist in themselves but only insofar as they appear to us spatiotemporally. Whether our concepts are likewise necessary conditions for our cognition of objects is something Kant will consider in the Transcendental Analytic to which we now turn.

Notes

1. *CPR* A27-28/B44 and A35-36/B52.
2. *CPR* A28/B44 and A36/B52. For Kant's general definition of "objective validity," see *CPR* A89-90/B122.
3. For example, since Newton thinks that space and time exist independently of the subject as things-in-themselves, he is a transcendental realist about space and time.
4. *CPR* A26/B42.
5. *CPR* A28/B44.
6. *CPR* A45-46/B63.

7. Kant considers the possibility of subjects that have forms of intuition different from our own. See *CPR* A37/B54 and B72. Although this is possible, they would not share a common world with us.

8. Friedrich Adolf Trendelenburg, *Logische Untersuchungen* (Leipzig, Germany: Hinzel, 1862), 163. See Gardner for a fairly neutral discussion of the objection in Gardner, *Kant and the Critique*, 107-111.

9. *CPR* A39/B56. As Dicker points out, Newton would likely not be impressed by the objection since he would not grant that space and time are nothing (i.e., are not real) in themselves. See Dicker, *Kant's Theory of Knowledge*, 29.

10. Buroker uses incongruent counterparts to argue against Trendelenberg's neglected alternative. See Buroker, *Kant's Critique*, 64-68.

11. Allison defends the former view whereas Dicker defends the latter. See Allison, *Kant's Transcendental Idealism*, 128-132 and Dicker, *Kant's Theory of Knowledge*, 46-48. Although we will largely follow Allison, it is important to note that he does not offer the only defense of Kant's position. For example, Hogan argues that the necessity that flows from our *a priori* cognition of space and time is incompatible with the "absolute contingency" of the world as it is in itself. See Hogan, "Kant's Copernican Turn," 37-38.

12. *CPR* Bxxvi.

13. For this example, see *CPR* A7/B11. Although Kant uses this sentence to illustrate conceptual containment, i.e., the concept of "extension" is contained within the concept of "body," what is important for our purposes is that no reference to intuition (pure or empirical) is required to formulate the judgment even if concept acquisition requires an *a posteriori* appeal to empirical intuition.

14. See *CPR* A8/B11-12, B15-17.

15. For this example, see *CPR* B16.

Part Two

The Transcendental Analytic

Chapter Five
Introduction to the Transcendental Analytic

Whereas the Transcendental Aesthetic is concerned with enumerating the *a priori* principles of sensibility, the Transcendental Analytic is concerned with enumerating the *a priori* principles of the understanding.[1] It is a transcendental *analysis* of the understanding. Understanding is the way in which we think about the objects that are given to us in intuition. Thinking is conceptual and in the Transcendental Analytic Kant wants to not only discover the *a priori* concepts of the understanding (what he will call "categories"), but also to justify their application to the objects we experience.

An important feature of Kant's view of human cognition is that it is *discursive*. This word derives from the Latin "*discursus*" which means to run through something. In the Transcendental Analytic, Kant describes how understanding runs through the diverse representations offered by sensibility classifying them under the concepts of the understanding.[2] In this respect, concepts rest on *functions*, or the "unity of the action of ordering different representations under a common one."[3] For example, in order to recognize different representations in sensibility as constituting the representation of a textbook these representations must be unified under the concept or common representation of a textbook. This unification requires *judgment* and the result is a proposition which is truth-evaluable and deals with the relations between concepts and intuitions, one concept and another, or the relation between a set of judgments. Kant's view, in this respect, prefigures the contemporary idea that experience is not imagistic but rather propositional.[4] Your experience of the textbook in your hands is not constituted simply by a series of fleeting images, but is rather constituted by the

judgment *that* you have a textbook in your hands. You must recognize what you
have in your hands *as* a textbook. This requires judgment applying concepts to
the diverse representations given in sensibility.

According to Kant, the objects of cognition must be both *given* in sensibility
(intuition) and *thought* through the understanding (concepts). For creatures like
us, intuitions and concepts are each necessary for cognition and only through
their unification can cognition arise. Kant believes that without intuition our
concepts are *empty*, i.e., they provide no information on existing states of affairs
but rather just lead to vacuous metaphysical speculation. Even though you can
think whatever you like as long as you do not contradict yourself, nothing in the
concept being thought guarantees that there is anything in experience that answers to the concept. Without concepts, however, our intuitions are *blind*, i.e.,
they are only sensory manifolds, disorganized representational contents. Seeing
without being able to recognize what you are seeing, however, is functionally
equivalent to blindness.[5]

By recognizing these two separate sources of cognition, Kant makes a dramatic break with the philosophers that precede him in the Modern period.
Though their starting points differ, both rationalists and empiricists believe there
is a continuum between intuitions and concepts.[6] Rationalists like Leibniz hold
that concepts are cognitively fundamental and they "intellectualize" appearances
by claiming that what is given in sensible intuition is only a more confused form
of conceptual knowledge. Empiricists like Locke, in contrast, hold that sensible
intuition is cognitively fundamental and they "sensitize" our concepts by claiming that they are all ultimately the result of reflecting upon what is given in sensible intuition.[7]

Kant's break with his predecessors goes more deeply than this, however,
once one recognizes the debt that rationalism owes to Plato and the debt empiricism owes to Aristotle. Plato thought everything we learn is the result of re-
membering things that are already present in our minds from birth. This view is
reflected in how rationalists embrace innate ideas or concepts that are present in
our minds from birth. Although sensible experience might be useful in helping
us to remember these concepts, these concepts are ultimately independent of
these sensible experiences.[8] In contrast, empiricists owe a debt to Aristotle insofar as they deny the existence of ideas not derivable from sense experience. Philosophers like Berkeley and Hume even go so far as to deny the existence of
general ideas in the Lockean sense (empirical concepts for Kant). Whereas the
rationalist cannot account for how innate ideas apply to the world without the
intervention of God, empiricists cannot account for the unity of our experience
since they overlook the role of judgment in constituting our experience.[9] Although Kant will argue that we do possess certain concepts *a priori* (contrary to
empiricism), he will attempt to show how we come to acquire them as well as
how they apply to the world without the intervention of God (contrary to rationalism).

The above considerations are directly relevant to Kant's theory of transcendental idealism. Although Kant has established the fact that we can only cognize

objects insofar as they appear to us spatiotemporally in the Transcendental Aesthetic, he has not established that we can only cognize objects insofar as they are in accordance with our concepts of them. The latter, however, is equally important to Kant's theory of transcendental idealism since, without our concepts, cognition of objects would be impossible. One would be left simply with blind spatiotemporal intuitions, i.e., an incomprehensible array of representational content. Consequently, the discursivity thesis is intimately connected to Kant's theory of transcendental idealism and both reflect Kant's Copernican turn.[10] Assuming objects conform to our cognition of them, we cognize them only insofar as they appear to us, i.e., insofar as they are given to us spatiotemporally and insofar as they are thought in accordance with our concepts of them.

Now that we have talked about how Kant's project in the Transcendental Analytic relates to his more general goals in *CPR*, we must examine the project itself in greater detail. Generally considered, the Transcendental Analytic becomes progressively less abstract in each of its stages. Kant's starting point, however, could not be more abstract. He begins by looking to pure general logic which he characterizes as the "form of thinking" in order to discover the categories or our *a priori* concepts of objects.[11] Kant's logical table of judgment is meant to encompass all of the functions of thinking within a judgment where the understanding is characterized as a "faculty for judging."[12] For Kant, although we might sometimes think illogically (e.g., when making an invalid argument) and we often make false judgments, we never think alogically. Regardless of whether our judgments are true or false, Kant argues that our judgments always have the forms that he enumerates. Without them, we could not think at all. Whereas the logical table of judgments contains the rules for thinking generally, the table of categories contains the rules for thinking about objects specifically. Kant's Metaphysical Deduction (chapter six) aims to show that the categories just are these forms of judgment though directed at objects specifically rather than at thinking in general. In this chapter, we will also solve a puzzle left over from the last one, viz., how Kant's theory of judgment allows for propositions that do not possess subject/predicate form. As we will see, the subject/predicate form is only *one* of *three* different judgments of relation that Kant outlines in the logical table of judgments. By referring to the other two, we will be able to draw the analytic/synthetic distinction in a way that avoids Quine's final criticism of Kant's analytic/synthetic distinction.

Although the Metaphysical Deduction might justify our possession of the categories, it does not establish *that* the categories actually apply to the objects that we use them to think about. This task is left to the Transcendental Deduction and Kant provides two versions of the Transcendental Deduction in the A and B editions of *CPR*. We will deal with each of these versions in different chapters (chapter seven and eight respectively). Kant hopes to establish that the categories actually apply to the objects of experience by showing that the categories are necessary conditions for the possibility of the objects themselves. In these chapters, we will also start to deal with an important problem for Kant's transcendental idealism that has not yet been mentioned, viz., what affects us in sensibility according to Kant? Is it the thing-in-itself? If so, it seems as if Kant would have to apply the categories beyond the conditions necessary for their meaningful application (viz., appearances in space and time). Is it the appearance in space and time? If so, then it seems as if appearances would be their own causes, an absurd proposition by Kant's own lights.[13] To paraphrase an early criticism of Kant: without the thing-in-itself one cannot enter into Kant's system, but with the thing-in-itself one cannot remain.[14] We will argue that the key to overcoming this dilemma lies in the Transcendental Deduction.

Kant's use of the term "deduction" in the above contexts has its root in law. At the beginning of the Transcendental Deduction, Kant draws a distinction between "*quid facti*" questions (what are the facts?) and "*quid juris*" questions (what is legal?). When someone is accused of a crime, there is a distinction to be drawn between establishing what the accused actually did (*quid facti*) and establishing whether these actions were legal (*quid juris*). In much the same way, in the Transcendental Analytic, there is a distinction to be drawn between establishing what *a priori* concepts of objects we possess (Metaphysical Deduction) and establishing whether they have *legitimate* application to the objects of our experience (Transcendental Deduction).[15]

Whereas the Metaphysical Deduction deduces *what* the categories are from the logical table of judgments, the Transcendental Deduction establishes *that* the categories are objectively valid, i.e., that objects of experience are possible only through the categories.[16] In this respect, the Metaphysical Deduction and Transcendental Deduction of the Transcendental Analytic mirror the Metaphysical Expositions and Transcendental Expositions of the Transcendental Aesthetic. Whereas both the Metaphysical Deduction and the Metaphysical Expositions are concerned with exhibiting our concepts (of objects or space and time) *a priori*, the Transcendental Deduction and Transcendental Expositions are concerned with imposing substantial formal constraints on what we intuit (conceptual or spatiotemporal).[17] At the end of the Metaphysical Deduction, Kant faces the problem that there may be no fit between the objects we sense in empirical intuition and our *a priori* concepts of them.[18] The Metaphysical Deduction only establishes the subjective conditions for our thinking about objects, but not yet that these categories are objectively valid.[19] Kant demonstrates the latter by showing that the categories are necessary conditions for the objects of experience. Even if this project is successful, however, Kant must also explain *how* the categories apply to objects as they are given in empirical intuition. At first blush, there seems to be a huge chasm between the understanding and sensibility. As a faculty of judgment, the understanding is active and conceptual. In contrast, sensibility is passive and relies on intuition. How can the two relate to one another? Kant's answer is to give each of the categories a schema or "*a priori* time-determination in accordance with rules."[20] Since the schemata are rules, they are still conceptual. Since they have a temporal component, they are also sensible (time as an *a priori* form of intuition). Consequently, the schemata are "homogenous" with both the understanding as well as sensibility.[21]

Although the Schematism (chapter nine) explains how the categories can relate to empirical intuition, Kant now needs to explain how the schematized categories are necessary for the experience of objects in empirical intuition. Even though the Transcendental Deduction, if successful, establishes that the categories are necessary for the experience of objects in empirical intuition, Kant deals with the categories as a group and not individually in their schematized form. Consequently, Kant still needs to explain how *each* schematized category is necessary for our experience of objects in empirical intuition. Kant carries out this latter task in the Principles of Pure Understanding which aim to establish certain synthetic *a priori* judgments based upon these schematized categories, i.e., they are "rules of the objective use of the categories."[22] Each of the principles contains a transcendental argument, i.e., an argument that shows that a kind of experience we unquestionably have would be impossible unless a certain principle were true.[23] Put differently, each of the principles contains a *progressive* argument which begins from a fact of experience that even the skeptic would have to accept and attempts to discover the necessary conditions for its possibility. In a reversal of his *regressive* strategy in the Transcendental Expositions, in each of the Principles, Kant concludes that a certain fact of experience requires that a corresponding synthetic *a priori* principle be true where the latter incorporates a certain schematized category. Perhaps, the most famous example comes in the Second Analogy where Kant holds that our experience of any alteration (e.g., a ship altering its location by moving downstream) requires that this alteration occur in accordance with the law of the connection of cause and effect (viz., the rule for the objective use of the category of cause and effect).

Since Kant provides explicit "proofs" of the principles only in the B edition, we will focus on the B edition arguments and corresponding principles. The reader should note, however, the significant differences between the A edition and B edition versions of these principles as well as the arguments that go to support them. In both editions, however, the Axioms of Intuition (chapter ten) provide rules for the objective use of the schematized categories of quantity. The Anticipations of Perception (also chapter ten) provide rules for the objective use of the schematized categories of quality. The Analogies provide rules for the objective use of the schematized categories of relation (chapter eleven). Finally, the Postulates of Empirical Thought (chapter twelve) provide rules for the objective use of the schematized categories of modality. In the Postulates, Kant also provides a famous argument, added in the B edition, entitled the "Refutation of Idealism." There he rejects both Berkeleyan (dogmatic) as well as Cartesian (skeptical) forms of idealism. Much to his dismay, Kant was widely depicted as a Berkeleyan by his critics after the publication of the A edition and he clearly wanted to set his critics straight in the B edition.[24]

As one can see from the above discussion, whereas Kant's project in the Transcendental Analytic begins from the most abstract possible starting point (general logic as the form of thought), it becomes progressively less abstract. The Metaphysical Deduction explains how the forms of thought *generally* (logical table of judgments) might be employed to think about objects *specifically* (table of categories). Whereas the Transcendental Deduction establishes that the categories are objectively valid *collectively*, the Schematism explains how *each* category might relate to empirical intuition while the Principles explains how *each* schematized category can be incorporated into a synthetic *a priori* proposition whose truth is assumed for the possibility of particular experiences that we most certainly have.

Notes

1. *CPR* A62/B87.

2. See Buroker, *Kant's Critique*, 81. Although Kant holds that God's understanding is intuitive, ours is discursive. Rosenberg marks the difference by noting that whereas we can think a manifold of representations only by thinking of these representations in relation to one another, God can grasp the manifold of representations "all at once." Rosenberg, *Accessing Kant*, 92.

3. *CPR* A68/B93.

4. See Savile, *Kant's Critique*, pp. 34-35.

5. See *CPR* A51/B75. See also Burnham's and Young's discussion of this important passage in Burnham and Young, *Kant's Critique*, 64.

6. Altman, *A Companion to Kant's Critique*, 89.

7. *CPR* A271/B327. Although Kant will largely accept the Lockean view of empirical concept formation and even thanks Locke at *CPR* A86/B118-19, he rejects the idea that all of our concepts are ultimately empirical. Furthermore, whatever empirical concepts we form are always under the condition of the categories. See Altman, *A Companion to Kant's Critique*, 88-89.

8. For example, just as the sensible experience of figures drawn in the sand helps the slave boy to remember a geometrical formula in Plato's *Meno*, so too does Descartes' experience of the wax in the Second Meditation help him to see through his "mind's eye" the essential feature of the wax.

9. See Buroker, *Kant's Critique*, 74-75 and Savile, *Kant's Critque* 35-36. When it comes to the epistemic role that God plays in rationalism, think of Descartes' account, in Meditation Six, of how the veracity of our clear and distinct perceptions of the external world depend upon God's benevolence. As Altman notes, empiricists like Hume readily grant that the *subjective* association of sensible ideas is simply incapable of providing us with the *objective* experience of material objects that exist independently of our perceptions of them and are related in accordance with causal laws. As Kant will argue, however, our experience is of the latter kind. See Altman, *A Companion to Kant*, 87.

10. Allison makes this point in Allison, *Kant's Transcendental Idealism*, 12-13.

11. *CPR* A54/B78.

12. *CPR* A69/B94.

13. Recall Kant's claim in the Preface to *CPR* that it is absurd to think that there should be an appearance without anything that appears. See *CPR* Bxxvi-xxvii.

14. F.H. Jacobi, *David Hume über den Glauben, oder Idealismus und Realismus. Ein Gespräch*, (Breslau, Germany: Gottlieb Löwe. 1787), 223.

15. *CPR* A84/B116-17. For a nice summary see Burnham and Young, *Kant's Critique*, 71.

16. This is similar to how Winkler defines "objective validity" and he cites several passages in support of this definition, e.g., *CPR* A93/B125-126. He distinguishes this from "objective reality." A concept is objectively real just in case its object is really possible. In the case of the categories, Winkler holds that Kant proves their objective reality by establishing their objective validity. See Winkler, "The Enterprise of Deduction," 69-70.

17. Savile notes this similarity. See Savile, *Kant's Critique*, 39.

18. Kant notes that from the perspective of human cognition, however, such a possibility is "empty nugatory, and without significance" since appearances that do not fall under the categories would be nothing for us. *CPR* A90/B123.

19. Gardner notes this worry. See Gardner, *Kant and the Critique*, 129 and 136.

20. *CPR* A145/B184.

21. *CPR* A137/B176.

22. *CPR* A161/B200.

23. Burnham and Young make this point. See Burnham and Young, *Kant's Critique*, 59.

24. Christian Garve and Johann Feder discuss these criticisms in their review of *CPR* in the *Göttingische Gelehrte Anzeigen*, January 19, 1782.

Chapter Six
Metaphysical Deduction

Quote

All intuitions, as sensible, rest on affections, concepts therefore on functions. By a function, however, I understand the unity of the action of ordering different representations under a common one. Concepts are therefore grounded on the spontaneity of thinking, as sensible intuitions are grounded on the receptivity of impressions. Now the understanding can make no other use of concepts than that of judging by means of them. . . All judgments are accordingly functions of unity among our representations, since instead of an immediate representation a higher one, which comprehends this and other representations under itself, is used for the cognition of the object. [A68-69/B93-94]

If we abstract from all content of judgment in general, and attend only to the mere form of the understanding in it, we find that the function of thinking in that can be brought under four titles, each which contains under itself in three moments. [A70/B95]

The same function that gives unity to the different representations *in a judgment* also gives unity to the mere synthesis of different representations *in an intuition*, which expressed generally, is called the pure concept of the understanding. The same understanding, therefore, and indeed by means of the very same actions through which it brings the logical form of a judgment into concepts by means of the analytical unity, also brings a transcendental content into its representations by means of the synthetic unity of the manifold of intuition in general, on account of which they are called pure concepts of the understanding that pertain to objects *a priori*. . . In such a way there arise exactly as many pure concepts of the understanding which apply to objects of intuition in general *a priori*, as there were logical functions of all possible judgments in the previous table; for the understanding is completely exhausted and its capacity entirely measured by these functions. [A79/B104-5]

Synopsis

In the Metaphysical Deduction, Kant attempts to deduce, *a priori*, the rules ("categories" or "pure concepts") that the understanding uses to organize the representational content of sensibility. As rules, these categories determine how we must perceive the world around us and the objects of intuition must conform to these categories in order to be cognized. According to Kant, it is because of the categories that we perceive and judge the objects around us as actual substances that are causally related to one another. Even so, the categories operate at a much higher level of generality than our empirical concepts. For example, you probably perceive the object in your hands not merely as a substance with accidents (category), but rather as a textbook that is (hopefully) not too soporific. Kant will argue, however, that your judgment about the textbook would be impossible were it not for the categories. Although Kant is not able to establish this thesis until later in the Transcendental Analytic, he does provide a deduction of the categories themselves in this section.

The Metaphysical Deduction appears in a chapter titled, "On the Clue to the Discovery of all Pure Concepts of the Understanding."[1] The "clue" Kant is referring to are the functions of thinking in judgment described in the first quote above. In order to see how the functions of judgment provide the clue for discovering the pure concepts of the understanding, we first need to understand what the functions of judgment are. As mentioned in the last chapter, when Kant talks about the logical functions of judgment he is referring to pure general logic. This logic is pure since it is not derived from the empirical psychology of creatures like us. It is general since it abstracts from all content of thought. It considers just the form of thinking *a priori* and enumerates the rules for thinking generally.[2] Since we come to discover these forms of thought *a priori*, they in no way depend upon any contingent feature of our empirical psychology and so we can conclude that any creature cognitively constituted as we are (discursive cognition) will share these same forms of thought. For Kant, that we think in accordance with the forms of pure general logic is a brute fact about creatures cognitively constituted like us.[3] In the second quote above, Kant describes the logical table of judgments that enumerates these different forms of thought. He breaks the functions of judgment up under four "titles": quantity, quality, relation, and modality. Under each title are three "moments." For example, under the title of quantity are the moments: universal, particular, and singular. When we make any judgment producing a truth-evaluable proposition that judgment will have at least one moment from each title, regardless of the content of that judgment.[4] Kant holds that the logical table of judgments enumerates all possible relations of thought that might occur in a judgment. As premise one claims, the table is both *complete* and *a priori*.[5] Whether it is complete, however, is a source of controversy, one we will return to at the end of this chapter.

In order to illustrate Kant's idea, consider the judgment that "The professor is bombastic." This judgment is singular since I am talking about a particular professor. It is affirmative, since I am affirming that the professor is something (bombastic) rather than not something (not bombastic which does not necessarily mean he is humble).[6] It is categorical, because I am saying this of the professor. Lastly, the statement is assertoric, since I am merely saying that the professor *is* bombastic rather than that he is necessarily or possibly bombastic (although the professor is this way, with a degree of restraint, he could have been otherwise). As mentioned before, and as stated in premise one below, these forms hold true of the judgment regardless of the content. The functions of the judgment would still be the same even if we replaced "professor" and "bombastic" with the variables, "A" and "B," since the table of judgments serves only to describe the relations of thoughts to one another without regard to the content of those thoughts.

The key to the Metaphysical Deduction comes in premise five, where Kant tells us why the functions of judgment are the clue for discovering the pure concepts of the understanding. In the third quote above, Kant explains that the very same functions that unite concepts through judgment unite the manifold of intuition in general through pure concepts of the understanding. This means that the very same functions that are expressed in judgment will also be expressed in the pure concepts since the only way in which representations of any sort can be united is through these functions. The difference is that the pure concepts are necessarily related to intuition, whereas judgments are not. Whereas the logical table of judgments is meant to describe general logic, the table of categories is meant to describe transcendental logic. The latter is transcendental since it is concerned with the *a priori* conditions for thinking about objects.[7] Just as general logic enumerates the rules of thinking generally, transcendental logic enumerates the "rules of the pure thinking of an object."[8] Assuming that the table of judgments provides a complete and *a priori* list of all possible functions in judgment and that the very same functions are operative in the pure concepts, then the table of categories will provide a complete and *a priori* list of all possible pure concepts of the understanding.

The application of the functions of judgment to intuition provides Kant with the pure concepts of the understanding, or categories understood as the concepts of an object in general.[9] If Kant's deduction is successful, then for every function of judgment on the logical table of judgments, there will be a corresponding category on the table of categories. Pure general logic and transcendental logic are considering the same judgments from different points of view. Whereas the former is concerned with examining the formal features of these judgments, the latter is concerned with examining the features of these judgments that allow them to be about objects.[10]

To illustrate this idea, again consider the example that "The professor is bombastic." Since this judgment has to do with an object of intuition, it should take a moment from each of the four titles in the table of categories much as it took a moment from each of the four titles in the logical table of judgments. With respect to the categories of quantity, the judgment involves unity since my various representations of the professor (clad in tweed, loudmouthed, wildly gesticulating) are united in the representation of a single thing much as from the standpoint of logical form, the judgment predicates something of a single subject. The judgment is not about several professors (plurality) or all professors (totality) thankfully, but only about the particular professor currently lecturing to himself. When it comes to the categories of quality, the judgment takes the professor to be something rather than nothing. The professor *is* bombastic much as from the standpoint of logical form, the judgment is affirming something of a logical subject. Besides reality and negation, however, Kant also has the category of limitation. This category is applied when one is considering the degree of a particular sensation, e.g., the loudness of the professor's voice. With regard to the categories of relation, the judgment is claiming that the professor possesses a certain quality and so an accident (being bombastic) inheres in the substance (the professor) in much the same way as the predicate (being bombastic) is attached to the subject (the professor) via the logical table of judgments.[11] It does not claim anything about the causal efficacy of the professor (e.g., that he is causing my headache) or how the professor might stand in causal community with other substances (e.g., the chalk in his hand or the lectern he is pounding). Finally, when it comes to the categories of modality, the judgment concerns something that exists at a particular time much as from the perspective of logical form, the judgment asserts that something *is* a certain way. That the professor is bombastic is not a necessary fact about the world. The professor might not have existed at all or at least could have been more humble. Since the bombastic professor exists, he is possible as well. The judgment, however, claims not merely that the professor might be bombastic but that, regrettably, he is so.[12]

The connection between the logical forms of judgments of relation and the categories of relation can help Kant to overcome two significant worries: 1) Hume's skepticism concerning the source of our idea of causation, and 2) Quine's concern that Kant's analytic/synthetic distinction is limited to propositions of subject/predicate form. To begin with Hume's worry, he believes that our idea of causation (or necessary connection) can only arise *a posteriori* from the constant conjunction of resembling events which leads the mind through custom or habit to expect one event upon the occurrence of the other. This customary transition of thought or habit is the impression from which our idea of causation is copied. In contrast, Kant attempts to show that our concept of causation has an *a priori* source.

According to Kant, the hypothetical relation "If P then Q" corresponds to cause and effect when interpreted in a metaphysical sense as a category. This is not to say that all hypothetical relations entail causal relations. One could, for example, make a hypothetical judgment such as that "If Socrates is a bachelor, then Socrates is a man." This does not mean that being a bachelor *causes* Socrates to be a man. Rather, part of what it means to be a bachelor is that one is a man. Such "if. . . then. . ." judgments express a ground-consequence relation in which the antecedent provides logical grounds for the consequent. This logical relation, however, should be distinguished from the causal relation which involves a metaphysical relationship between the cause and the effect. For example, take the causal judgment that "If Socrates drinks hemlock, then Socrates dies." In this case, we would want to say that drinking the hemlock is the *cause* of Socrates' demise.

What exactly is the relationship between the two kinds of judgment? Although we have already explained the relationship between some of the forms of judgment and their corresponding categories, of all the categories, it is perhaps most important that the category of cause and effect have an *a priori* source since this will be a key component in Kant's response to Hume. Put simply, the hypothetical judgment provides the generic form of a subordination relation (consequence subordinate to logical ground) which is then realized in particular by causal subordination (effect subordinate to cause). We can explain this in terms of counterfactual asymmetry. Whereas it follows from the fact that Socrates is a bachelor that he is a man, it does not follow from the fact that Socrates is a man that he is a bachelor (he could be married). Likewise, whereas it follows from the fact that Socrates drinks hemlock that Socrates dies, it does not follow from the fact that Socrates dies that he drinks hemlock (there are many ways to kill a man). If this makes sense, then Kant has already done something that Hume considered impossible, viz., providing a way of deriving the concept of causation *a priori* without appeal to experience. All that is left is to determine whether the category of causation is objectively valid. This is something Kant begins to deal with in the Transcendental Deduction, though we will not get a complete explanation until the Analogies of Experience (chapter eleven).

Once one conjoins Kant's discussion of the judgments and categories of relation to what has already been said concerning the analytic/synthetic distinction in chapter four, one can also overcome Quine's worry that Kant's account of the analytic/synthetic distinction only allows for propositions that have subject/predicate form. The categorical judgment (subject/predicate) is only the first of Kant's three judgments of relation. The hypothetical judgment connects two propositions via the relation of ground to consequent. The disjunctive judgment connects two or more propositions via disjunction. According to Kant, every proposition that does not have subject-predicate form is ultimately built up out of propositions that do have this form.[13] It seems consistent with what Kant says that a hypothetical proposition containing two categorical propositions will be analytic just in case one need not make any essential appeal to intuition (either pure or empirical) but only to the component propositions themselves in order to make the hypothetical judgment. In this respect, our account of hypothetical judgment is much the same as Kant's account of categorical judgment except that in the former case *propositions* are being conjoined whereas in the latter case *concepts* are being conjoined to form categorical propositions.

The two propositions involving Socrates mentioned above provide clear examples of analytic and synthetic propositions that do not have subject/predicate form. The judgment that "If Socrates is a bachelor, then Socrates is a man" is an example of an analytic hypothetical proposition. Here it seems that a grasp of the two constituent propositions plus the global form of judgment is sufficient to form the hypothetical proposition without any essential appeal to intuition.[14] An example of a synthetic hypothetical judgment would be that "If Socrates drinks hemlock, then Socrates dies." This is a causal proposition which would require appeal to intuition in order to form the structure and content of the proposition.[15]

Even if one accepts Kant's derivation of the category of causation from the hypothetical form of judgment as well as the proposed responses to Hume and Quine, is there any reason to think that Kant's logical table of judgments and so the table of categories are complete? Is the first premise of the below argument really true? If not, and if there really are more logical functions of thought would not there be more corresponding categories besides the ones that Kant mentions? At this point, it is important to note that Kant's conception of logic is far closer to Aristotle than to philosophers like Boole and Frege.[16] From the perspective of contemporary truth-functional and quantificational logic, there are many problems that one might have with Kant's logical table of judgments and the corresponding table of categories.[17] As mentioned at the outset of this book, however, our concern will not be with problems *external* to Kant's philosophical perspective, but rather with problems *internal* to it.

With respect to the latter, a problem that several commentators mention is that Kant does not consider conjunctive judgments as a separate moment under the title of relation.[18] For example, Kant was certainly aware of judgments like "The textbook is long and boring." In this case, two predicates ("is long" and "is boring") are attributed to a single subject (the textbook). Should not Kant, by his own lights, have to account for this relation? Recall the three judgments of relation that Kant includes on his table: categorical, hypothetical, and disjunctive. The central difference between categorical judgments on the one hand and hypothetical as well as disjunctive judgments on the other is that categorical judgments are affirmed or denied irrespective of their relationship to other judgments. Likewise, each component of a conjunctive judgment is affirmed or denied irrespective of its relationship to the other components. The affirmation or negation of one component has no impact on the affirmation or negation of another. For example, the textbook may be long though thoroughly engaging. Conversely, it might be short though nonetheless tedious. Consequently, for Kant, the conjunctive judgment does not constitute a separate moment of thought from categorical judgments.[19] In what way do the hypothetical and disjunctive judgments constitute separate moments of thought? In both cases, the judgments related are considered "problematically," i.e., they are themselves neither affirmed nor denied but only the connection between them.[20] In hypothetical judgments, affirmation of the logical ground entails *affirmation* of the consequent (e.g., "If Socrates is a bachelor, then Socrates is a man"). In disjunctive judgments, however, affirmation of one of the disjuncts entails *denying* the others (e.g., Socrates is married or Socrates is unmarried).[21] For Kant, the components of disjunctive judgments are mutually exclusive and jointly exhaustive of the possibilities. Consequently, hypothetical and disjunctive judgments really do constitute separate moments of thought.

Even if the logical table of judgments is complete and the table of categories derived from it *a priori* is complete as well, Kant still has not established that the categories, or the ways we think about objects *a priori*, are objectively valid, i.e., that objects of experience are possible only through the categories. This is a task that Kant takes up in the Transcendental Deduction and one that we start explaining in the next chapter.

Reconstruction

1) The logical table of judgments provides a complete and *a priori* list of the functions by which the understanding can judge in general.
2) Judgments are functions of unity among our representations.
3) If the logical table of judgments provides a complete and *a priori* list of the functions by which the understanding can judge in general and judgments are functions of unity among our representations, then there are no other ways in which representations can be unified except for the functions enumerated in the logical table of judgments.
4) From (1), (2), and (3), there are no other ways in which representations can be unified except for the functions enumerated in the logical table of judgments (modus ponens).
5) If there are no other ways in which representations can be unified except for the functions enumerated in the logical table of judgment, then the same functions that unify judgments also unify the manifold of intuition in general through pure concepts of the understanding.
6) From (4) and (5), the same functions that unify concepts through judgment also unify the manifold of intuition in general through pure concepts of the understanding (modus ponens).
7) If the logical table of judgments provides a complete and *a priori* list of the functions by which the understanding can judge in general and the same functions that unify concepts through judgment also unify the manifold of intuition in general through pure concepts of the understanding, then the table of categories forms a complete and *a priori* list of pure concepts of the understanding.
8) From (1), (6) and (7), the table of categories forms a complete and *a priori* list of the pure concepts of the understanding (modus ponens).

Notes

1. Kant describes this project as a "metaphysical deduction" only later in *CPR*. See *CPR* B159.

2. *CPR* A50-55/B74-79.

3. This is true of all the formal features of cognition. See *CPR* B145-46.

4. When it comes to propositions being truth-evaluable, Kant lays out two conditions for truth: 1) the proposition must not contradict itself or any laws of the understanding. See *CPR* A59/B84. This makes the proposition a candidate for truth, 2) the proposition must be in agreement with its object. See *CPR* A58/B82. This shows that Kant subscribes to some form of a correspondence theory of truth. See also *CPR* A191/B236 and A821/B849 on this latter point.

5. *CPR* A64-65/B89.

6. Kant distinguishes between infinite judgments which *affirm* a negative property of a subject (e.g., the soul is non-mortal) and negative judgments which *deny* that a subject has a certain property (e.g., the soul is not immortal). Just because something is non-mortal does not entail that it is immortal (it could be an inanimate rock) whereas negating that something is not immortal entails that it is immortal. For Kant's rather confusing discussion see *CPR* A71-72/B97. For a fairly clear discussion of the issue see Allison, *Kant's Transcendental Idealism*, 141.

7. See Kant's definition of "transcendental" at *CPR* A11-12/B25.

8. *CPR* A55/B80.

9. *CPR* B128.

10. Altman, *A Companion to Kant's Critique*, 98.

11. As Altman notes, rationalism conflates the distinction between the subject/predicate relation (general logic) and the substance/property relation (transcendental logic). See Altman, *A Companion to Kant's Critique*, 102. Kant will rely on this distinction to criticize rationalists' claims concerning the nature of the soul in the Paralogisms (chapter fifteen).

12. Altman uses the example that "the door is open" to illustrate both the logical table of judgments as well as the categories pp. 95-96 and 99-101.

13. Hanna refers to the categorical predication as the "*Ur*-form" of all judgment. See Hanna, *Kant and Analytic Philosophy*, 62.

14. Notice in this case, much as with the judgment that "bodies are extended," even if the component propositions (or concepts) are empirical that nevertheless the proposition itself is analytic since the judgment generating this proposition does not require appeal to intuition.

15. Although we are describing the "third thing" required for the unification of concepts/propositions in synthetic judgments as simply being intuition, Kant himself describes this "third thing" as having three aspects: (1) inner sense whose *a priori* form is time, (2) imagination's synthesis of representations, and (3) the unity of apperception. See *CPR* A155/B194. Although (2) and (3) are important aspects of Kant's theory of synthetic judgment (and we will discuss both imagination and apperception at greater length in the next two chapters), (1) seems insufficient for synthetic geometrical judgments which require appeal to the pure intuition of space. This is why we describe synthetic judgment as requiring appeal to intuition generally rather than merely to the intuition of time.

16. Kant does make some modifications to Aristotle's logical forms by adding the class of singular judgments and infinite judgments. For more on why Kant makes these breaks from Aristotle, see Dicker, *Kant's Theory of Knowledge*, 54-55.

17. For a description of some of these problems, see Buroker *Kant's Critique*, 85-93.

18. For example, see Dicker, *Kant's Theory of Knowledge*, 59 and Buroker, *Kant's Critique*, 88.

19. Here we are following Allison's solution to the problem and one should also note his more general discussion of the completeness of the categories. See Allison, *Kant's Transcendental Idealism*, pp. 136-146.

20. See *CPR* A73-75/B98-100.

21. Disjunction is exclusive for Kant which is, of course, very different from the inclusive disjunction of truth-functional logic.

Chapter Seven
The A Transcendental Deduction

Quote

For this unity of consciousness would be impossible if in the cognition of the manifold the mind could not become consciousness of the identity of the function by means of which this manifold is synthetically combined into one cognition. Thus the original and necessary consciousness of the identity of oneself is at the same time a consciousness of an equally necessary unity of the synthesis of all appearances in accordance with concepts, i.e., in accordance with rules that not only make them necessarily reproducible, but also thereby determine an object for their intuition, i.e., the concept of something in which they are necessarily connected; for the mind could not possibly think of the identity of itself in the manifoldness of its representations, and indeed think this *a priori* if it did not have before its eyes the identity of its action, which subjects all synthesis of apprehension (which is empirical) to a transcendental unity, and first makes possible their connection in accordance with *a priori* rules. Further, we are now also able to determine our concepts of an *object* in general more correctly. All representation, as representations, have their object, and can themselves be objects of other representations in turn. Appearances are the only objects that can be given to us immediately, and that in them which is immediately related to the object is called intuition. However, these appearances are not things in themselves, but themselves only representations, which in turn have their object, which therefore cannot be further intuited by us, and that may therefore be called the non-empirical, i.e., transcendental object = X. [A108-109]

Both extremes, namely sensibility and the understanding, must necessarily be connected by means of this transcendental function of the imagination, since otherwise the former would be sure yield appearances but no objects of an empirical cognition, hence there would be no experience. Actual experience, which consists in the apprehension, the association (the reproduction), and finally the recognition of the appearances, contains in the last and highest (of the merely empirical elements of experience) concepts that make possible the formal unity of experience and with it all objective validity (truth) of empirical cognition. These grounds of the recognition of the manifold, so far as they concern merely the form of an experience in general, are now those categories. On them is grounded, therefore, all formal unity in the synthesis of the imagination, and by means of the latter also all of its empirical use (in recognition, reproduction, association, and apprehension) down to the appearances, since the latter belong to our consciousness at all and hence to ourselves only by means of these elements of cognition. [A124-25]

Synopsis

Although Kant answers the *quid facti* question of *what* the categories are in the Metaphysical Deduction, he must still answer the *quid juris* question of whether the categories have *legitimate* application to their objects. The Transcendental Deduction aims to show that the categories deduced in the Metaphysical Deduction are objectively valid. He tries to do this by proving that they are necessary conditions for the possibility of objects of experience. Whereas God plays the role of providing a *quid juris* of our *a priori* concepts for rationalists (for the latter innate ideas), empiricists deny there are any *a priori* concepts for which a *quid juris* might be needed. If Kant's Metaphysical Deduction is successful, however, then there are *a priori* concepts (the categories) for which the *quid juris* question must be answered. Kant will not answer this question by appealing to divine intervention and will also attempt to show that by the empiricist's own lights, the categories are required for our experience of objects.

What does the empiricist mean by our "experience of objects?" Empiricists like Berkeley and Hume are empirical idealists, which is to say that they affirm the reality of sensible ideas and forbid inferences to anything beyond them. For them, our experience of objects is reducible to the contents of consciousness itself as a unified set of representations. The question then becomes: how is our consciousness unified? For Berkeley, the answer is simple: consciousness is unified by the fact that all of its representations are modifications of a single mind (immaterial thinking thing). Hume rejects this view, however, since we possess no impression of a mind to which these representations could be attributed. This creates a huge problem for Hume and one that he recognizes in the Appendix to the *Treatise of Human Nature*. He wants to hold that consciousness is a bundle or unity of successive representations. Each of the representations within the bundle is supposed to be distinct from the others. According to Hume, distinct representations are distinct existences. Hume also holds that the mind never perceives any real connection among distinct existences. If this is true, however, then there cannot be any real connection among our representations and so no bundle of perceptions. In other words, Hume's view on the unity of consciousness undermines itself.[1] One might retreat to the idea that representations can merely be associated with one another without being really connected. This is not sufficient, however, for a unity of consciousness. Imagine two students, call them Mary and John. Whenever Mary thinks about her homework John feels fear and loathing. Whenever John feels fear and loathing Mary thinks about her homework. Although these two representations are associated with one another, they are not unified in one consciousness since neither Mary nor John thinks both about the homework while feeling fear and loathing.[2]

Kant breaks from the empiricist by holding that the unity of consciousness depends upon our experience of objects where these objects are not reducible simply to the contents of consciousness. In a very important way, objects of experience are necessary for the unity of consciousness. At the same time, however, the unity of consciousness is necessary for the objects of experience. Without consciousness of objects, we could not recognize diverse representations as belonging to a single consciousness. Likewise, without the unity of consciousness, we could not recognize diverse representations as individual objects. For Kant, subjects and objects are interdependent. This is a point we will return to again in the next chapter.

In the A edition Preface to *CPR*, Kant claims that the Transcendental Deduction contains both a subjective and an objective phase.[3] Whereas the subjective phase is meant to explain *how* the understanding functions in our experience of objects, the objective phase is meant to show *that* the categories are necessary conditions for the possibility of objects of experience. Kant's primary target is clearly the latter. Some commentators hold that the A Transcendental Deduction is so tilted toward the former, however, that it seems little more than an exercise in psychology.[4] Furthermore, Kant's own statement of where to find the deduction (*CPR* A92-93) is of little help since this passage does more to articulate the problem of the Transcendental Deduction than it does to solve it. This leaves commentators casting about in the 35 pages of the A Transcendental Deduction for an argument.

Above, we have identified two quotations that we think expose the central argument of the A Transcendental Deduction. As will become clear, however, there are several other passages that are equally relevant. In the first of the above quotes, the argument begins by assuming that there is a unity of consciousness where this is understood as a necessary unity of one's representations. Following the quote, we begin our reconstruction below in the same way. This unity is necessary since without it there would be no *single* consciousness but rather only a manifold of diverse representations (Hume's problem). Since this unity is necessary, whatever brings about this unity must be *a priori*. We already know that the categories are *a priori* functions of unity or rules of synthesis from the Metaphysical Deduction (see chapter six). The central idea is that the categories, as *a priori* rules of synthesis, are required to produce the unity of consciousness (premise two), but they do so by unifying objects of experience (premise five). The *a priori* rules for the unity of consciousness are the same as those for the unity of objects of experience.[5] For Kant, the unity of consciousness is what provides us with our relationship to a unified object of experience.[6] Since the categories are required for the unity of objects of experience, they are going to be objectively valid of them as well.

Kant says that all of our representations must be "ordered, connected, and brought into relations" through time, which is the form of all appearances in general (see chapter one).[7] In other words, our representations must be synthesized. Here it is evident that Kant concedes the Humean point that the representations themselves do not provide the relations they bear to one another. How we make sense of our representations is not settled by the representations themselves. For example, that the book on the table is not part of the table while the leg of the table is a part of it is not settled by the book, the table, or the leg.[8] Making sense of these representations requires synthesis since without it we only have jumbled and unrelated representations, not unified objects of experience. One might think of it like a jigsaw puzzle. In order to experience the unified picture, one must bring the various pieces together according to a concept (the picture on the box). Likewise, Kant thinks that in order to experience a unified object, one must bring the various representations of the object together according to the categories.[9] As the second quote above notes, the synthesis of these different representations is a function of the imagination.[10] The imagination has a foot in the understanding as well as in sensibility. Essentially, imagination just is the understanding insofar as it relates to sensibility.[11] The imagination, however, always combines representations in accordance with rules where the pure concepts of the understanding are the *a priori* rules of synthesis. This is not something new. In the Metaphysical Deduction, Kant describes the categories as guiding the imagination in unifying our representations insofar as these representations have to do with objects. The categories express the exact same functions of unity in intuition as the logical forms do in judgment.[12] For our representations to be related to an object means that they are related to one another in a rule-governed way.[13]

The synthesis Kant describes is three-fold. First, there is the synthesis of apprehension in intuition where the manifold (or disorganized representational content) of intuition is unified into a single representation in a given moment.[14] Second, there is the synthesis of reproduction in the imagination through which apprehended representations are unified with one another over time.[15] Imagination allows us to hold in our minds apprehended representations that are no longer present in intuition and connect them to those we are currently apprehending. Finally, there is the synthesis of recognition in the concept whereby these temporally ordered representations are recognized in the concept of an object and so brought to the unity of consciousness.[16] It is at this point that Kant mentions "transcendental apperception." This is the formal unity of consciousness that precedes the representational content of consciousness and allows one to think of these representations as one's own.[17] Thinking requires concepts and so in order to think of these temporally ordered representations as ours requires that they be recognized under concepts. Most generally, in order for there to be a unity of consciousness, transcendental apperception must be able to recognize these temporally ordered representations as falling under the categories or the understanding's concepts of objects in general. Recognizing these representations under concepts is how we think of these representations as our own.

Through the three-fold synthesis, the A Transcendental Deduction offers a provisional account of how the categories serve to determine the objects given in sensible intuition. In line with the opening passages of the Transcendental Analytic, it is only through the unification of concepts (in this case the categories) and sensible intuition that the cognition of objects arises. It is important not to think of these different syntheses as being independent processes. Rather, much like a Chinese box, they are nested within one another.[18] The unity of consciousness assumes the synthesis of recognition in a concept which itself assumes the reproduction in imagination while the latter assumes the apprehension in intuition. To illustrate Kant's idea, consider the sentence you are reading right now. Each of the twelve words of the sentence must be apprehended individually, but if each word were apprehended by a distinct consciousness (e.g., you read one word, then pass it off to your friend who reads another), there would be no consciousness of the whole sentence. It seems clear that the words must all be represented by one consciousness in order for there to be consciousness of the sentence, but how does this happen? As each word is apprehended, one must also represent the words that one has already read as a string of words. They must be reproduced in memory along with whatever word of the sentence you are currently apprehending. Finally, in order to cognize this set of twelve words as a sentence, one must recognize that they fall under the concept of a sentence. It is through the reproduction of these words and their recognition in a concept that one is conscious of the string of words as a sentence.[19]

In addition to objects being synthesized in these three ways by imagination in accordance with the categories, Kant also claims in the first quote above, that all objects of experience correspond to what he calls the transcendental object. This is the concept of an object "corresponding to and also distinct from the cognition."[20] The idea here is that there must be something thought of as distinct from ourselves to which the unity of our representations corresponds. That thing which is thought of as corresponding to the unity of our representations is always one and the same thing ($= X$), though the unity of representations that is related to this object may be very different in different cases. For example, the subject might have a unified whole of representations under the concept of a textbook or a table, but in each of these cases the subject must think of some object as corresponding to that unity of representations such that there is some object distinct from the subject that the subject is experiencing.

Premise four makes the crucial point that the objects of experience are nothing more than these apprehended representations reproduced in imagination, and recognized under the concept of an object to which the transcendental object $=$ X corresponds. This leads to the crux of the argument in premise five. If the categories are assumed for each of these syntheses as *a priori* rules of synthesis, then they are also assumed for the possibility of objects of experience. This is the *quid juris* that the Transcendental Deduction is meant to establish, viz., that the categories have legitimate application to the objects of experience. If the categories are necessary conditions for the objects of experience, then they are objectively valid of them.

Notice that, unlike rationalists, Kant does not rely on the benevolence of God to insure the objective validity of our *a priori* concepts. The fact that we must think of something, distinct from ourselves, as corresponding to a unified whole of representations in order for that unified whole to count as an object of experience is also an important departure from the empirical idealism of philosophers like Berkeley and Hume who believe that an object of experience can be reduced to the contents of consciousness. In order for something to count as an object of experience, according to Kant, it must be thought of as distinct from the unity of consciousness. Although we have talked about how Kant's view in the Transcendental Deduction provides a response to empiricists like Berkeley and Hume, what about Locke? Locke is not an empirical idealist in the same way as philosophers like Berkeley and Hume since he thinks that an object of experience constrains our perceptions of it. The problem is that his view assumes the object unites our sensible ideas without explaining how we come to attribute these sensible ideas to the object in the first place.[21] Kant's doctrine of the three-fold synthesis along with his conception of the transcendental object fills this lacuna in Locke's theory. Experience of unified objects is not somehow given and then later interpreted by the mind; rather our representations of objects must be worked into experience of unified objects. This idea ties into Kant's Copernican turn. The objects of experience appear as objects of experience because they are cognized as objects of experience (object conforms to cognition). The objects of experience are not cognized as objects of experience because they appear as objects of experience (cognition conforms to object).

There are several problems that commentators have with the A Transcendental Deduction. As mentioned above, one might worry that it is too much an exercise in psychology to convincingly establish the objective validity of the categories. The connection between the Metaphysical Deduction and the A Transcendental Deduction is also unclear since Kant's theory of judgment is completely absent from his discussion of synthesis in the A Transcendental Deduction.[22] Finally, the A Transcendental Deduction seems more interested in describing the conditions of unified *consciousness* rather than the conditions of unified *self*-consciousness (i.e., being able to reflect upon the unified consciousness we possess). The latter is equally important, however, in describing the kind of conscious life creatures like us enjoy. Just as Hume's theory is insufficient to guarantee the unity of consciousness, Kant's theory in the A Transcendental Deduction seems insufficient to guarantee the unity of self-consciousness.[23]

Reconstruction

1) The unity of consciousness is the consciousness of the necessary unity of all one's representations.

2) If the unity of consciousness is the consciousness of the *necessary* unity of all one's representations, then these representations must be synthesized by imagination in accordance with the categories, i.e., the *a priori* rules of synthesis.

3) From (1) and (2), these representations must be synthesized by imagination in accordance with the categories (modus ponens).

4) These representations are synthesized by being apprehended in intuition, reproduced in imagination, and recognized in the concept of an object to which the transcendental object = X corresponds where the result of this three-fold synthesis is an object of experience.

5) If these representations must be synthesized by imagination in accordance with the categories, and they are synthesized by being apprehended in intuition, reproduced in imagination, and recognized in the concept of an object to which the transcendental object = X corresponds where the result of this three-fold synthesis is an object of experience, then the categories are necessary conditions for the possibility of objects of experience.

6) From (3), (4), and (5), the categories are necessary conditions for the possibility of objects of experience (modus ponens).

Notes

1. Hume, *Treatise*, 636. See also Rosenberg, *Accessing Kant*, 55.

2. This example is adapted from Robert Wolff, *Kant's Theory of Mental Activity* (Cambridge, MA: Harvard University Press, 1963), 108-9.

3. *CPR* Axvi-xvii.

4. For example, see Altman, *A Companion to Kant's Critique*, 122 and Strawson, *The Bounds of Sense* (London: Methuen & Co, 1966), 31-32.

5. Altman makes this point. See Altman, *A Companion to Kant's Critique*, 121.

6. See *CPR* A109.

7. *CPR* A99.

8. This example is from Altman, *A Companion to Kant's Critique*, 124.

9. This example is from Rosenberg, *Accessing Kant*, 130. See also Kant's example of representing a house in the B edition Transcendental Deduction. *CPR* B162.

10. Kant makes the same point earlier in the Metaphysical Deduction. See *CPR* A78/B103-4.

11. Rosenberg makes this point in Rosenberg, *Accessing Kant*, 119.

12. *CPR* A78-79/B103-5.

13. Dicker makes this point in Dicker, *Kant's Theory of Knowledge*, 103.

14. *CPR* A98-100.

15. *CPR* A100-2.

16. *CPR* A103-114. Although Kant only mentions imagination explicitly in this synthesis, given Kant's general account of synthesis in the A Transcendental Deduction, we know the other two are functions of the imagination as well.

17. *CPR* A106-7. See also B132. Kant contrasts transcendental apperception with empirical apperception. Whereas the latter is just a stream of representations in inner sense, the former is what makes it possible for us to be aware of this stream as our own.

18. H.J. Paton uses this metaphor. See H.J. Paton, *Kant's Metaphysic of Experience*, 2 vols. (New York: Macmillan Publishing, 1936) I:354-55.

19. This example is inspired by one offered by William James. If twelve men are each given one word of a twelve word sentence, this could not result in consciousness of the whole sentence. See William James, *Principles of Psychology* (New York: Henry Holt, 1890), I.160. The basic idea, however, can be traced back to an argument Kant himself makes. See Kant, *Metaphysik Mrongovius,* 107-287 in *Lectures on Metaphysics,* trans. Karl Ameriks and Steve Naragon (Cambridge: Cambridge University Press, 1997), originally from 1782-1783, 29:905.

20. *CPR* A104.

21. Altman raises this worry. See Altman, *A Companion to Kant,* 116.

22. Guyer sees this as the main problem with the A edition Transcendental Deduction. In the Metaphysical Deduction, the categories are applied through judgment. In the A edition Transcendental Deduction, however, Kant does not connect apperception to judgment and so it is unclear how apperception involves application of the categories. See Paul Guyer, "The Deduction of the Categories: The Metaphysical and Transcendental Deductions," in *The Cambridge Companion to Kant's Critique of Pure Reason*, 133-34.

23. Buroker raises this worry. See Buroker, *Kant's Critique*, 115.

Chapter Eight
The B Transcendental Deduction

Quote

In the above proposition, therefore, the beginning of a *deduction* of the pure concepts of the understanding has been made, in which, since the categories arise *independently from sensibility* merely in the understanding, I must abstract from the way in which the manifold for an empirical intuition is given, in order to attend only to the unity that is added to the intuition through the understanding by means of the category. In the sequel (§26) it will be shown from the way in which the empirical intuition is given in sensibility that its unity can be none other than the one the category prescribes to the manifold of a given intuition in general according to the preceding §20; thus by the explanation of its *a priori* validity in regard to all objects of our senses the aim of the deduction will first be fully attained. [§21, B144]

The manifold that is given in a sensible intuition necessarily belongs under the original synthetic unity of apperception, since through this alone is the *unity* of the intuition possible (§17). That action of the understanding, however, through which the manifold of given representations (whether they be intuitions or concepts) is brought under apperception in general, is the logical function of judgments (§19). Therefore all manifold, insofar as it is given in *one* empirical intuition is *determined* in regard to one of the logical functions for judgment by means of which, namely, it is brought to a consciousness in general. But now the *categories* are nothing other than these very functions for judging, insofar as the manifold of a given intuition is determined with regard to them (§13). Thus the manifold in a given intuition also necessarily stands under categories. [§20 B143]

Thus even the *unity of the synthesis* of the manifold, outside or within us, hence also a *combination* with which everything that is to be represented as determined in space or time must agree, is already given *a priori*, along with (not in) these intuitions, as conditions of the synthesis of all *apprehension*. But this synthetic unity can be none other than that of the combination of the manifold of a given *intuition in general* in an original consciousness, in agreement with the categories, only applied to our sensible intuition. Consequently all synthesis, through which even perception itself becomes possible, stands under the categories, and since experience is cognition through connected perceptions, the categories are conditions of the possibility of experience, and are thus also valid *a priori* of all objects of experience. [§26 B161]

Synopsis

There are several changes that Kant makes in the B Transcendental Deduction. First, whereas the A Transcendental Deduction was largely a *subjective* deduction explaining *how* the understanding functions in our experience of objects, the B Transcendental Deduction is largely an *objective* deduction showing *that* the categories are objectively valid of the objects of experience. Although this is the same conclusion he argues for in the A Transcendental Deduction, the argumentative order of the deduction is reversed which brings into relief its different focus. Whereas the A Transcendental Deduction begins with the unity of consciousness and ends with the objects of experience, the B Transcendental Deduction begins with the objects of experience and then considers what the necessary conditions are for our cognition of them. This helps to remove the impression that the Transcendental Deduction is merely an exercise in psychology. Another difference between the two deductions is that Kant's theory of judgment is a central feature of the B Transcendental Deduction which helps to connect the latter to the Metaphysical Deduction. A third difference between the two deductions is that the B Transcendental Deduction deals not only with the conditions for the unity of consciousness, but also with the conditions for the unity of self-consciousness.[1] Consequently, Kant's B Transcendental Deduction, if successful, will be a more accurate description of the kind of conscious experience creatures like us actually possess. Finally, the argumentative structure of Kant's B Transcendental Deduction is far clearer in the text than the A Transcendental Deduction. In the first of the above quotes, Kant makes clear that the deduction will be given in two phases with the second phase (§26) presupposing the success of the first (§20). Whereas the §20 argument aims to prove that the manifold of intuition in general stands necessarily under the categories insofar as it is represented as united, the §26 argument builds upon this conclusion by aiming to prove that the categories are necessary conditions for the possibility of objects of experience. In other words, whereas the argument in §20 aims to show that the categories are necessary for the unity of the manifold *in general*, the argument in §26 aims to show that the categories are necessary for the unity of empirical manifold *in particular*. In the below reconstruction of the combined argument, premises (1)-(9) belong to the §20 argument, whereas the remaining premises come from the §26 argument. Unlike the A Transcendental Deduction, the heart of Kant's B Transcendental Deduction is actually given in the passages he cites. This is not to say, however, that all the premises of the B Transcendental Deduction are given in these sections.

In order to understand the starting point of Kant's B Transcendental Deduction, one must first understand what an object is for Kant. His definition is not at all surprising given what he said in the A Transcendental Deduction. In §17 of the B Transcendental Deduction, Kant holds that an object is "that in the concept of which the manifold of a given intuition is united."[2] This should remind one of the synthesis of recognition in a concept from the A Transcendental Deduction. For Kant, an object is the representation of a united manifold of intuition and like Kant we begin our reconstruction below under the assumption that there are objects of experience that fall under this definition. As the second premise of the below argument makes clear, the unification and representation of this manifold, however, are only possible through transcendental apperception which brings our representations under a single consciousness. In §16-17 of the B Transcendental Deduction, Kant spends a lot more time discussing transcendental apperception than he did in the A Transcendental Deduction. Although Kant does not use the phrase "transcendental apperception" in the B edition, he uses several phrases that stand for the exact same concept, e.g., "pure apperception," "original apperception," and the "original synthetic unity of apperception." What he is describing is the "*I think*" that accompanies all of my representations since without it these representations could not be thought of as mine.[3] In both editions, transcendental apperception stands in contrast to empirical apperception.[4] Empirical apperception is the unity of consciousness at a given time. Although this is a unity of consciousness, it is not a unity of consciousness over time. The latter requires transcendental apperception (self-consciousness) recognizing that all these moments of empirical apperception (unities of consciousness) are themselves moments in the conscious life of a single individual. Unfortunately, Kant does not do a good enough job in the A Transcendental Deduction distinguishing the unity of consciousness at a time from the unity of consciousness over time which requires self-consciousness.[5] To illustrate Kant's point, consider the following example: This morning I was aware of the coffee cup in my hand. This afternoon, I was aware of the bombastic professor in my class. Right now, I am aware of the sentence I just read. Each of these representations of a unified object of experience (mug, professor, and sentence) corresponds to a distinct moment of empirical apperception or unity of consciousness. Without transcendental apperception, however, there would be no way for me to recognize all of these moments as belonging to a single conscious life. Consequently, self-consciousness is required to truly describe the kind of unity that my conscious life possesses.

After talking about the role that transcendental apperception has to play in uniting my conscious life, he goes on to ask how transcendental apperception goes about doing this? He gives his answer in the §20 (second quote above). In the fourth premise of the argument, Kant holds that representations, in general,

are united through the logical functions of judgment. Going back to the Metaphysical Deduction, one might recall that these logical functions of judgment are
the clue for discovering the categories or pure concepts of the understanding. In
fact, as premise seven of the argument notes, the categories just are these logical
functions of judgment as applied to an object of intuition in general. If we follow Kant's line of thought closely here, it becomes apparent that since the logical functions of judgment are needed for transcendental apperception to unify its
representations in a single consciousness whatever they might be, and the categories just are those logical functions of judgment when applied to intuition
generally, since objects just are unified manifolds of intuition, these objects will
require the categories for their unity. Kant describes this as the *intellectual* synthesis since it has to do with intuition in general not with the form (space and
time) or content (sensation) of human intuition in particular.[6]

The second phase of the B Transcendental Deduction in §26 (third quote
above) assumes the conclusion of the argument in §20 but also claims in premise ten below that what is true of intuition in general must also be true of our
form of intuition in particular (spatiotemporal). One can think of this in terms of
types and tokens. If it is true of textbooks as a type of thing that they are boring,
then this will also be true of any token textbook (e.g., the one that you are holding). Our form of intuition is simply a token of the more general type "intuition." In §24, Kant argues that much as the manifold of intuition in general is
subject to the categories for its unity so too is the manifold of pure intuition
(space and time) subject to the categories for its unity. Kant refers to this as the
figurative synthesis of intuition where the *intellectual* synthesis described above
is a condition for its possibility.[7] As premise twelve notes, perception just is the
empirical consciousness of this unity. In other words, perception is the representation of the unity of the manifold of empirical intuition *a posteriori*. At this
point, Kant describes perception in terms of the synthesis of apprehension from
the A Transcendental Deduction.[8] Whereas the A edition argues that the synthesis of apprehension, along with the other forms of synthesis, are required for the
possibility of objects of experience, the B edition deduction argues that the synthesis of apprehension unifies a manifold of empirical intuition where this unification presupposes the figurative synthesis of pure intuition which itself presupposes the intellectual synthesis of intuition in general where each form of
synthesis is subject to the categories. Consequently, a three-fold synthesis subject to the categories shows up in both the A and B edition Transcendental Deductions, though in somewhat different guises. In addition, whereas the imagination is at the forefront of Kant's account of synthesis in the A Transcendental
Deduction, in the B Transcendental Deduction it is deemphasized in favor of
transcendental apperception and the faculty of judgment.[9] In the last steps of the
§26 argument, Kant claims that since experience is cognition through connected
perception and since the categories are required for perception, they will be required for the possibility of experience. One might also note that the categories
will be required for the connection of perceptions in experience as well (e.g.,
causal claims).[10] Since the categories are required for any experience whatso-

ever, the categories will be necessary conditions for the possibility of any object of experience, i.e., they are objectively valid. Tying this back into the starting point of the argument, insofar as an object of experience is the representation of a united manifold of empirical intuition and the categories are required for this unity, the categories are going to be necessary conditions for the possibility of objects of experience.

Although the B Transcendental Deduction is a significant improvement over the A Transcendental Deduction, there are still some problems as well as some questions that are left unanswered. One classic objection to the Transcendental Deduction (in either edition) is that it does not allow for dreaming or hallucinations since these are not experiences of objects. As C.I. Lewis quipped, "Did the sage of Königsberg have no dreams?"[11] The idea is that if representations can only be unified by referring to objects of experience, then it seems as if we could not have dreams where representations are clearly unified though they do not refer to objects of experience. Unfortunately, this is not a question that Kant can answer at the end of the Transcendental Deduction, though it is one that he takes up when he gets to the Refutation of Idealism (chapter twelve). The main idea is that the possibility of dreams and hallucinations relies upon us having experience of an objective world. The categories do not distinguish dreams from reality but rather chaos from order even if this order is a dream or hallucination.[12] There are other unanswered questions at the end of the Transcendental Deduction. For example, although the Transcendental Deduction might answer the *quid juris* question by establishing *that* the categories have legitimate application to the objects of experience, *how* are they applied to the objects of experience? The subjective A Transcendental Deduction goes some way toward explaining how the understanding functions in experience, but given the radical heterogeneity between the categories (intellectual) and intuitions (sensible), it is nevertheless unclear exactly how the former are supposed to apply to the latter. This is a topic that Kant takes up in the Schematism (next chapter). In addition, the Transcendental Deduction at best shows that the categories in *general* are objectively valid though it does not show that any *specific* category is objectively valid. This is a topic that Kant will take up in the Principles (chapter ten through twelve).[13]

At the end of the day, the Transcendental Deductions establish that the categories have legitimate application to the objects of experience since these objects are themselves possible only through the categories. An interesting conclusion that can be derived from combining the A and B Transcendental Deductions (i.e., the subjective and objective deductions) is that objects and subjects mutually condition one another. Subjects and objects are fundamentally interdependent. Arguably, understanding the interdependence of the unity of the subject and the unity of the object is the key to understanding the whole Transcendental Deduction.[14] In the subjective deduction, Kant begins with subjects and gets objects. In the objective deduction he begins with objects and gets subjects. Regardless of which way we start we see that the other one is necessary. Subjects and their synthetic activity are required in order to have unified manifolds of intuition (objects). Conversely, the representations of the unified manifolds (objects) are required in order for there to be a subject that recognizes itself as identical over time. Without the representational content provided by these objects through affection, one could not be self-consciousness (see also the Refutation of Idealism in chapter twelve). There would not be any subject because subjectivity requires representations to be unified within one consciousness by transcendental apperception in accordance with the categories. Without that you just have a bare activity of the *I think* (transcendental apperception) without anything being thought. Absent the unity of consciousness the subject would not be related to an object, but absent the relation to an object there would be no unity of consciousness. Adapting one of Kant's own quotes to make the point, one commentator quips that "self-consciousness without perceptions is empty; inner sense without apperception is blind."[15]

We will argue in the conclusion to Part Two that the interdependence of subjects and objects provides a way of understanding Kant's theory of affection without committing him to affection by things-in-themselves (which would violate the constraints placed on the application of the categories) or affection by appearances (which would make the effects of affection their own causes). Kant discusses the cognitive constraints on the categories at greater length in the Schematism to which we will now turn. The main idea is that the categories only have legitimate cognitive application within the bounds of sense. Although they can be used to think of things-in-themselves beyond these bounds, they can no longer serve a cognitive function.

Reconstruction

1) There are objects of experience where an object is the representation of a united manifold of intuition (definition of "object" from B137).
2) If the manifold of intuition is represented as united, then transcendental apperception must unite the manifold of intuition in a single consciousness (see §17).
3) From (1) and (2), transcendental apperception must unite the manifold of intuition in a single consciousness (modus ponens).
4) The logical functions of judgment are the means by which representations, in general, are united by transcendental apperception (see §19).
5) If transcendental apperception must unite the manifold of intuition in a single consciousness and the logical functions of judgment are the means by which representations, in general, are united by apperception, then the logical functions of judgment are required for transcendental apperception to unite the manifold of intuition in a single consciousness.
6) From (3), (4) and (5), the logical functions of judgment are required for transcendental apperception to unite the manifold of intuition in a single consciousness (modus ponens).

7) The categories are these functions of judgment with regard to the manifold of intuition in general (from the Metaphysical Deduction).

8) If the logical functions of judgment are required for transcendental apperception to unite the manifold of intuition in a single consciousness and the categories are these functions of judgment with regard to the manifold of intuition in general, then the manifold of intuition in general stands necessarily under categories insofar as that manifold is represented as united.

9) From (6), (7), and (8), the manifold of intuition in general stands necessarily under categories insofar as that manifold is represented as united (modus ponens).

10) If the manifold of intuition in general stands necessarily under categories insofar as that manifold is represented as united, then the manifold of sensible intuition (spatiotemporal) stands necessarily under the categories insofar as that manifold is represented as united (see §24).

11) From (9) and (10), the manifold of sensible intuition (spatiotemporal) stands necessarily under the categories insofar as that manifold is represented as united (modus ponens).

12) Perception is the empirical consciousness of this unity.

13) If the manifold of sensible intuition (spatiotemporal) stands necessarily under the categories insofar as that manifold is represented as united and perception is the empirical consciousness of this unity, then the categories are necessary conditions for the possibility of perception.

14) From (11), (12), and (13), the categories are necessary conditions for the possibility of perception (modus ponens).

15) Experience is cognition through connected perceptions.

16) If the categories are necessary conditions for the possibility of perception and experience is cognition through connected perceptions, then the categories are required for the possibility of experience.

17) From (14), (15), and (16), the categories are required for the possibility of experience (modus ponens).

18) If the categories are required for the possibility of experience, then they are necessary conditions for the possibility of objects of experience.

19) From (17) and (18), the categories are necessary conditions for the possibility of objects of experience (modus ponens).

Notes

1. Dicker makes this point. See Dicker, *Kant's Theory of Knowledge*, 130.
2. *CPR* B137.
3. It is important to note that Kant is not inferring his existence as a simple thinking thing from the fact that he thinks. He will challenge this Cartesian inference in the Paralogisms (chapter fifteen).

4. Compare the contrast between transcendental and empirical apperception in the A edition of *CPR* (A106-7) with the contrast between pure and empirical apperception in the B edition (B131-32). See also Altman's discussion of the difference between transcendental and empirical apperception. Altman, *A Companion to Kant's Critique*, 126.

5. Rosenberg argues that both Descartes and Hume make this error, viz., inferring from (1) I think X & I think Y & I think Z to (2) I, who think X = I, who think Y = I, who think Z. See Rosenberg, *Accessing Kant*, 124. Insofar as Kant's A Transcendental Deduction makes the same error, it is important that he avoid it in the B edition.

6. *CPR* B151.

7. *CPR* B151.

8. *CPR* B160-61.

9. Imagination does still have a role in driving synthesis in the B Transcendental Deduction. This is important since transcendental apperception belongs solely to the understanding whereas imagination bridges the gap between the understanding and sensibility. See *CPR* B151-52.

10. See Kant's example of perceiving water freezing. *CPR* B162-63.

11. C.I. Lewis, *Mind and the World Order: Outline of a Theory of Knowledge* (Mineola, NY: Dover, 1956), 221. Königsberg was Kant's hometown in Prussia.

12. Beck makes this point. See Lewis White Beck, "Did the Sage of Königsberg Have no Dreams?," in *Kant's Critique of Pure Reason: Critical Essays*, 109-114.

13. Allison emphasizes the incompleteness of the B Transcendental Deduction and how it must be supplemented by both the Schematism and Principles. See Allison, *Kant's Transcendental Idealism*, 201. Guyer makes a similar point. See Guyer, "The Deduction of the Categories," 146-150.

14. Altman seems to think so. See Altman, *A Companion to Kant's Critique*, 130.

15. Altman, *A Companion to Kant's Critique*, 129. Compare with *CPR* A51/B75, "Thoughts without content are empty, intuitions without concepts are blind."

Chapter Nine
Schematism

Quote

In all subsumptions of an object under a concept the representations of the former must be *homogeneous* with the latter, i.e., the concept must contain that which is represented in the object that is to be subsumed under it. . . Now pure concepts of the understanding, however, in comparison with empirical (indeed in general sensible) intuitions are entirely unhomogeneous, and can never be encountered in any intuition. Now how is the *subsumption* of the latter under the former, thus the application of the category to appearances possible since no one would say that the category, e.g., causality, could also be intuited through the senses and is contained in the appearance. . . Now it is clear that there must be a third thing, which must stand in homogeneity with the category on the one hand and the appearance on the other, and makes possible the application of the former to the latter. This mediating representation must be pure (without anything empirical) and yet *intellectual* on the one hand and *sensible* on the other. Such a representation is a *transcendental schema*. . . Now a transcendental time-determination is homogenous with the *category* (which constitutes its unity) insofar as it is *universal* and rests on a rule *a priori*. But it is on the other hand homogenous with the *appearance* insofar as *time* is contained in every empirical representation of the manifold. Hence an application of the category to appearances becomes possible by means of the transcendental time-determination which, as the schema of the concept of the understanding, mediates the subsumption of the latter under the former. [A137-39/B176-78]

Synopsis

In the Transcendental Deduction Kant argued *that* the categories have legitimate application to objects of experience. In the Schematism, Kant intends to explain *how* the categories are applied to objects given in empirical intuition. This question might seem strange. After all, is there any meaningful sense in which one might possess a concept but not be able to apply it?[1] It is important to note that Kant's problem is not with the *applicability* of the categories (this was already established in the Transcendental Deduction), but rather with empirical conditions for their application.[2] As the first premise below notes, the problem is that the categories and empirical intuition are not homogenous with one another. Concepts, including the categories, are not homogenous with intuition in at least two ways: 1) concepts are general representations whereas their instances given in intuition are particular representations, and 2) concepts are intellectual representations whereas intuitions are sensible representations.[3] The problem is particularly acute for the categories. Given their *a priori* origin in the logical table of judgments, the categories are extremely general representations that possess absolutely no sensible content. While this is not a problem for a philosopher like Leibniz who holds that sensation is just a confused mode of conceptual thinking, it is a serious problem for Kant given his bifurcation of sensibility and understanding.[4]

Assuming that the Transcendental Deduction is successful, however, there must be some way of understanding the categories such that what is given in intuition can conform to them. Kant suggests that there is some third thing which mediates between a category on the one hand and empirical intuition on the other.[5] This intermediary must be homogeneous with both. In other words, it must both particularize as well as sensitize the categories. He calls this the *schemata*.

To understand this problem it may help to consider a more familiar example. The legislature is the branch of government that makes laws. People (alas) commit crimes. These crimes have to be captured by those laws in some fashion. If you simply tried to apply the law as written by the legislature to concrete cases, however, the law would be too general and would not allow for discrimination between individual cases. To resolve this problem we have a separate branch of government that is involved in interpreting those laws such that they can be applied to concrete cases, viz., the judiciary. So, just as laws written by the legislature are not homogenous with specific crimes that are committed (i.e., as written those laws are too general to be applied to the criminal acts), so too are the categories of the understanding heterogeneous with empirical intuition (i.e., the nature of the former is different in kind from the latter so as to prohibit application). Additionally, just as the judiciary mediates between the legislature and the crimes committed in such a way so as to allow application of laws to crimes, the schemata acts as an intermediary between the categories and empirical intuition.

There are two ways in which concepts can be said to apply to objects: 1) a concept applies to an object when it falls under the concept as one of its instances, 2) a concept applies to an object if the way in which the object is used is determined by the concept functioning as a rule.[6] Focusing on (2), Kant argues in premise six that since the categories are the *a priori* rules of synthesis (something we know from the Metaphysical and Transcendental Deductions) and since the schemata must be homogeneous with the categories, the schemata must rest upon the *a priori* rules of synthesis. When it comes to empirical intuition, in premise eight he argues that since all appearances are in time (something established in the Transcendental Aesthetic) and the schemata must be homogeneous with empirical intuition, then the schemata must have a temporal character. Consequently, the schemata must rest upon the *a priori* rules of synthesis and must have a temporal character if they are to be both homogenous with the categories and empirical intuition. The crux of the argument comes in premise ten. If the schemata rest upon *a priori* rules of synthesis and have a temporal character, then the schemata allow empirical intuitions (temporal) to be subsumed under categories (*a priori* rules of synthesis). By possessing aspects that are common to both empirical intuition and the categories, the schemata explain *how* the categories are applied to objects in empirical intuition.

In the above quote, Kant says that the schemata are transcendental time-determinations of the categories. They are transcendental in that they are conditions for the possibility of experience. With regard to time, each of the schematized categories involves a temporal component. This is what *sensitizes* the categories.[7] Lastly, they are determinations insofar as the categories are going to be able to determine something with regards to time. The categories are applied to empirical intuition by being understood as thoughts about time. The schemata *particularize* the categories as concepts of an object in general to determinate modes of sensible presentation.[8] Since particular images are never going to be fully adequate to a general concept, the schematized categories are not themselves particular images, but are rather procedures for generating images.[9] Kant's view of schemata allows him to avoid a problem that Berkeley poses for Locke's theory of abstract ideas. Locke believes the abstract idea (or concept) of a triangle, for example, represents all triangles (since it is the general representation of a triangle) and none of them (since it is not identical to any particular instance of a triangle) at the same time.[10] If one thinks of the abstract idea as an image, Berkeley notes that one simply cannot frame this contradictory image in one's mind.[11] Kant's schemata do not face this worry since they are not themselves images, but rather just procedures for their production. Since he believes that both the pure concepts (categories) as well as empirical concepts will possess schemata, Kant's theory of concepts can avoid the problem that faces Locke's theory of abstract ideas.[12]

Since the schemata have a foot both in the understanding (concepts) as well as in sensibility (intuition), it is not surprising Kant holds that imagination is what generates the schemata since it too has a foot in both parts of human cognition.[13] In particular, given the fact that the schemata are transcendental time-determinations, the function of the imagination in generating schemata is close to the one described in the figurative synthesis of the B Transcendental Deduction. The schemata offer a procedure for constructing the formal intuition of time.[14]

At this point, an example might well be useful. For the category of causality, Kant gives the schema of "the real upon which, whenever it is posited, something else always follows. It therefore consists in the succession of the manifold insofar as it is subject to a rule."[15] If something is a cause, then it is something real (a substance), which when posited, something else always (rule-governed) follows (time via succession). So the schematized category is going to have a rule based component, and also a temporal component. It offers a procedure for constructing the formal intuition of rule-governed temporal succession. If we step back for a moment, we can reflect on how Kant arrived at the schematized category of causation. In the Transcendental Analytic, Kant has moved from the hypothetical relation as a purely logical function of judgment, to cause and effect as a category of the understanding, and then to the schematized category as a transcendental time-determination. An interesting point that Kant makes at the end of the Schematism is that only the schematized categories can provide cognition of objects. When discursive creatures like us use unschematized categories to make theoretical claims beyond the bounds of sensible intuition (space and time), they have "only a logical significance" and are merely "functions of the understanding for concepts, but do not represent any object."[16] In other words, when one deploys an unschematized category beyond the bounds of sense in a theoretical context, one does nothing more than signify the corresponding function of thought represented in the logical table of judgments.[17] Although one can *think* what one wants using these logical forms, this will not result in the *cognition* of any object. This limitation on the cognitive significance of the categories will have important implications for the problem of affection which we will return to in the final chapter of Part Two.

Whereas the Schematism is meant to show how the categories are applied to objects given in empirical intuition, the Principles of Pure Understanding provide rules for the objective use of these schematized categories. In the next three chapters, we will reconstruct the arguments that Kant gives to justify these synthetic *a priori* principles.

Reconstruction

1) Categories and empirical intuitions are not homogenous with one another.
2) If categories and empirical intuitions are not homogenous with one another, then some third thing (schemata) mediates between categories and empirical intuition by being homogeneous with both of them.
3) From (1) and (2), schemata mediate between categories and empirical intuitions by being homogeneous with both of them (modus ponens).
4) Categories are *a priori* rules of synthesis.

5) All appearances are in time.
6) If the schemata are homogenous with categories and the categories are *a priori* rules of synthesis, then the schemata must rest upon *a priori* rules of synthesis.
7) From (3), (4), and (6), schemata must rest upon *a priori* rules of synthesis (modus ponens).
8) If the schemata are homogeneous with empirical intuition and all appearances are in time, then the schemata must have a temporal character.
9) From (3), (5), and (8), schemata must have a temporal character (modus ponens).
10) If the schemata must rest upon *a priori* rules of synthesis and have a temporal character, then the schemata allow empirical intuitions (temporal) to be subsumed under categories (*a priori* rules of synthesis).
11) From (7), (9), and (10), the schemata allow empirical intuitions to be subsumed under categories (modus ponens).

Notes

1. This objection is raised by, among others, Jonathan Bennett. See Jonathan Bennett, *Kant's Analytic* (Cambridge, Cambridge University Press, 1966), 150.

2. This is Allison's response. See Allison, *Kant's Transcendental Idealism*, 203.

3. Buroker makes this distinction. See Buroker, *Kant's Critique*, 139.

4. Rosenberg notes this difference. See Rosenberg, *Accessing Kant*, 142.

5. Buroker notes that this problem is a version of Plato's "third man" argument from the *Parmenides*. See Buroker, *Kant's Critique*, 136.

6. Rosenberg, *Accessing Kant*, 150.

7. It is important to note that by making the categories sensible, Kant is not reducing them to *a posteriori* reflections on sensible data as Locke would have it. For Kant, the categories will still be *a priori*; they will just be supplemented by an *a priori* temporal component.

8. Rosenberg makes this point. See Rosenberg, *Accessing Kant*, 149.

9. *CPR* A140/B179.

10. Locke, *Essay*, IV.8.9.

11. Berkeley, *Principles*, Introduction §13.

12. For empirical concepts, Kant uses the example of the concept of a dog. See *CPR* A141-42/B180-81. Dicker thinks that Kant might still face Berkeley's objection if the images generated by the schemata are not fully determinate. See Dicker, *Kant's Theory of Knowledge*, 216.

13. *CPR* A140/B179.

14. Sarah Gibbons makes this point. See Sarah Gibbons, *Kant's Theory of Imagination: Bridging Gaps in Judgment and Experience* (Oxford: Oxford University Press, 1994), 56-57.

15. *CPR* A144/B183.

16. *CPR* A147/B186-87. Kant gives an example using the unschematized category of substance which he characterizes as signifying nothing more than the relation between

subject and predicate, i.e., the first relation of thinking in a judgment from the logical table of judgments.

17. Kant makes this point explicitly at *CPR* A242.

Chapter Ten
Axioms and Anticipations

Axioms of Intuition: All intuitions are extensive magnitudes (B202).

Quote

All appearances contain, as regards their form, an intuition in space and time, which grounds all of them *a priori*. They cannot be apprehended, therefore, i.e., taken up into empirical consciousness except through the synthesis of the manifold through which the representations of a determinate space or time are generated, i.e., through the composition of that which is homogenous and the consciousness of the synthetic unity of this manifold (of the homogenous). Now the consciousness of the homogeneous manifold in intuition in general, insofar as through it the representation of an object first becomes possible, is the concept of a magnitude (*Quanti*). Thus even the perception of an object, as appearance, is possible only through the same synthetic unity of the manifold of given sensible intuition through which the unity of the composition of the homogenous manifold is thought in the concept of a *magnitude*, i.e., the appearances are all magnitudes and indeed *extensive magnitudes*, since as intuitions in space or time they must be represented through the same synthesis as that through which space and time in general are determined. [B202-3]

Synopsis

As mentioned in the introduction to Part Two, Kant describes the Principles of Pure Understanding as rules for the objective use of the categories.[1] They are synthetic *a priori* judgments that describe how the categories are applied for the possibility of objects of experience. The Principles are meant to supplement both the Transcendental Deduction and the Schematism. Whereas the Transcendental Deduction treats the categories as a group, the Principles discuss the objective validity of the categories individually. Whereas the Schematism provides a way of understanding how the categories can be applied to empirical intuition, the Principles enumerate the synthetic *a priori* rules for applying the schematized categories to empirical intuition. Each principle offers a synthetic *a priori* rule that explains how an individual category (or set of categories) is employed for the possibility of experience. As mentioned above, Kant claims in the Introduction to *CPR* that the central problem the book is meant to address is how synthetic *a priori* judgments are possible. Since Kant only fully answers this question in the Principles, it should be considered the heart of his project. The Principles are broken into four sections corresponding to the four titles of the table of categories: Axioms of Intuition (quantity), Anticipations of Perception (quality), Analogies of Experience (relation), and Postulates of Empirical Thought (modality). In the Axioms and the Anticipations, there is only one principle for the categories of quantity and another for the categories of quality. Each principle, however, incorporates all three categories under the respective title within the principle. The reason that Kant uses the plural form is because the Axioms are meant to provide the fundamental principle for the many axioms of geometry while the Anticipations are meant to provide the fundamental principle for the many principles of the mathematics of infinitesimals. The Axioms and Anticipations are meta-mathematical principles.[2] The Axioms, Anticipations, and Analogies are all progressive arguments insofar as they assume that our experience possesses certain undeniable features and then attempt to show that certain synthetic *a priori* propositions must be true in order for our experience to possess those features. Although the Postulates contain an important argument in the B edition called the "Refutation of Idealism," Kant does not provide arguments for but rather just definitions of the rules for the objective application of the categories of possibility, existence, and necessity.

We have already mentioned that the Axioms and Anticipations are mathematical principles. What Kant means is that these principles secure the amenability of reality to different sorts of measurement. They show that the world as it appears is geometrically and arithmetically mathematizable. Given the constraints Kant places on the legitimate application of the schematized categories, these principles do not hold (as Descartes thought) of the world as it might be in itself.[3] Specifically, Kant thinks these principles are required to represent the magnitude of an object in empirical intuition (both with respect to its spatiotemporal extent as well as the intensity of the sensations it produces). That the objects of experience possess these features is not something Kant questions (this is what makes the arguments progressive). Rather, he will argue that if they are to possess these features, then certain synthetic *a priori* principles must be true. The principle of the Axioms is listed above in bold and we have done the same thing for the principle of the Anticipations below.

While the Axioms and Anticipations are *mathematical* principles, Kant holds that the Analogies and Postulates are *dynamical* principles. Whereas the mathematical principles are *constitutive* since they are intuitively certain, the dynamical principles are *regulative* since they concern the relations of things that are given as existing in empirical intuition. While we can be certain *a priori* that any object given in empirical intuition will have the kinds of magnitude that the Axioms and Anticipations describe, we cannot be certain *a priori* that anything will actually be given in empirical intuition or to what other objects this object will be related spatiotemporally.[4]

In the Axioms of Intuition, Kant demonstrates that all intuitions, whether they are pure or empirical, are going to have extensive magnitude. An extensive magnitude is one where the representations of its parts make possible the representation of the whole.[5] He begins his argument by explaining that the consciousness of a homogeneous manifold in pure intuition requires composition of the parts of space (or time) with one another. As spatial (or temporal) parts, they are all of the same kind and so homogeneous with one another. The synthetic unity of the manifold of pure intuition simply is the unification of these parts with one another.

The key to the argument comes in premise two since this is where Kant incorporates the schematized category. In the above quote, he says that the composition described in the first premise requires the concept of magnitude. Magnitude, as the schematized category of quantity, is the *a priori* rule of synthesis by which these spatial (or temporal) parts are unified with one another.[6] It stipulates that the representation of an extensive magnitude requires the successive addition of its homogenous parts. As all schemata, the concept of magnitude is an *a priori* rule of synthesis with a temporal (succession) component. Although it might seem strange that the three categories of quantity would only have one schema, if one looks at the three categories closely, one can see how they are all involved in this schema. One must begin with individual parts (unity), adding them together successively (plurality), in order to represent a whole extensive magnitude (totality). This idea is not entirely new of course. It should remind one of the three-fold synthesis of the A Transcendental Deduction as well as the figurative synthesis of the B Transcendental Deduction insofar as it is operating at the level of pure intuition. To illustrate his idea at the level of pure intuition, Kant offers the example of drawing a line in thought. It requires "successively generating all its parts from one point," i.e., considering a point where the line begins and then successively thinking of the other parts of space that the line passes through.[7]

It follows from this that the consciousness of the homogeneous manifold in pure intuition requires both the composition of the parts of space (or time) and the concept of magnitude for that composition. Premise five is another important move in the argument. Since any representation of an object in empirical intuition is spatiotemporal (something we know from the Transcendental Aesthetic), whatever is required for the consciousness of a homogeneous manifold in pure intuition will also be required for the representation of an object in empirical intuition. More specifically, what is required for the composition of a whole in pure space and time (e.g., the line) will also be required for the composition of a whole object in empirical space and time. Therefore, the representation of an object in empirical intuition is going to require the successive addition of the object's spatial and temporal parts as well as the concept of magnitude for this synthesis. As premise eight notes, if *both* the manifold of pure intuition and the manifold of empirical intuition require this kind of composition, then "*all* intuitions are extensive magnitudes" (the principle of the Axioms of Intuition).

In what way do the Axioms of Intuition serve as a meta-mathematical principle for the axioms of geometry? One way of thinking about this is in terms of the Pythagorean Theorem. It holds that the square of the two legs of a right triangle add up to the square of the hypotenuse. We can know that the theorem is true both of the right triangle we construct *a priori* in geometrical space as well as of a right triangle we experience out in the world *a posteriori*, e.g., a ship's sail, since both the geometrical lines as well as the lines of the sail are extensive magnitudes. Both the geometrical figure and the sail are constructed in the exact same way, viz., through the successive addition of parts that leads to the representation of the whole. What is true of the geometrical figure (the relations between the lengths of the sides) must be true of the sail as well since both are objects in space constructed in the exact same way.[8]

One worry with the Axioms is that Kant's position on measurement seems to contradict the position he argued for in the Transcendental Aesthetic. In the former, he claims that the parts of an extensive magnitude in space and time precede the whole, but in the latter he claims that space and time are singular wholes that precede their parts.[9] When philosophers get into trouble, they typically try to make a distinction before they change the subject. Let us see if Kant can overcome this problem using the former strategy without appeal to the latter. It seems as if a distinction can be drawn between the *indeterminate* representation of space and time (unsynthesized manifold) that Kant is discussing in the Transcendental Aesthetic and the *determinate* representations (synthesized manifolds) he is discussing in the Axioms of Intuition (and elsewhere in the Transcendental Analytic).[10] In fact, Kant says explicitly in the above quote that he is concerned with the latter. To illustrate, consider that while geometrical space is a singular whole that precedes its parts, the drawing of a line is a determinate limitation of this otherwise indeterminate space where the parts of the line do precede the whole (e.g., when drawing a line in thought).

Reconstruction

1) The consciousness of a homogeneous manifold in pure intuition requires composition (synthesis) of the manifold of pure intuition (as extensive magnitude).

2) By definition of the schematized category, the concept of magnitude (quantity) is required for the composition of the manifold of pure intuition.

3) If the consciousness of a homogeneous manifold in pure intuition requires composition of the manifold of pure intuition and by definition of the category, the concept of magnitude (quantity) is required for the composition of the manifold of pure intuition, then the consciousness of a homogenous manifold in pure intuition requires composition of the manifold in accordance with the concept of magnitude.

4) From (1), (2), and (3), the consciousness of a homogenous manifold in pure intuition requires composition of the manifold in accordance with the concept of magnitude (modus ponens).

5) Whatever is required for the consciousness of a homogenous manifold in pure intuition is also required for the representation of an object in empirical intuition.

6) If the consciousness of a homogenous manifold in pure intuition requires composition of the manifold in accordance with the concept of magnitude and whatever is required for the consciousness of a homogenous manifold in pure intuition is also required for the representation of an object in empirical intuition, then the representation of an object in empirical intuition requires composition of the manifold (as extensive magnitude) in accordance with the concept of magnitude.

7) From (4), (5), and (6), the representation of an object in empirical intuition requires composition of the manifold (as extensive magnitude) in accordance with the concept of magnitude (modus ponens).

8) If the consciousness of a homogenous manifold in pure intuition and the representation of an object in empirical intuition both require composition of the manifold in accordance with the concept of magnitude, then all intuitions are extensive magnitudes.

9) From (4), (7), and (8), all intuitions are extensive magnitudes (modus ponens).

Anticipations of Perception: In all appearances the real, which is an object of the sensation has intensive magnitude, i.e., a degree (B207).

Quote

Perception is empirical consciousness, i.e., one in which there is at the same time sensation. Appearances, as objects of perception, are not pure (merely formal) intuitions, like space and time (for these cannot be perceived in themselves). They therefore also contain in addition to the intuition the materials for some object in general (through which something existing in space or time is represented), i.e., the real of the sensation, as merely subjective representation, by which one can only be conscious that the subject is affected, and which one relates to an object in general. Now from the empirical consciousness to the pure consciousness a gradual alteration is possible, where the real in the former entirely disappears, and a merely formal (*a priori*) consciousness of the manifold in space and time remains; thus there is also possible a synthesis of the generation of the magnitude of a sensation from its beginning, the pure intuition = 0 to any arbitrary magnitude. Now since sensation in itself is not an objective representation, and in it neither the intuition of space nor that of time is to be encountered, it has, to be sure, no extensive magnitude, but yet it still has a magnitude (and indeed through its apprehension, in which the empirical consciousness can grow in a certain time from nothing = 0 to its given measure), thus it has an *intensive magnitude*, corresponding to which all objects of perception, insofar as they contain sensation, must be ascribed an *intensive magnitude*, i.e., a degree of influence on sense. [B207-8]

Synopsis

In the Anticipations of Perception, Kant argues that all of our sensations have an intensive magnitude. Unlike extensive magnitude, which concerns appearances in a quantitative manner (i.e., spatiotemporal extension), intensive magnitude concerns our appearances in a qualitative manner (i.e., degree of intensity). Extensive magnitudes are additive in a way that intensive magnitudes are not. For example, when you add one gallon of water at 50 degrees to another gallon of water at 100 degrees, although you get two gallons of water (extensive magnitude) you do not have two gallons of water with a temperature of 150 degrees (intensive magnitude).[11] As the first premise below notes, for Kant, all magnitudes are either extensive or intensive. Sensation, which is the result of being affected by objects, is the matter of appearance. As the second premise points out, the matter of appearance has a magnitude distinct from its spatiotemporal form. Here, think of any sensation like a color, taste, smell, or sound. It will always have a degree of intensity (e.g., hot pink as more intense than soft pink) different from the spatiotemporal character of the thing producing this sensation (e.g., a pink elephant or flamingo). Extensive magnitudes depend on spatiotemporal form since they require the successive addition of spatiotemporal parts. Intensive magnitudes, in contrast, are not dependent in this way on the form of appearances. So Kant can infer in premise six that the matter of appearance has an intensive magnitude. The key to the argument is premise seven which holds that the schematized category of reality, which falls under the categories of quality, is the means by which we represent this intensive magnitude. It is what allows us to think of intensive magnitude and when applied to sensation cognize it. The objects of empirical intuition possess a *reality* in producing sensations that is irreducible to their spatiotemporal form. Kant's view, in this respect, marks a distinct break from other philosophers of the Modern period. For Descartes and Locke, the nature of matter is exhausted by extension (i.e., filling space). For Kant, however, this conception of matter is all form (extensive magnitude) with no content (intensive magnitude).[12] Much as we can know *a priori* that any object given in empirical intuition will have an extensive magnitude, we can also know *a priori* that the sensations it produces will have an intensive magnitude or "a degree of influence on sense" (the conclusion of Kant's argument in the Anticipations). Both claims are intuitively certain *a priori* which returns us to Kant's description of the Axioms and Anticipations as mathematical principles.

Although Kant's focus on reality in the Anticipations might seem to ignore the other categories of quality, if one turns back to the Schematism and compares what Kant says there to what he says in the Anticipations, one can see that the other schematized categories of quality are not irrelevant.[13] As Kant says in the above quote, the intensity of any sensation can diminish gradually until it disappears. Representation of the absence of sensation (i.e., "nothing = 0") requires the category of negation. Likewise, the representation of a determinate quality on a continuum (e.g., hot pink on the continuum of shades of pink) requires the schematized category of limitation. Incorporating these other categories also helps to explain how the Anticipations are the meta-mathematical principle for the mathematics of infinitesimals. The idea is that intensive magnitudes are *continuous*, i.e., no degree of sensation is ever the smallest (e.g., the lightest shade of pink). The quality of the sensation is always capable of further diminution. Although Kant believes that extensive magnitudes are also continuous (no region of space is ever the smallest, no moment of time is ever the shortest), he chooses the Anticipations to make this point about infinitesimals.[14] The central conclusion of Kant's argument in the Anticipations, however, is that the real, the object of sensation represented by the schematized category of reality, has an intensive magnitude, i.e., a degree of influence on sense.

One worry for Kant's view in the Anticipations is that it seems to assume a causal theory of perception that is at odds with his theory of affection.[15] Sensations, the matter of appearance, are supposed to be produced by objects affecting us in sensibility. If these sensations are produced by non-spatiotemporal things-in-themselves, however, then as we learned in the Schematism, the category of causation would have to be illegitimately applied beyond the bounds of sense. Notwithstanding this limitation, it taxes the imagination to conceive of how something outside of space and time could possibly produce effects within space and time. One response is to hold that things-in-themselves might be in space and time (Trendelenberg's neglected alternative). The final chapter of Part One, however, argued against this option. Another option is to hold that appearances are themselves the causes of affection. This would make appearances (here the matter of appearance) their own causes, which is equally taxing to imagine if not downright absurd. Although we are not in a position to solve this problem right now, we will return to this issue in the final chapter of Part Two. As we will argue, the solution to this problem hinges on the interdependency of subjects and objects which was a central thesis of the Transcendental Deduction.

Reconstruction

1) Magnitudes are either extensive or intensive.
2) The matter of appearance (object of sensation) has a magnitude independent of its form (space and time).
3) Extensive magnitude depends on the form of appearance (space and time).
4) If the matter of appearance has a magnitude independent of its form and extensive magnitude depends on this form, then the matter of appearance has a magnitude which is not an extensive magnitude.
5) From (2), (3), and (4), the matter of appearance has a magnitude which is not an extensive magnitude (modus ponens).
6) From (1) and (5), the matter of appearance has an intensive magnitude (disjunctive syllogism).
7) The schematized category of reality is necessary for the consciousness of intensive magnitude.
8) If the matter of appearance has an intensive magnitude and the schematized category of reality is necessary for the consciousness of intensive magnitude, then in all appearances the real, which is an object of the sensation has intensive magnitude, i.e., a degree.
9) From (6), (7), and (8), in all appearances the real, which is an object of the sensation has intensive magnitude, i.e., a degree (modus ponens).

Notes

1. *CPR* A161/B200.

2. See Paul Guyer, *Kant and the Claims of Knowledge* (Cambridge: Cambridge University Press, 1987), 190-91 and Rosenberg, *Accessing Kant*, 165-66.

3. Savile, *Kant's Critique*, 66-67.

4. See *CPR* A160-62/B199-202 and A178-79/B220-22.

5. *CPR* A162/B203.

6. *CPR* A142-43/B182.

7. *CPR* A162-63/B203.

8. See *CPR* A165-66/B206-7. For this particular example, see Dicker, *Kant's Theory of Knowledge*, 63-64.

9. See the third Metaphysical Exposition of space and the fourth Metaphysical Exposition of time. Wolff, among others, raises this worry. See Wolff, *Kant's Theory of Mental Activity*, 62.

10. This is Arthur Melnick's response (following Patton). See Arthur Melnick, *Kant's Analogies of Experience* (Chicago: University of Chicago Press, 1974), 18. Dicker makes a similar response. See Dicker, *Kant's Theory of Knowledge*, 64.

11. Buroker makes this point. See Buroker, *Kant's Critique*, 157.

12. Rosenberg makes this point. See Rosenberg, *Accessing Kant*, 164-65.

13. *CPR* A143/B182.

14. *CPR* A169/B211.

15. See Dicker's discussion of the problem of affection as it relates to the Anticipations of Perception. Dicker, *Kant's Theory of Knowledge*, 69-70.

Chapter Eleven
Analogies of Experience

First Analogy: in all change of appearances substance persists, and its quantum is neither increased nor diminished in nature (B224).

Quote

All appearances are in time, in which, as substratum (as persistent form of inner intuition), both *simultaneity* as well as *succession* can alone be represented. The time, therefore, in which all change of appearances is to be thought, lasts and does not change; since it is that in which succession or simultaneity can be represented only as determinations of it. Now time cannot be perceived by itself. Consequently it is in the objects of perception, i.e., the appearances, that the substratum must be encountered that represents time in general and in which all change or simultaneity can be perceived in apprehension through the relation of the appearances to it. However, the substratum of everything real, i.e., everything that belongs to the existence of things, is *substance*, of which everything that belongs to existence can be thought only as a determination. Consequently that which persists, in relation to which alone all temporal relations of appearances can be determined, is substance in the appearance, i.e., the real in the appearance, which as the substratum of all change always remains the same. Since this, therefore, cannot change in existence, its quantum in nature can also be neither increased nor diminished. [B224-25]

Synopsis

Whereas the Principles are the heart of Kant's project in *CPR*, the Analogies of Experience are the heart of Kant's project in the Principles since it is here that Kant finally offers an answer to Hume's skepticism concerning causation. As you might recall, Hume's skepticism with respect to causation (and other issues) is what originally awoke Kant from his dogmatic slumber and inspired him to write *CPR*. There are three principles in the Analogies with each principle corresponding to a different category of relation. An "analogy" is when we say that a relation between one pair of things has a structural similarity with a relation between a second pair of things. College entrance exams are (in)famous for including these kinds of analogies. For example, a bibliophile is to books as a philosopher is to. . . wisdom, of course! The Analogies explain the relations between objects or events in a way structurally similar to the way general logic governs the relation between concepts or propositions.[1] For example, in the First Analogy, Kant holds that properties are to substances as predicates are to subjects (both are modifications of something else that does not change). Whereas categorical judgments have only to do with the relations of concepts, however, the category of substance has to do with the relationship between an independently existing thing and its properties. The schematized version of this category gives it a temporal interpretation, viz., "the persistence of the real in time" which serves as a substratum for changes in time.[2] In the First Analogy, Kant gives us the rule for the objective use of the schematized category of substance in empirical intuition.

As a progressive argument, the First Analogy begins with an undeniable fact about our experience, viz., that appearances stand in temporal relations of simultaneity and succession.[3] When I perceive a leaf and the branch it is attached to, I perceive these objects at the same time (simultaneity). When I perceive a leaf changing color, I perceive a change in the states of an object over time (succession). The central question is what allows me to distinguish between objects (simultaneous appearances) and events (successive appearances)? If such relations are to occur, then there must be something persistent in the appearance that does not change, some constant by reference to which we can represent appearances as related in these ways. For example, if the leaf did not *persist* through the change of *its* color, there would be no sense of *it* changing color. As another example, consider time-lapse photography. Each photograph represents a particular moment, and each one is successive to another. Let's say these photographs were combined to make a flipbook. Each photograph in the flipbook is related, but not merely because they are photographs. They are related because of the content of the photographs themselves, i.e., the same scene being shot over time. If the photographs were of completely unrelated scenes, there would be no sense of them representing a single temporal sequence. It is that which persists within the pictures that give this impression.

We know that *something* must persist through the changing of appearances, and the second premise gives us three options for what persists. Either what persists is time itself, apprehension of the manifold of appearance (an option Kant mentions immediately after the above quote), or by definition of the schematized category above, substance. The basic structure of each of Kant's arguments in the Analogies follows the same format. Kant starts with a feature of our temporal experience. He then asks what makes this feature possible. In each case, he offers (1) time itself, (2) apprehension, or (3) application of the relevant relational category as possible explanations. After dispensing with the first two options, he explains how the third option is successful in explaining what makes this feature of our temporal experience possible.

How does Kant dismiss the first option? As he says in the above quote, time itself cannot be perceived and so cannot be the persistent in appearance. Time is not an *object* of empirical intuition like the leaf in the above example but rather a *form* of empirical intuition. When it comes to the second option, in the same way as each photograph in a flip-book represents a particular moment and each photograph is successive to and different from the previous photograph, the apprehension of the manifold of empirical intuition offers a synopsis of the manifold at a particular moment and each synopsis is successive to and different from the previous synopsis.[4] Since apprehension is *successive* and changing, however, it cannot help us to distinguish between successive (events) and simultaneous (objects) appearances. Apprehension simply is not the right kind of thing to serve as the persistent in all change of appearances. Just like time, apprehension is a feature of the subject. After dismissing these options in premises four and five, he turns to the nature of the object as a substance in premise six.

This is the crux of the argument. The persistent has to be substance, which, by definition of the schematized category ("persistence of the real in time") persists through all change of appearances. The schematized category of substance allows us to think of something persisting in appearance and when applied to empirical intuition cognize it. In premise seven, Kant claims that since substance persists through all change of appearances, it remains the same throughout all these changes. In other words, its quantum (amount) cannot be increased or diminished in nature where nature is understood as the sum total of these appearances.[5] The idea is that although the states of substances *change* (i.e., one state goes out of existence and is replaced with another), the substances that underlies these changes only suffer *alteration* (i.e., they remain in existence through all change of states).[6]

Unlike the rationalists, Kant does not try to establish the existence of substance from mere concepts.[7] Although the schematized category of substance is *a priori*, the existence of substance can only be established *a posteriori* by applying this category to what is given in empirical intuition. At the same time, unlike the empiricists, this does not make substance unknowable (Locke) or its existence dependent upon perception (Berkeley). All we need to know about substance is that it is "the way in which we represent the existence of things (in appearance)."[8] To hold that the existence of substance depends on perception is to get things backwards. Substances do not exist *because* we perceive them. Rather, we perceive them *because* they exist. There must be things that persist regardless of whether we perceive them since they are a condition of our perceiving objects at all.[9] When it comes to the empiricists, there is finally Hume's own view that the ideas of persistence and duration are mutually supporting fictions.[10] Although Kant would agree that persistence and duration are mutually supporting, he would reject the idea that they are fictions. With respect to persistence, objects persist if and only if duration can be measured.[11] With respect to duration, however, Kant has taken himself to have established the objective validity of the schematized category of substance (persistence of the real in time) through his arguments in the Transcendental Analytic.[12]

One worry with Kant's argument in the First Analogy shows up in premise seven. Why should the fact that in any change of appearance substance persists imply that its quantum neither increases nor diminishes in nature, i.e., that substances never arise or perish absolutely? The reason why Kant makes this claim is pretty clear once one recalls his comments concerning natural science in the Introduction to *CPR*. He claims there that in order for pure natural science to be possible it must have certain synthetic *a priori* principles. One that he mentions is that "in all alterations of the corporeal world the quantity of matter remains unaltered."[13] The principle he is defending in the First Analogy just is a version of the law of conservation of mass.[14] It seems that as long as substances overlap in their existence with one another, however, that there would never be a case of change without substance persisting, but that the total amount of substance in the world could always be variable. The problem is that Kant is inferring from the *persistence* (existence at some times) of substance to its *permanence* (existence at all times or sempiternality), but this inference seems illegitimate.[15]

But in the Transcendental Aesthetic, as you might recall, Kant argues that all times belong to one singular and successive time. If the empirical *unity* of time is to be maintained, all experience must take place within the *same* temporal continuum. For any experience of something arising, there must be a determinate point in time at which this arising occurs within the temporal continuum. This requires connecting the experience of arising with something that exists prior to it within the continuum whereby one could locate the moment at which the new substance arises. If a substance arises *absolutely* (and so adds to the quantity of substance), then it arises from an empty time wherein there is *nothing* out of which the substance arises. Besides being no object of possible experience, empty time offers no connection to any prior *existence* within the successive temporal continuum and so offers no way of connecting the temporal continuum associated with the new substance that arises with the temporal continuum of the substances with which it is supposed to overlap in a common time. In this respect, it is important to note that although simultaneous *events* (two events happening at the same time) are unproblematic for Kant, simultaneous *times* (two times happening at the same time) are absurd. The idea of substances arising absolutely seems to require the latter insofar as it requires a time at which the two times overlap (are simultaneous), but in doing so it violates the empirical unity of time. For Kant, substances cannot arise or perish absolutely if the empirical unity of time is to be maintained since the idea of temporally overlapping times violates this empirical unity.[16]

Once one recognizes that substances cannot be experienced to either arise or perish absolutely within a common time, it is easy to see how Kant could claim that the quantum of substance is neither increased nor diminished in nature. An increase in the quantum of substance would require substance to arise absolutely (thus adding to the overall quantum) whereas diminishing the quantum of substance would require substance to perish absolutely (thus subtracting from the overall quantum). Since substance can neither arise nor perish absolutely, it is not simply relatively persistent but rather absolutely permanent.

Reconstruction

1) Appearances stand in temporal relations of simultaneity and succession.
2) If appearances stand in temporal relations of simultaneity and succession, then either time itself, or apprehension, or (by definition of the schematized category) substance persists in all change of appearances.
3) From (1) and (2), either time itself, or apprehension, or substance persists in all change of appearances (modus ponens).
4) Not time, since time itself cannot be perceived (form of intuition).
5) Not apprehension, since this is always successive (A182/B225).
6) From (3), (4), and (5), in all change of appearances substance persists (disjunctive syllogism).
7) If in all change of appearances substance persists, then in addition to persisting its quantum (amount) of substance is neither increased nor diminished in nature.
8) From (6) and (7), in all change of appearances substance persists and its quantum is neither increased nor diminished in nature (modus ponens).

Second Analogy: All alterations occur in accordance with the law of the connection of cause and effect (B232).

Quote

I perceive that appearances succeed one another, i.e., that a state of things exists at one time the opposite of which existed in the previous state. Thus I really connect two perceptions in time. Now connection is not the work of mere sense and intuition, but is here rather the product of a synthetic faculty of the imagination, which determines inner sense with regard to temporal relations. This, however, can combine the two states in question in different ways, so that either one or the other precedes in time; for time cannot be perceived in itself, nor can what precedes and what follows in objects be as it were empirically determined in relation to it. I am therefore only conscious that my imagination places one state before and the other after, not that the one state precedes the other in the object; or in other words, through the mere perception the *objective relation* of the appearances that are succeeding one another remains undetermined. Now in order for this to be cognized as determined, the relation between the two states must be thought in such a way that it is thereby necessarily determined which of them must be placed before and which after rather than vice versa. The concept, however, that carries a necessity of synthetic unity with it can only be a pure concept of understanding, which does not lie in the perception and that is here the concept of the *relation of cause and effect*, the former of which determines the latter in time, as its consequence, and not as something that could merely precede in the imagination (or not even be perceived at all). Therefore it is only because we subject the sequence of the appearances and thus all alteration to the law of causality that experience itself, i.e., empirical cognition of them [i.e., alterations] is possible; consequently they themselves, as objects of experience, are possible only in accordance with this law. [B232-34]

Synopsis

In the above quote, the argument for the Second Analogy begins with an indisputable feature of our experience, viz., that we perceive alteration or the objective successions of appearances. In other words, Kant's claim is that we have knowledge of events (e.g., a leaf changing color). This premise assumes a distinction between two types of succession which will only become explicit in premise seven. An objective succession of appearances is a perception of succession. Kant thinks that the experience of any event is going to be an example of experiencing an objective succession. This stands in contrast to the mere subjective succession of apprehension which is a succession of perceptions. That apprehension is always successive simply reiterates a point made in the First Analogy above.[17] Since apprehension is always successive, however, it is an open question as to whether or not the states of the object apprehended are successive as well since they might be simultaneous. What is the relationship between the two kinds of succession? For Kant, the subjective apprehension of appearances (succession of perceptions) is undetermined in time unless it is the apprehension of an objective succession of appearances (perception of succession).[18]

Sometimes the subjective succession of apprehension is not determined in time. Let us return to the idea of a flipbook. Each photograph represents a particular moment, and each one is successive to another. Taking photographs of something is analogous to the apprehension of that thing and so we can use the example of a flipbook to illustrate Kant's example of apprehending a house.[19] Our successive snapshots of the house can start from the roof and work down to the foundation or vice versa. They could also start from the right and work to the left or vice versa. The order of our apprehension of the house is reversible. Though the snapshots will be successive, the order of that succession is up to the person taking the photos since there is nothing in the house that determines the temporal order in which the person has to take the photographs. As we will see in the Third Analogy, the subjective succession of apprehension in this case does not rely on an objective succession of appearances, but rather on their objective *simultaneity*. It is the objective simultaneity of the appearances that explains the fact that the subjective succession of these appearances is reversible.[20]

Next, consider our apprehension of a boat moving downstream.[21] We must photograph the boat upstream before we can photograph it downstream. The order of the photographs in our flipbook is determined in time. This is an example of apprehending an objective succession since the order of the appearances that the subject is apprehending is determined in time (ship is first upstream then downstream). The objective succession of the appearances determines the subjective apprehension of these appearances making the latter irreversible. It is important to note that the objective succession of the appearances is not derived from the irreversibility of our apprehension of these appearances, but rather the irreversibility of our apprehension of these appearances is derived from their objective succession. Although we will discuss this at greater length below, this is why the second option under premise four does not work. Whereas in the case of the house one is not apprehending the alteration of something (the house stays the same), in the case of the boat one is apprehending alteration (the ship alters its location). With the apprehension of the house all of the appearances apprehended are perceptually available for the whole time period the house is being apprehended. The same cannot be said for the ship.[22] Something is *happening* in the latter case that is not happening in the former. Put slightly differently, one is apprehending an *event* in the case of the ship (its movement downstream) whereas one is not in the case of the house.

Kant's argument in the Second Analogy is progressive. As mentioned above, he believes it is an indisputable feature of our experience that we perceive events and that when we are apprehending an event, the order of the successive appearances (objective) determines the temporal order of the apprehension of these appearances (subjective). Since Kant is providing his response to Hume's skepticism with regard to causation in the Second Analogy, before claiming something is "indisputable" it is important to see whether Hume would assent to it. Hume does not deny that we perceive events.[23] For Hume, in our perception of events, the order of our sensible ideas, copied from the original impressions, reflects the order of the original impressions. If this order is repeated often enough, we come to expect one event upon the appearance of its usual attendant. It is this expectation based on habitual association that serves as the impression from which we copy our idea of necessary connection.[24] It is important to note, however, that Hume is far more concerned with whether there is a necessary connection between events than what the necessary conditions are for our perception of a given event. When it comes to the latter, Hume seems to identify events with instantaneous states of affairs rather than as objective successions of appearances. This is why Hume often uses the term "object" and "event" interchangeably.[25] Kant hopes to undercut Hume's argument by showing that an event must be understood as an objective succession of appearances if it is to be represented as an event at all.[26]

Returning to Kant's argument, in the second premise, he claims that if we perceive an objective succession of appearances (i.e., an event), then the succession of appearances is necessary. The idea is that there must be some explanation for why the subjective succession of apprehension has a determinate time-order. If the objective succession is necessary, of course, this would explain why the subjective succession of apprehension is irreversible. Hume would certainly disagree with this premise, but without it there is no way of accounting for why our experience of the ship is different from our experience of the house, i.e., of why our experience of events is different from our experience of objects. In order to perceive an event, the appearances that constitute the event must be determined in time. Insofar as the determination of the appearances in time that constitute the event is a necessary condition for our perception of the event, Hume's account simply cannot explain how we perceive the events that we clearly do perceive. His fatal error, it would seem, is the conflation of "event" and "object."

If we admit that the objective order of appearances is necessary, where does this necessity come from? Something must be determining the temporal order of these appearances. In premise four, Kant introduces the usual suspects. Following a pattern set in the First Analogy, Kant asks whether time itself, the succession of apprehension, or the relevant schematized category can explain the necessity of the objective succession of appearances. Let us consider each option in turn.

Kant dismisses the first option in premise six. As he says in the above quote, "time cannot be perceived in itself, nor can what precedes and what follows in objects be as it were empirically determined in relation to it." This point should already be familiar from the First Analogy. The sixth premise simply applies this insight in the present context by noting that since time itself cannot be perceived we cannot determine the objective order of appearances relative to it.

When it comes to the second option, Kant says in the above quote, "through the mere perception the *objective relation* of the appearances that are succeeding one another remains undetermined." This seems to rule out the second option. Apprehension is always successive (the succession of perceptions) regardless of whether a house (perception of simultaneity) or a ship (perception of succession) is being apprehended. As the seventh premise makes clear, furthermore, even when the subjective succession of apprehension is irreversible (i.e., is a perception of succession), this does not explain why the objective succession of appearances apprehended is necessary. This is to put the cart before the horse. It is the necessity of the objective succession of appearances (e.g., the movement of the ship downstream) that explains why the subjective succession of apprehension has an irreversible order (perceive ship upstream and only then downstream). Put slightly differently, it is the necessary order of the appearances that constitute an event that explains why we perceive them in the way that we do, not vice-versa. Ultimately, the subjective succession of apprehension cannot explain the necessary time-order of the objective succession of appearances.

As we know from Hume, even if there is an order to the appearances, we do not perceive any necessary connection between them that would explain why this order is necessary. Could there be a causal rule, based upon an inductive inference from perception *a posteriori*, by which we could determine the objective succession of appearances? Kant agrees with Hume that if the rule is *a posteriori*, the relation of cause and effect could not be necessary. Since the rule would be known *a posteriori*, it would be contingent and *contingent* rules cannot provide *necessary* orders of succession.[27]

Much as is the case for Hume, the answer must lie in the mind. Kant's answer, however, will differ significantly from Hume's own. For Kant, Hume's account of experience is nothing more than a "play of representations" since Hume rejects that the objective succession of appearances is necessary.[28] As we have seen though, this is required for the subjective succession of apprehension to have a determinate time-order. What about Kant's own view? Premise eight is the crux of the argument and is in many ways the crux of *CPR* as a whole. Whereas Hume attempts to derive his idea of necessary connection *a posteriori* from the customary transition of thought produced by habitual association, in the Metaphysical Deduction, Kant shows that we possess a concept of causation, or idea of necessary connection to use Hume's terms, *a priori*. The Transcendental Deduction establishes that this concept (along with the other categories) is objectively valid. He later gives this concept a temporal form in the Schematism, viz., "the real upon which, whenever it is posited, something else always follows. It therefore consists in the succession of the manifold insofar as it is subject to a rule."[29] In the Second Analogy, Kant completes his response to Hume. For the objective succession of appearances to be necessary, the understanding must apply the schematized category of causation to the appearances through an act of judgment.[30] This concept of causation must be *a priori* in order for it to carry the necessity that is required for objective succession. The idea then is that judgment generates the objective succession of appearances in accordance with an *a priori* rule (schematized category of causation) such that the succession is necessary.[31] In other words, it is only through application of the schematized category of causation that the appearances that constitute an event are necessarily ordered in time. This is the basic point Kant is trying to make in the second half of the above quote.

This may seem counterintuitive. After all, don't the states of affairs that constitute an event possess their order irrespective of the subject experiencing them? How can the subject be involved? The answer lies in Kant's theory of transcendental idealism. We cognize objects only insofar as they appear to us spatiotemporally and in accordance with our concepts of them. The states of affairs ordered in time are not things-in-themselves but are rather relations of appearances. These relations must be determined in accordance with the subject's concepts, in this case cause and effect. Kant believes that events just are

alterations of substances and so it follows that all alterations must occur in accordance with the law of cause and effect which is the conclusion of Kant's argument. Much as the principle of the First Analogy goes to support the conservation of mass, the Second Analogy goes to support the law of inertia. The law
of inertia holds that an object will stay in uniform motion or rest unless it is affected by an outside force. Insofar as any change in motion can be considered an
alteration, the principle of the Second Analogy provides a synthetic *a priori*
foundation for the empirical law's claim that this change must have an external
cause.[32]

What does it mean for all alterations to occur in accordance with the law of
cause and effect? For Kant, this means that every alteration (event) necessarily
has a cause such that the succession of appearances that constitute the alteration
has a necessary temporal order. Put in terms of a response to Hume, in order to
perceive an event at all, this event must be caused by something else. When
Hume tries and fails to find a necessary connection between events *a posteriori*,
he overlooks the possibility that experience of any event at all will itself presuppose such a necessary connection *a priori*.

Take the event of Socrates' death. That Socrates died when he did and that
he drank hemlock (another event) are both contingent. He might have accepted
exile and died years later for different reasons. What is not contingent, however,
is that when Socrates' died his death necessarily had a cause (in his case the
drinking of hemlock). Likewise, when the ship alters its location on the river (an
event), this alteration must have a cause as well (e.g., the motion of the water
which is another event). Although we do not know *what* the cause of any given
event will be *a priori*, we do know *a priori* that any event will have a cause.
This is what makes the Second Analogy a dynamical principle. Although it is
certain *a priori*, its application requires that some event be given in empirical
intuition such that this event can be related to a cause from which it follows necessarily.

With all the talk of *succession* in the Second Analogy, it might come as a
surprise that Kant thought that, for the most part, causes and effects are *simultaneous*.[33] Take Kant's own example of a ball lying on a pillow. In this case, the
ball-shaped impression on the pillow is simultaneous with the ball sitting on the
pillow. Since the two are simultaneous with one another, what makes one the
cause and the other the effect? Kant's answer is that there is a counterfactual
asymmetry between the two.[34] Although the ball-shaped impression on the pillow follows from the ball lying on it, the ball lying on the pillow does not follow
from the ball-shaped impression. Many other things could have caused the ball-
shaped impression on the pillow besides the ball (e.g., someone's bald head). If
the relationship were symmetrical, then regardless of whether you assumed a
ball-shaped impression or a ball lying on a pillow, the other would follow.

Even though there may not be a time *lapse* in simultaneous causation, there
is a determinate causal *order*. The same is true of any alteration regardless of
whether there is time lapse or not. The death of Socrates at t_2 follows from him

drinking hemlock at t_1, though Socrates' drinking hemlock does not follow from him being dead. Many other things can kill a man besides hemlock. As mentioned in the Metaphysical Deduction, the same kind of counterfactual asymmetry is originally found in hypothetical judgments. What Kant is doing here is trading on this *analogy* between the relation in the logical form of judgment and the relation in its corresponding schematized category.

Kant's argument in the Second Analogy also provides an important supplement to the First Analogy. A consequence of his view in the former is that substances cannot arise from an empty time since this would be an example of an event that does not have a cause.[35] As you might recall, one of the objections to the First Analogy is that substances might arise or perish absolutely thus adding to or subtracting from the total quantity of substance. If Kant's argument in the Second Analogy is sound, however, then the absolute arising of substance would violate the causal principle that the argument establishes. Likewise, it would violate the unity of time for the reasons mentioned in our discussion of the First Analogy. Consequently, the fact that all alteration is subject to the law of cause and effect is required to maintain the empirical unity of time.

One famous objection to the Second Analogy is the claim that it involves "a non-sequitur of numbing grossness."[36] Put simply, the objection is that Kant *identifies* (1) the *conceptual* necessity that, where events are concerned, the subjective succession of apprehension must follow the same order as the objective succession of appearances being apprehended with (2) the *causal* necessity of the objective succession of the appearances themselves. In other words, the way in which the subjective succession of apprehension is necessary (irreversible) is identified with the way in which the objective succession of the appearances apprehended is necessary (causal). As premise seven makes clear, however, Kant is not identifying the irreversibility of the subjective succession of apprehension with the causal necessity of the objective succession of the appearances being apprehended. The schematized category of causation is not applied to the subjective succession of apprehension in order to determine it in time, but rather to the appearances apprehended in order to insure the necessity of their objective succession. Crucially, the latter is what explains the fact that we apprehend the appearances in an irreversible order.[37]

Before we leave the Second Analogy, however, let us consider one more objection that Hume might raise for Kant's view. Can we not at least conceive of events occurring without causes, e.g., things just popping into existence? If conceivability entails possibility, then is it not at least possible that Kant's causal principle is false? If it is possibly false, then in what sense is it necessarily true?[38] Here it is important to emphasize the synthetic *a priori* nature of the causal principle. Kant agrees with Hume that the causal principle is not analytic and one cannot demonstrate it by manipulating general concepts.[39] This is why Kant's argument is progressive and starts from a fact of experience that even Hume would have to accept. That Kant is talking about a synthetic *a priori* principle and not an analytic *a priori* principle allows him to admit that although it is not *logically* necessary (since it is consistently deniable) it is *materially* necessary (given the conditions of our experience). In other words, although Hume's counterexample is conceivable it is not something that creatures like us could ever experience since it would violate the empirical unity of time which is contrary to our experience of time. Even though Kant does not bring up the distinction between these two forms of necessity until the Postulates (next chapter), it should suffice for present purposes to note that Hume's objection is only sufficient to show that Kant's causal principle is not logically necessary, though it is insufficient to show that his principle is not materially necessary. In this way, Kant's causal principle is quite contemporary insofar as he holds that causal necessity is not equivalent to logical necessity.

Reconstruction

1) I perceive events (i.e., objective successions of appearances or alterations).
2) If I perceive events, then the succession of the appearances is necessary.
3) From (1) and (2), the objective succession of appearances is necessary (modus ponens).
4) If the objective succession of appearances is necessary, then either time itself, or the subjective succession of apprehension, or (by definition of the schematized category) the law of the connection of cause and effect determines the temporal order of the appearances.
5) From (3) and (4), either time itself, or the subjective succession of apprehension, or the law of the connection of cause and effect determines the temporal order of the objective succession of appearances (modus ponens).
6) Time itself cannot be perceived and so we cannot determine on its basis the temporal order of the appearances.
7) The subjective succession of apprehension cannot determine the temporal order of the appearances apprehended since its own irreversible order depends upon the objective succession of appearances being necessary.
8) From (5), (6), and (7), the law of the connection of cause and effect determines the temporal order of the objective succession of appearances (disjunctive syllogism).
9) If the law of the connection of cause and effect determines the temporal order of the objective succession of appearances, then all alterations occur in accordance with the law of the connection of cause and effect.
10) From (8) and (9), all alterations occur in accordance with the law of the connection of cause and effect (modus ponens).

Third Analogy: All substances insofar as they can be perceived in space as simultaneous, are in thorough-going interaction (B256).

Quote

Things are *simultaneous* if in empirical intuition the perception of one can follow the perception of the other *reciprocally* (which in the temporal sequence of appearances, as has been shown in the case of the second principle, cannot happen). Thus I can direct my perception first to the moon and subsequently to the earth, or, conversely, first to the earth and then subsequently to the moon, and on this account, since the perceptions of these objects can follow each other reciprocally, I say that they exist simultaneously. Now simultaneity is the existence of the manifold at the same time. But one cannot perceive time itself and thereby derive from the fact that things are positioned at the same time that their perceptions can follow each other reciprocally. The synthesis of the imagination in apprehension would therefore only present each of these perceptions as one that is present in the subject when the other is not, and conversely, but not that the objects are simultaneous, i.e., that if the one is then the other also is in the same time, and that this is necessary in order for the perceptions to be able to succeed each other reciprocally. Consequently, a concept of the understanding of the reciprocal sequence of the determinations of these things simultaneously existing externally to each other is required in order to say that the reciprocal sequence of perceptions is grounded in the object, and thereby to represent the simultaneity as objective. Now, however, the relation of substances in which the one contains determinations the ground of which is contained in the other is the relation of influence, and, if the latter reciprocally contains the ground of the determinations of the former, it is the relation of community or interaction. Thus the simultaneity of substances in space cannot be cognized in experience otherwise than under the presupposition of an interaction among them; this is therefore also the condition of the possibility of the things themselves as objects of experience. [B256-58]

Synopsis

Whereas the Second Analogy begins with our experience of objective succession, the Third Analogy begins with our experience of objective simultaneity. Put in terms of an example from the Second Analogy, the Third Analogy is concerned with the *a priori* conditions for our experience of the house. The example that Kant uses in the Third Analogy is our experience of the earth and the moon as existing simultaneously. As he says in the above quote, our perception of the moon can follow the perception of the earth and vice-versa. Just as the parts of the house are perceptually available throughout the entire time we perceive the house, so too are the earth and the moon perceptually available through the entire time we perceive these two substances. "On this account," Kant holds that the two substances exist at the same time. The earth and the moon are objectively simultaneous in the same way that the parts of the house were in the Second Analogy.

What accounts for this objective simultaneity? Again, Kant considers the usual suspects in premise four. Either it is time itself, the subjective succession of apprehension, or the relevant relational category (in this case causal community). Just like the previous arguments, Kant dismisses the first option in the above quote saying, "But one cannot perceive time itself and thereby derive from the fact that things are positioned at the same time that their perceptions can follow each other reciprocally." As premise six notes, time itself cannot be perceived and so we cannot establish on its basis that the two substances exist at the same time. Likewise, apprehension will not work. In the above quote, Kant explains that "The synthesis of the imagination in apprehension would therefore only present each of these perceptions as one that is present in the subject when the other is not, and conversely, but not that the objects are simultaneous." We apprehend things one at a time and successively. Just because the moon is being apprehended at a given time does not reveal that the earth exists at that same time or vice-versa. Just because the earth is apprehended in the next moment, furthermore, this does not entail that it existed in the previous one when you were apprehending the moon. As the seventh premise notes, since the subjective succession of apprehension only presents us with one substance at a time we cannot establish on its basis that the two substances exist at the same time. Put in terms familiar from the Second Analogy, the subjective succession of apprehension cannot explain the objective *simultaneity* of appearances since apprehension is always *successive*. Even though the subjective succession of apprehension is reversible when objectively simultaneous substances are being apprehended (something we already know from the house example), it is the objective simultaneity of these substances that explains this reversibility, not vice-versa.

The key to the argument comes in premise eight. Since the other options have failed, the schematized category of community must provide the *a priori* rule whereby these substances can be determined to exist at the same time. Kant describes the schematized category of community or "the reciprocal causality of substances with regard to their accidents" as "the simultaneity of the determinations of the one with those of the other, in accordance with a general rule."[40] The idea is that the experience of the earth and the moon as objectively simultaneous (much as the parts of the house in the Second Analogy) requires that these substances stand in causal community with one another. For Kant, this perception of coexisting substances is the result of a two-way causal interaction between substances. Whereas the Second Analogy could be described as an argument for the necessity of one-way causal sequences (category of causation), e.g., between the alteration of the ship's location and the current, the Third Analogy provides an argument for the necessity of two-way causation where each substance contains the grounds for determinations of the other substance. For example, the tides on earth are an effect of the moon's gravitational pull whereas the orbit of the moon is an effect of the earth's gravitational pull. Their causal community, not only with one another but also with us as embodied cognitive subjects, makes possible our representation of these two substances as existing simultaneously. Whereas the First Analogy provides a metaphysical foundation for the conservation of mass and the Second Analogy provides a metaphysical foundation for the law of inertia, the Third Analogy provides a metaphysical foundation for universal gravitation.[41] Given how the three Analogies go to support Newton's laws, one can view their synthetic *a priori* principles as showing how a pure natural science is possible.

Are the substances Kant is discussing in the Third Analogy, however, identical to the substances he is talking about in the First Analogy? In the latter, Kant argues that substance is permanent. In the Third Analogy, Kant also insists that there must be "matter everywhere" in order to preclude the experience of empty space. Kant's problem with the experience of empty space is that it would compromise the empirical unity of space since perceptions of appearances in space would be "broken off" from one another.[42] This mirrors Kant's reasoning for the permanence of substance in the First Analogy, i.e., that it is necessary to preclude the experience of empty time where the latter would compromise the empirical unity of time. Kant seems to be suggesting that substance must be both sempiternal and omnipresent, i.e., that there is one big substance.

This stands in stark contrast, however, to the substances related by the category of community in the Third Analogy. Although the earth and the moon have been around for a long time and will (hopefully) continue to exist for a long time to come, neither of them are permanent. Both could, in principle, be annihilated.[43] Even though the matter from these substances would continue to exist in a different form, Kant describes the earth and the moon *themselves* as substances standing in causal community. The earth and the moon are not just modifications of one sempiternal and omnipresent substance, but must have their own distinct ontological status in order for the causal community of the Third Analogy to make sense.[44] Consequently, it seems that Kant requires that there are relatively persistent substances in addition to a sempiternal and omnipresent substance in the Analogies. Kant is using "substance" equivocally in the Analogies.[45] The relatively persistent substances of the Third Analogy (e.g., moon and earth) do not meet the standards of substance in the First Analogy, while the omnipresent and sempiternal substance that does meet the standards of the First Analogy cannot serve the function required by the Third Analogy. Is this a huge problem for Kant? Perhaps it is, but it is important to remember that the schematized category of substance is itself neutral between these two conceptions of substance. As we already know, it holds that substance is the "persistence of the real in time." This persistence can, however, be sempiternal or relative, omnipresent or discreet.[46]

Since Kant seems committed to the existence of one big substance, one might wonder whether the Analogies can establish that every event has an external cause. If there is only one big substance, then how could alterations of this substance (i.e., events) have causes outside of this substance?[47] Here it is important to take Kant's need for relatively persistent substances in the Third Analogy seriously. They are required for causal community where the latter is required for our perception of objective simultaneity. Objects like the sun and the moon cannot simply be *accidents* of one big substance but must be *substances* in their own right if they are to participate in the kinds of causal relations that our awareness of objective simultaneity requires. This raises another problem. What are true causes for Kant? Are they the causal powers of substances as the central example in the Third Analogy suggests (gravitational forces of the earth and moon) or are they events (understood as the alterations of substances) as the central example in the Second Analogy suggests (ship's motion caused by water's motion)? If Kant's theory of causation is substance-based rather than event-based, then can Kant's substance-based model really offer a response to Hume's event-based model especially since Hume seems to view events as instantaneous states-of affairs? Are Kant's view and Hume's view really two ships passing in the night?[48] As mentioned above, Hume often conflates events and objects. Kant's argument against Hume in the Second Analogy hinges on the idea that events must be understood in terms of objective successions of appearances and that Hume must accept this analysis if he is to distinguish between the perception of the ship's motion (event) and the perception of the house (object). If Hume is forced to accept that an event is an objective succession of appearances, then Kant would seem to have a response to Hume in the Second Analogy regardless of whether the event is caused by another event (Second Analogy) or the causal powers of substance (Third Analogy).

In closing, it is important to note that the three Analogies are interdependent. The argument of the First Analogy, which proves that substance persists, assumes that we experience successive and simultaneous appearances in its first premise. Our experience of objective succession is explained in the Second Analogy and our experience of objective simultaneity is explained in the Third Analogy. The Second and Third Analogies also provide us with the causal rules required for the reencountering and reidentification of enduring objects. Without a causal order to our world, we could not recognize substances as persistent.[49] Conversely, the experience of objective succession in the Second Analogy (alteration of substance) and objective simultaneity in the Third Analogy (causal community of substances) is going to require the persistent substance that Kant proves in the First Analogy. The three Analogies are internally related to one another in such a way that if the argument for one of the Analogies is flawed, it will have ramifications for the other two Analogies. They stand or fall together and one cannot be taken independently of the others.

The best way to see their interconnection is by understanding how they collectively go to support the general principle of the Analogies, which holds in the A edition that: "As regards their existence, all appearances stand *a priori* under rules of the determination of their relation to each other in *one* time."[50] In other words, and as alluded to above, the Analogies aim to insure the empirical unity of time. This is the foundational fact of our experience that Kant hopes to explain in the Analogies. They guarantee that we cognize all appearances as either objectively successive (Second Analogy) or simultaneous (Third Analogy) in a common time that persistent substance (First Analogy) underpins.[51]

Reconstruction

1) The perception of one substance can follow the perception of another substance reciprocally (e.g., sun and moon).
2) If the perceptions of these substances can follow one another reciprocally, then these substances are objectively simultaneous.
3) From (1) and (2), these substances are objectively simultaneous (modus ponens).
4) If these substances are objectively simultaneous, then either time itself, or the subjective succession of apprehension, or (by definition of the schematized category), the category of community determines that these substances exist at the same time.
5) From (3) and (4), either time itself, or the subjective succession of apprehension, or the category of community determines that these substances exist at the same time (modus ponens).
6) Time itself cannot be perceived and so we cannot establish on its basis that the two substances exist at the same time.
7) The subjective succession of apprehension only presents us with one substance at a time and so cannot establish that the two substances exist at the same time.
8) From (5), (6), and (7), the category of community provides the *a priori* rule whereby these substances can be determined to exist at the same time (disjunctive syllogism).
9) If the category of community provides the *a priori* rule whereby these substances can be determined to exist at the same time, then all substances, insofar as they can be perceived in space as simultaneous, are in thoroughgoing interaction (i.e., causal community).
10) From (8) and (9), all substances, insofar as they can be perceived in space as simultaneous, are in thoroughgoing interaction (modus ponens).

Notes

1. Burnham and Young define "analogy" this way. See Burnham and Young, *Kant's Critique*, 115. Unfortunately, Kant's own discussion of what he means by an "analogy" is rather obscure. See *CPR* A179-180/B222-23.

2. *CPR* A144/B183.

3. The argument we are reconstructing is sometimes called the "time-substrate" argument. Burnham and Young locate two other arguments for the principle of the First Analogy: the duration argument (*CPR* A183/B226-27) and the *ex nihilo* argument that

nothing comes from nothing (*CPR* A188/B231). When discussing the objections and responses to Kant's argument we will discuss these other arguments elliptically. See Burnham and Young, *Kant's Critique*, 117-18.

4. Recall the synthesis of apprehension from the A Transcendental Deduction. See A98-100. Kant uses the term "synopsis" in connection with this synthesis at *CPR* A94/B127.

5. *CPR* A114.

6. Kant distinguishes between "change" [*Wechsel*] which has to do with states and "alteration" [*Veränderung*] which has to do with substances. Kant restates the First Analogy in these terms at the beginning of the Second Analogy. See *CPR* B232-33. See also Rosenberg, *Accessing Kant*, 205.

7. Kant makes this point at *CPR* A184-85/B227-28.

8. *CPR* A186/B229. See also Gardner, *Kant and the Critique*, 174.

9. Altman makes this point. See Altman, *A Companion to Kant's Critique*, 150.

10. Hume, *Treatise*, 1.2.3.

11. *CPR* A183/B226.

12. Rosenberg raises this issue. See Rosenberg, *Accessing Kant*, 202-3.

13. *CPR* B17.

14. Savile makes this point and further discusses these issues. See Savile, *Kant's Critique*, 70.

15. Unfortunately, many commentators who note that Kant's argument for the permanence of substance is problematic also conflate persistence [*Beharrlichkeit*] and permanence [*Beständigkeit*]. Kant's starting point is the former, though he seemingly wants to conclude the latter. See, for example, Altman, *A Companion to Kant's Critique*, 148, Buroker, *Kant's Critique*, 167 and Dicker, *Kant's Theory of Knowledge*, 145.

16. Rosenberg offers this solution to the problem. See Rosenberg, *Accessing Kant*, 210. See *CPR* A188-89/B231-32. See also *CPR* A186/B229 for more on the relationship between the sempiternality of substance and the unity of time. Philosophers like Strawson and Dicker argue that a universe of temporally overlapping substances can insure the empirical unity of time. If Kant is right, however, this view would undermine the very conception of unity it is meant to insure. See P.F. Strawson, *The Bounds of Sense*, 128-132 and "Kant on Substance," in *Entity and Identity: and Other Essays* (Oxford: Oxford University Press, 1997), 268-280, especially 274. See Dicker, *Kant's Theory of Knowledge*, 160-62.

17. *CPR* A189/B234.

18. *CPR* A193/B238.

19. *CPR* A192-93/B237-38.

20. Rosenberg makes this point. See Rosenberg, *Accessing Kant*, 227.

21. *CPR* A192/B237.

22. Rosenberg, *Accessing Kant*, 219.

23. Hume, *Enquiry*, 7.59. It has long been objected that Kant cannot assume we can identify events. Kant's target, however, is Hume and the latter does assume that we can identify events. Here, I am following Allison who traces this objection back to Kant's contemporary, Salmon Maimon. See Allison, *Kant's Transcendental Idealism*, 252-53. Kant will argue, however, that Hume has failed to understand the nature of these events.

24. See Hume, *Enquiry*, 7.59.

25. For example, see Hume, *Enquiry*, 5.35.

26. Guyer argues that Kant's concern is not with establishing that the temporal order of events is necessary, but rather with establishing that the temporal order of the appearances that go to constitute an event is necessary. An event (daybreak) might well precede another event in time (sunset) without the former being the cause of the latter. See Guyer, *Kant and the Claims*, 259-262. Although Kant will agree that just because one event precedes another in time this does not entail that the former is the cause of the latter, he will argue that if an event occurs, it necessarily has a cause. To put this in terms of the example, that the sunset has a cause is necessary even though daybreak is not the cause. Of course, they both have a common cause, viz., the rotation of the earth relative to the sun (another event).

27. Kant discusses Hume's position at *CPR* A196/B241. See also Hume's criticism of probable causal rules based on induction. If such rules were to guarantee the necessity of causal inferences, they would have to assume that the future will resemble the past which itself would have to be established probabilistically. The defender of these rules is thus caught in a circle. Hume, *Enquiry*, 4.30.

28. *CPR* A194/B239.

29. *CPR* A144/B183.

30. Although we are emphasizing the point here, application of the schematized categories to appearances will always be a function of judgment. See *CPR* A132/B171.

31. See *CPR* A201-2/B246-47.

32. Savile, *Kant's Critique*, 78-79. Some philosophers, however, challenge whether the argument of the Second Analogy entitles Kant to claim that alterations have external causes. For example, see Kenneth Westphal, *Kant's Transcendental Proof of Realism* (Cambridge: Cambridge University Press, 2004), 152

33. *CPR* A203/B248.

34. Rosenberg puts the point this way. See Rosenberg, *Accessing Kant*, 227.

35. *CPR* A194/B239.

36. Strawson, *The Bounds of Sense*, 137.

37. Many commentators make this point including Guyer, *Kant and the Claims*, 247-48.

38. See Hume, *Treatise*, 1.3.3.

39. See *CPR* B19-24. For Hume, it cannot be a relation of ideas nor can it be demonstrated from reasoning *a priori*. See Hume, *Enquiry*, 4.20-23. Dicker notes this similarity. See Dicker, *Kant's Theory of Knowledge*, 163-64.

40. *CPR* A144/B183-84.

41. Savile, *Kant's Critique*, 81. For more on the relationship between the Principles and Newton's laws see Kant's 1786 work *The Metaphysical Foundations of Natural Science*. Michael Friedman discusses this connection at length. See Michael Friedman, *Kant and the Exact Sciences* (Cambridge, MA: Harvard University Press, 1992), chapters three and four.

42. *CPR* A213-14/B260-61.

43. This leads Buroker to conclude that macro-objects (e.g., the earth and the moon) cannot count as substances. See Buroker, *Kant's Critique*, 172-73. If there is no meaningful sense in which macro-objects are substances, however, then the Third Analogy is nonsense.

44. This runs contrary to Bennett's suggestion that the substances in the Third Analogy exist only adjectivally. Bennett, *Kant's Analytic*, 198.

45. Dicker also makes this point. See Dicker, *Kant's Theory of Knowledge*, 182. Other philosophers note that Kant sometimes speaks of substance as a bearer of properties but at other times as something permanent. These two conceptions, however, are not identical and one cannot infer from the former to the latter. See Bennett, *Kant's Analytic*, 182.

46. Although a full discussion of all the implications of this equivocation would take us too far afield, I argue elsewhere that it indeed poses some serious problems for Kant's view. See Bryan Hall, "A Dilemma for Kant's Theory of Substance," *British Journal for the History of Philosophy* (forthcoming).

47. As mentioned above, Westphal argues that the Second Analogy is insufficient to establish the claim that every event has an external cause. He goes on to argue that all three of the Analogies can be explained in terms of one big substance. See Westphal, *Kant's Transcendental Proof of Realism*, 152-164.

48. This is Eric Watkins' suggestion. See Eric Watkins, *Kant and the Metaphysics of Causality* (Cambridge, Cambridge University Press, 2005), chapter four.

49. Dicker makes this point. See Dicker, *Kant's Theory of Knowledge*, 125.

50. *CPR* A176.

51. Although Kant offers a separate proof for the general principle of the Analogies in the B edition of *CPR*, we are not reconstructing this argument since the arguments of the three Analogies together seem to support its conclusion that "Experience is possible only through the representation of a necessary connection of perceptions." If the arguments for the three Analogies are sound, then perceptions will be necessary connected with one another in one experience (a common time) through application of the three relational categories. See *CPR* B218-19.

Chapter Twelve
Postulates and Refutation of Idealism

Postulates of Empirical Thought

Quote

1. Whatever agrees with the formal conditions of experience (in accordance with intuitions and concepts) is *possible*.
2. That which is connected with the material conditions of experience (of sensation) is *actual*.
3. That whose connection with the actual is determined in accordance with general conditions of experience is (exists) *necessarily*. [A218/B265-66]

Synopsis

Unlike the other Principles, Kant does not offer "proofs" for the Postulates choosing instead to offer only an "elucidation" of each principle. Kant holds that the Postulates are nothing more than "definitions of the concepts of possibility, actuality, and necessity in their empirical use."[1] Since Kant himself does not offer proofs for the Postulates, we will dispense with attempting to reconstruct any kind of argument for these principles. Even so, Kant does offer an important argument in the Refutation of Idealism (between his discussion of the Second and Third Postulates) which will be reconstructed below.

As their name makes clear, in the Postulates of Empirical Thought, Kant is only interested in discussing the categories of modality in their *empirical* use.

Consequently, he is not concerned with logical possibility or necessity which would have to do with the form of thinking in general, but rather with our thinking about objects of possible experience. In addition, Kant holds that the Postulates do not at all "augment" the concept of the object they concern, but rather simply denote differences in the way the subject thinks about the object.[2] Although the Postulates are coextensive (i.e., concern the same set of objects), they are not synonymous (i.e., they have different meanings). The modal categories have different meanings insofar as they describe different cognitive relations or ways of considering objects, but they do not denote differences in the concepts of the objects so considered. For example, although we can consider a pink elephant either as possible, or actual, or necessary, the concept being considered (pink elephant) remains the same. All that changes is the way that the subject is considering that concept. Put in more contemporary terms, Kant's distinction between the three kinds of modality do not mark changes in the content of the proposition under consideration, but only the propositional attitude the judger takes toward that proposition.[3] For example, whether a subject takes it to be possible, actual, or necessary that "there is a pink elephant in the room," the content of the proposition does not change. All that changes is the attitude the subject takes toward the proposition.

As mentioned above, the First Postulate (possibility) has to do not simply with what a subject is capable of thinking generally (logical), but rather with what a subject is capable of thinking with regard to objects of experience (real). As long as an object agrees with the formal conditions of experience, it is really possible. In other words, if the object is locatable in the global space and time of human intuition (Transcendental Aesthetic), is extensively and intensively measurable (Axioms and Anticipations), and is governed by principles of substance and causality (Analogies), then it is possible.[4]

Unlike the First Postulate, the Second Postulate (actuality) requires perception, and anything that is connected with perception in accordance with the Analogies of Experience (i.e., the formal conditions of experience that have to do with relation) should be considered actual according to Kant.[5] This gives him the ability to affirm the reality of objects that are not themselves immediately perceived. Kant gives the example of "magnetic matter" to illustrate this point.[6] Although only the effects of magnetic matter can be perceived (e.g., the movement of iron filings), one can still affirm the actuality of magnetic matter (or in contemporary terms, a magnetic field) since it is connected with what is perceived in accordance with the Second Analogy's law of cause and effect.

As mentioned in the previous chapter, Kant does not consider his causal principle to be logically necessary (in thought) but only materially necessary (in experience). Kant draws this distinction explicitly in the Third Postulate (necessity).[7] Although we can never cognize the actuality of a substance or the alteration of a substance *a priori*, if some alteration is perceived (e.g., the movement of the iron filings), then it is materially necessary that this alteration have a cause (e.g., magnetic matter). This "hypothetical necessity" is limited to the alteration of substances.[8] In other words, the sole function of material necessity for Kant is to describe the kind of necessity that causal claims enjoy. As Kant says, "Necessity therefore concerns only the relations of appearances in accordance with the dynamical law of causality."[9] Whereas the Second Postulate holds that anything that is connected with perception in accordance with the Analogies is actual, the Third Postulate articulates the necessity of this connection.

Refutation of Idealism: The mere, but empirically determined, consciousness of my own existence proves the existence of objects in space outside me (B275).

Quote

> I am conscious of my existence as determined in time. All time-determination presupposes something *persistent* in perception. . . But this persisting element cannot be an intuition in me. For all the determining grounds of my existence that can be encountered in me are representations, and as such they themselves need something persisting distinct from them, in relation to which their change, and thus my existence in the time in which they change can be determined . . . Thus the perception of this persistent thing is possible only through a *thing* outside me and not through the mere *representation* of a thing outside me. Consequently, the determination of my existence in time is possible only by means of the existence of actual things that I perceive outside myself. Now consciousness in time is necessarily combined with the consciousness of the possibility of this time-determination: Therefore it is also necessarily combined with the existence of the things outside me, as the condition of time-determination; i.e., the consciousness of my own existence is at the same time an immediate consciousness of the existence of other things outside me.[10] [Bxxxix and B275-76]

Synopsis

The idealism that Kant attempts to refute here is what he calls "material idealism" which concerns the existence of objects outside of us. This type of idealism can be divided into two forms. First is the "problematic idealism" Kant finds in the writings of Rene Descartes who claims that the existence of external objects is "doubtful and indemonstrable." The second form is the "dogmatic idealism" of George Berkeley who holds that the existence of external objects is "false and impossible."[11] Berkeley believes that space cannot be transcendentally real (i.e., a mind-independent thing) since the existence of things depends on their being perceived. This leads Berkeley to affirm the empirical ideality of space as well as of everything in space (i.e., they are just sensible ideas). As Kant shows in the Transcendental Aesthetic, however, space need not be transcendentally real in order to be empirically real. Kant's transcendental idealism/empirical realism effectively undercut the grounds for Berkeley's form of empirical idealism.[12] As already mentioned, this did not keep early critics from accusing Kant of being a Berkeleyan, criticisms which might well have provided some impetus for the Refutation. Regardless of whether or not Kant successfully refutes Berkeley in the Transcendental Aesthetic, however, Kant still needs some way of refuting Descartes. Consequently, Kant's main target in the Refutation is Descartes. Given the fact that Berkeley's dogmatic idealism is modally stronger than Descartes' problematic idealism, however, refuting the latter will serve as an additional refutation of the former. Establishing the actuality of external objects is the surest proof of their possibility.

Kant begins by affirming what Descartes claims is indubitable, namely consciousness of my own existence as determined in time. Both would agree that I am empirically self-conscious of myself as existing in inner sense. In other words, I am aware of my own mental states as temporally ordered, i.e., as a stream of consciousness.[13] The second premise simply imports an idea already familiar from the First Analogy. Any awareness of representations having a time order requires that something persists through the change of these representations. Without this persistent, the empirical unity of time would be destroyed, but the awareness of my own existence as determined in time presupposes such an empirical unity. Either this persistent is something inside of me or it is something outside (distinct from) me.

When it comes to the first option, Kant would grant the Humean insight that at no point in our perception of ourselves do we ever come across a simple substance that persists. Rather, all we come upon are our own representations which are constantly changing.[14] As the fourth premise notes, inner sense is simply that stream of consciousness which requires its own persistent, distinct from itself, to determine its sequence. The representations that form this stream cannot provide their own order. Analogously, a river constantly flows and changes, but only relative to the river bed which is persistent. If the river bed were part of the river, it would then fail to be persistent. Without that river bed you would fail to have a river, much as one would fail to have a stream of consciousness were it not for something persistent distinct from that stream relative to which the representations in the stream are ordered in time.

This leaves the second option, i.e., that the persistent is something outside or distinct from myself relative to which these representations can be temporally ordered. What could serve this function? Again, the First Analogy provides the answer though with a spatial twist (anticipated in the Third Analogy) that insures the persistent is something distinct from me. Substances distinct from me in space underpin the empirical unity of time including consciousness of my own existence as determined in time. The crux of the argument comes in the fifth premise. As Kant notes in the above quote, and as we reiterate in the premise, the existence of things in space and not simply the representations of things in space is required for the determination of my own existence in time. If we were dealing merely with the representations of substances, these would be part of the stream of consciousness in inner sense and so would not persist through the change of representations. Again, mere representations do not a stream of consciousness make (i.e., a temporally ordered succession of representations) without substance persisting through the change of representations. Given his starting point, Kant can conclude that the consciousness of my own existence as determined in time proves the existence of objects in space outside me.

The Refutation serves as an important supplement to the Second Postulate that it follows. One might wonder how Kant's inferences to the unobserved in the Second Postulate are any different from the "always doubtful" inferences that transcendental realists (like Descartes and Locke) make from perceptions to external objects causing those perceptions in us.[15] If the Refutation is sound, however, then we have non-inferential awareness of the existence of objects outside of us and so further inferences to other objects are not problematic.[16] The problem was how to get beyond the veil of perceptions in the first place, but once one is there, there is no problem in making further inferences beyond that veil.

The Refutation also completes Kant's response to the objection that we would be incapable of dreaming if the Transcendental Deduction is sound (chapter eight). The idea behind the objection is that Kant only allows for a unity of representation when those representations refer to objects of experience, but dreams are unities of representation that do not refer to objects of experience. Consequently, they would be impossible under Kant's account. Given what Kant says in the Refutation, his response is pretty clear. The very possibility of dreams, hallucinations, or wild imaginings requires that there be an objective world (categorically structured substances in space and time). Not only does this world provide the raw material for my flights of fancy, but without it there would be no *me* to dream, hallucinate, or imagine. As we said earlier, the categories do not distinguish dreams from reality but rather chaos from order even if this order is a dream or hallucination. The fact that this world consists of persistent substances, however, does help us to distinguish between it and the world of dreams. A characteristic feature of the latter is that the objects within it do not persist since they exist within my dream only so long as I am dreaming them. Although we certainly have dreams, the world of dreams cannot insure the consciousness of my own existence as determined in time and neither would be possible were it not for my experience of an objective world.[17]

At this point, however, one might wonder what has happened to Kant's transcendental idealism? If things in space exist independently of my representations of them, aren't they things-in-themselves? If they are mere appearances, however, then how are they distinct from my representations?[18] Answering this question requires that we get clear on the exact relationship between objects and subjects, something we will return to in the next chapter.

Reconstruction

1) I am conscious of my own existence as determined in time.
2) If I am conscious of my own existence as determined in time, then something either inside me or outside me persists relative to which my own existence is determined in time.
3) From (1) and (2), something either inside me or outside me persists in the consciousness of my existence (modus ponens).
4) This persistent cannot be something inside me since representations in inner sense require something persistent *distinct* from themselves relative to which their sequence is determined.
5) From (3) and (4), this persistent is a thing outside me and not the mere representation of a thing outside me relative to which my own existence is determined in time (disjunctive syllogism).
6) If this persistent is a thing outside me and not the mere representation of a thing outside me relative to which my own existence is determined in time, then the mere, but empirically determined, consciousness of my own existence proves the existence of objects in space outside me.
7) From (5) and (6), the mere, but empirically determined, consciousness of my own existence proves the existence of objects in space outside me (modus ponens).

Notes

1. *CPR* A219/B266.
2. *CPR* A219/B266.
3. Dicker, *Kant's Theory of Knowledge*, 57.
4. This is the way Buroker puts things. See Buroker, *Kant's Critique*, 187.
5. *CPR* A225/B272.
6. *CPR* A226/B273.
7. *CPR* A226-27/B279.
8. *CPR* A228/B280.
9. *CPR* A227/B280.
10. Kant asks in the Preface to the B edition of *CPR* to replace the third sentence of the original proof with what is placed between the ellipses in the above quote.
11. For Kant's description of these two forms of idealism, see *CPR* B274.
12. *CPR* B69-70.
13. Descartes suggests that the contents of consciousness have a temporal order. See Descartes, *Meditations*, 2: 30-31.
14. Hume, *Treatise*, 1.4.6.
15. *CPR* A372.
16. Savile makes this point. Savile holds that Kant agrees with Berkeley both in his criticisms of Descartes and Locke as well as in his claim that our experience of the world is immediate. See Savile, *Kant's Critique*, 92-93 and 114. As Buroker notes, all that is

required for our cognition of these substances is the unification of concepts and intuition which is not inferential. See Buroker, *Kant's Critique*, 196-97. Berkeley's error, it seems, was his failure to recognize the necessary conditions for the very form of consciousness that (like Descartes and Locke) he takes for granted.

17. Buroker makes a similar point. See Buroker, *Kant's Critique*, 194.

18. Several commentators raise this worry with the Refutation. For example, see Gardner, *Kant and the Critique*, 185-87.

Chapter Thirteen
Conclusions from the Transcendental Analytic

After completing the Principles, Kant begins the final chapter of the Transcendental Analytic by noting: "We have now not only traveled through the land of pure understanding, and carefully inspected each part of it, but we have also surveyed it, and determined the place for each thing in it."[1] Although Kant has explained how cognition of objects is possible in the Transcendental Analytic, not all of our thoughts about objects result in cognition. To see this, one should note that the categories are objectively valid of objects in *empirical intuition*. This formulation noticeably excludes cognition of objects where that cognition would require going beyond the bounds of sense. Kant makes a distinction between the empirical use of pure concepts and their transcendental use and explains that the understanding is limited to the former. The transcendental use of a concept "consists in its being related to things in general and in themselves," whereas the empirical use consists "in its being related merely to appearances, i.e., objects of a possible experience."[2] For a concept to be related to an object in general or in itself, is for it to have no relation to the way in which an object is intuited. According to Kant, the transcendental use employs the categories in their unschematized form, and such utilization can never result in cognition. In fact, as we know from the Schematism, applying the categories in their unschematized form is no different than applying the logical functions of judgment. Although the latter allow us to think what we will (as long as we are consistent),

135

they do not allow us to cognize any object. The only legitimate use of the categories themselves is within the bounds of sense.[3]

When it comes to cognition then, our concepts are restricted to objects in sensible intuition. Nevertheless, objects beyond the bounds of sense can still be thought even if they cannot be cognized.[4] In order to mark the difference, Kant introduces two new terms to distinguish two kinds of objects, viz., "phenomena" which are objects of sense, and "noumena" which are either simply not objects of sensible intuition (negative sense) or are objects of a non-sensible intuition (positive sense).[5] For Kant, it is the positive not the negative noumenon that is problematic. The latter is just a "boundary concept" that marks the limit of sensibility.[6] Philosophers get in trouble, Kant thinks, when they overstep the bounds of sense and attempt to use the categories to cognize positive noumena, i.e., substances that exist independently of our sensible conditions. Since cognition requires the unification of intuition and concept, this kind of cognition would require non-sensible intuition, a kind of intuition that creatures like us do not possess.[7]

By wedding Kant's discussion of noumena to his arguments in the Transcendental Deduction, one can finally explain Kant's theory of affection without claiming that a positively noumenal thing-in-itself is the cause of affection (which would violate Kant's constraints on the legitimate application of the categories) or that the appearance itself is the cause of affection (which would make the effect of affection its own cause). This will allow us to solve a number of problems that plague Kant's theory of transcendental idealism and which we have mentioned throughout the book (most recently at the end of the Refutation).

Although most commentators assume that the affecting object must either be an appearance or a thing-in-itself, this is a false dilemma insofar as it ignores the possibility that appearances are not themselves particulars but rather *relations*.[8] Even though Kant often seems to refer to appearances as particulars, he also refers to them as relations.[9] Under the latter interpretation, we can view appearances as relations between phenomenal objects and phenomenal subjects, i.e., objects insofar as they appear to subjects and subjects insofar as they appear to themselves through these objects.[10] As we will argue, this is an *intrinsic* relation since neither phenomenal objects nor phenomenal subjects could exist outside of the appearance relation.

In the Transcendental Deduction Kant claims that appearances are the means by which subjects are immediately related to phenomenal objects in empirical intuition, but such objects of representation are undetermined unless these representations are united in the concept of what it is to be an object (categories).[11] The unification of representations requires synthesis and consequently the unity of consciousness (apperception) in the synthesis of them. According to Kant, "the unity that the object makes necessary can be nothing other than the formal unity of the consciousness in the synthesis of the manifold of representations."[12] For these unified representations, we think of some object of representation as corresponding to them. This is the "transcendental object = X," which is always one and the same thing: a transcendental placeholder for the object of representation. The concept of a transcendental object is necessary, however, so that there is something to which cognition is related.[13] This is where the positive/negative noumena distinction becomes relevant. Although they are distinct kinds of objects, both phenomena and positive noumena are viewed *substantively*. The former is an object that persists within the bounds of sense whereas the latter is an object which is thought to exist beyond these bounds. In contrast, both the transcendental object and the negative noumenon are viewed *conceptually*. One can understand the concept of a transcendental object = X from the A edition Transcendental Deduction as the concept of a *negative* noumenon that Kant explicitly introduces in the B edition of *CPR*.[14] Both are completely indeterminate concepts. Whereas the concept of a transcendental object is the thought of *something* wherein sensible representations are unified, the negative noumenon is the thought of this same *something* once all sensible representations are taken away.[15]

At this point, it might appear that Kant views the object of representation as a mere intentional object, i.e., one that depends wholly on the subject's mental activity. If so, then how is it different from Berkeley's view that a sensible object is just a collection of sensible ideas which depend wholly upon the subject's perception? It is important to point out that although the object of representation is possible only through the subject's activity, the subject of representation is itself possible only through the representations of objects. This is the lesson of the Refutation, but the basic point already occurs in the Transcendental Deduction. Without the synthetic unity of these representations, one would not be able to represent oneself as an identical subject enduring throughout these representations. As Kant says, "it is only because I can combine a manifold of given representations *in one consciousness* that it is possible for me to represent the *identity of the consciousness in these representations* itself."[16] The Refutation only adds that consciousness of my own existence as determined in time (i.e., the phenomenal subject) requires the existence of persistent substances (i.e., phenomenal objects) not their mere representation.

Consequently, the subject of representation makes the objects of representation possible by unifying these representations, but the synthetic unity of these representations make the subject of representation possible.[17] Since the subject of representation makes the object of representation possible, the object cannot be a thing-in-itself. Instead, the object of representation is a phenomenal object that is possible only through the relation it bears to a subject of representation. Similarly, since the object of representation makes the subject of representation possible, the subject of representation cannot be a thing-in-itself, i.e., a positively noumenal substance capable of existing on its own. Instead, the subject of representation is the phenomenal self which is only possible through the relations it bears to phenomenal objects. Kant maintains his transcendental idealism with regard to all objects of representation given that they are nothing once one abandons the perspective of the subject of representation. But since the objects of representation make the subject of representation possible, the objects of representation cannot be mere creatures of the mind. Kant maintains his empirical realism with regard to all objects of representation. If the "thing-in-itself" that is required to enter into Kant's system can be understood simply in terms of a concept (transcendental object or negative noumenon) rather than a substance that exists independently of the conditions of sensibility (positive noumenon), then the mere possession of this concept should not require one to leave Kant's system.[18] Although we must *think* of something (conceptual) as grounding affection in the phenomenal object, this should not entail that there must *be* something (substance) beyond the phenomenal object that actually causes affection.[19]

Even so, it seems almost paradoxical to say that the phenomenal object could serve as one of the relata in the appearance relation while at the same time not possessing any nature independently of the appearances whereby it appears. Once one recognizes the *intrinsic* nature of the appearance relation, however, we believe the apparent paradox resolves itself. To say that the phenomenal object is exhausted by relations is not to say that the phenomenal object is not an object (or relatum of the appearance relation), but rather that the phenomenal object cannot exist outside of these relations. Failure to recognize the intrinsic nature of the appearance relation is what leads philosophers to search for relata beyond the bounds of sense. Once one recognizes, however, that the relata of the appearance relation cannot exist beyond the bounds of sense, one need not go beyond the phenomenal world in order to find the relata of the relation, i.e., the object of affection. This also helps to explain why Kant often talks about phenomena in both relational and objectival terms. Below is a revised diagram of the relationship between subject and object that takes its intrinsic nature into account.[20]

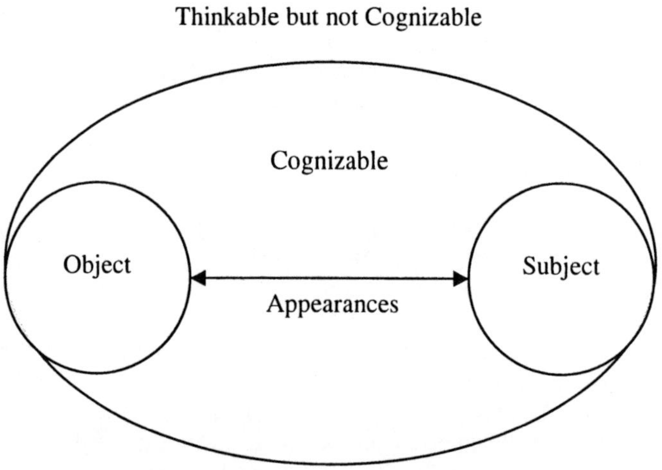

Figure 3: Relationship between Subject and Object (Revised)

If Kant's arguments in the Transcendental Analytic are successful, then he has also completed his positive argument for transcendental idealism. Whereas the Transcendental Aesthetic establishes that we can cognize objects only insofar as they appear to us spatiotemporally and not as they might be in themselves, the Transcendental Analytic establishes that we can only cognize these objects insofar as they conform to our concepts of them (most importantly the categories). Since space and time as well as the categories are contributions of the subject to her experience, the objects of experience are nothing once we leave behind the sensible and conceptual conditions of the subject (transcendental idealism). At the same time, however, we can affirm the reality of these objects within the bounds of sense and to which our concepts have legitimate application (empirical realism).

The Transcendental Analytic also completes Kant's positive case for synthetic *a priori* cognition. We can know certain things about objects (synthetic) without appeal to experience (*a priori*) since these objects must conform to our *a priori* concepts of them (the categories). Kant derives these *a priori* concepts of objects in the Metaphysical Deduction and establishes *that* they apply to objects in the Transcendental Deduction. The Schematism explains *how* these *a priori* concepts can be applied to appearances in empirical intuition while the Principles enumerates certain synthetic *a priori* judgments based on these schematized categories that serve as rules for the application of the latter to appearances in empirical intuition. The kind of synthetic *a priori* cognition that Kant establishes in the Principles shows how both pure mathematics (Axioms and Anticipations) as well as pure natural science (Analogies) are possible, his goal from the very beginning.[21]

In the Appendix to the Transcendental Analytic, Kant spends most of his time ruthlessly criticizing Leibniz, though what he says is also relevant to other philosophers of the Modern period. Although we have already discussed many of these criticisms above, they bear repeating before we leave Kant's positive project behind. If Kant's arguments to this point are sound, then human cognition is discursive, i.e., it requires the unification of sensible intuitions and concepts. For Kant, sensibility (the faculty of intuition) and understanding (the faculty of concepts) are two *distinct* sources of cognition. Whereas he describes the nature of the former in the Transcendental Aesthetic, he describes the nature of the latter in the Transcendental Analytic. The shared error of both rationalism and empiricism was not recognizing that these are distinct sources of cognition. Rationalists like Leibniz tried to intellectualize sensibility believing that this allows for the cognition of things-in-themselves through mere concepts. Empiricists like Locke tried to sensitize the understanding which caused them to reject the very idea of *a priori* cognition. By recognizing the two different sources of cognition, Kant can allow for synthetic *a priori* cognition (contra Locke) while at the same time limiting our cognition to appearances within the bounds of sense (contra Leibniz).[22]

Whereas the Transcendental Analytic can be viewed as the final part of Kant's positive project, the Transcendental Dialectic can be viewed as Kant's negative project. In other words, while the Transcendental Analytic articulates the legitimate use of the categories, the Transcendental Dialectic articulates the illegitimate use of the categories and explains the kinds of illusions that arise once reason traverses the bounds of sense. To return to the opening metaphor of this book, while the Transcendental Aesthetic and Transcendental Analytic contain Kant's positive comments on reason in its broad sense (how it might be used correctly in supplying the principles of cognition *a priori*), the Transcendental Dialectic contains Kant's negative comments on reason in its narrow sense (how it can fall into error when applying these principles beyond the bounds of sense). Consequently, the Transcendental Dialectic completes Kant's *critique* of pure reason.

Notes

1. *CPR* A235/B294.
2. *CPR* A238-39/B298. As we will see in the next chapter, Kant does not always use "transcendental" this way.
3. *CPR* A246/B303.
4. *CPR* B146.
5. *CPR* B307.
6. *CPR* A255/B310-11.
7. *CPR* B308-9.
8. Most commentators make this assumption and their interpretations break down into two main camps. The first defends a "one-world" interpretation of Kant's distinction between appearances and things-in-themselves. For example, Allison argues that one can consider the *same* object from two different standpoints or aspects, both as appearance as well as thing-in-itself. See Allison, *Kant's Transcendental Idealism*, 52-53. The second camp defends a "two-world" interpretation of Kant where appearances and things-in-themselves are ontologically distinct from one another. For example, James van Cleve argues for a virtual object interpretation of Kantian appearances whereby they are constructed from noumenal subjects and their cognitive acts. See James van Cleve, *Problems from Kant* (New York: Oxford University Press, 1999), especially 8-12 and 154-55. Although our accounts differ markedly, Rae Langton has also argued that appearances are relations within a one-world context. See Rae Langton, *Kantian Humility: Our Ignorance of Things in Themselves* (Oxford, Oxford University Press, 1998), 19.
9. See *CPR* A20/B34 where Kant refers to appearances as objects. See *CPR* B66-67 where he refers to appearances as relations.
10. See *CPR* B157-58 where Kant says that we only cognize ourselves insofar as we appear to ourselves.
11. *CPR* B146-47.
12. *CPR* A105.
13. *CPR* A108-9. One might notice how the transcendental object (locus for objectivity) and transcendental apperception (locus of subjectivity) are interconnected in this passage.

14. Here, I am following Allison, *Kant's Transcendental Idealism*, 63. There are several points where Kant uses "transcendental object" and "noumenon" interchangeably. See *CPR* A250-52, A288/B344-45, and A358. It is important to note that Kant claims at *CPR* A253, however, that the transcendental object *cannot* be called a noumenon. Gerd Buchdahl overcomes the seeming contradiction by noting that the distinction between negative and positive noumena is only implicit in this section of the A edition. Once one has this distinction in mind, however, there is little problem seeing how the transcendental object could be equivalent to the negative noumenon (indeterminate concept) while certainly different from a positive noumenon (non-sensible substance). See Gerd Buchdahl, *Dynamics of Reason: Essays on the Structure of Kant's Philosophy* (Oxford: Blackwell Publishing, 1992), 84-85.

15. Rosenberg characterizes the relationship between the two concepts somewhat differently. Whereas the concept of a negative noumenon results from abstracting away the sensible conditions whereby an object can be given, the concept of the transcendental object results from abstracting away the conceptual conditions whereby an object can be thought. See Rosenberg, *Accessing Kant*, 252-53.

16. *CPR* B133.

17. See also Sebastian Gardner's discussion of how subject and object make one another possible in Gardner, *Kant and the Critique*, 157-160.

18. See *CPR* A256/B312 where Kant seems to identify the negative noumenon with the thing-in-itself. In addition, see *CPR* A494/B522 where Kant holds that "we may call the merely intelligible cause of appearances in general the transcendental object." See also *CPR* A390 and A393. In the latter, Kant holds we may think of the transcendental object as the cause of outer appearances though we lack any acquaintance with this cause or any positive concept of it.

19. Rosenberg holds that when talking about the "causes" of affection, all Kant needs is the ground/consequent relation and not the cause/effect relation. See Rosenberg, *Accessing Kant*, 284.

20. I discuss Kant's solution to the problem of affection at greater length in Bryan Hall, "Appearances and the Problem of Affection in Kant," *Kantian Review* 14, no. 2 (January, 2010): 38-66.

21. *CPR* B20.

22. *CPR* A271/B327.

Part Three

The Transcendental Dialectic

Chapter Fourteen
Introduction to the Transcendental Dialectic

Much as the Transcendental Aesthetic isolated sensibility *a priori* and the Transcendental Analytic isolated understanding *a priori* such that reason, in its broad sense, could supply certain principles of cognition *a priori*, the Transcendental Dialectic isolates reason itself *a priori* (i.e., the narrow sense of "reason"). Whereas the Transcendental Analytic deals with the understanding's *legitimate* use of the categories within the bounds of sense as applied to appearances, the Transcendental Dialectic deals with reason's *illegitimate* use of the categories beyond the bounds of sense as applied to things-in-themselves. As Kant puts it, the Transcendental Dialectic is a critique of the understanding and reason with regard to their "hyperphysical use," i.e., the misapplication or "dialectical" use of the understanding's pure concepts by reason beyond the bounds of sense.[1] For Kant, the main problem with traditional metaphysics is that its questions can only be answered by applying concepts, which only have proper application within the bounds of sense, beyond the bounds of sense. If Kant is right, we simply cannot know if immortal souls (Paralogisms), free causes (Third Antinomy), or God (Ideal) exist from the theoretical perspective regardless of how important these ideas might be from the perspective of traditional metaphysics.[2] This results in a kind of epistemic humility. Although we can know a great deal both *a priori* and *a posteriori* about objects within the bounds of sense, the nature of things beyond the bounds of sense is forever closed off to creatures cognitively constituted like us.

Kant believes the transcendent use of the categories beyond the bounds of sense results in "transcendental illusion."[3] Like perceptual illusion (e.g., sticks appearing bent in water), transcendental illusion is perpetual, natural, and inevitable.[4] The Transcendental Dialectic aims to uncover the fallacious inferences that reason is predisposed to make which result in application of the categories beyond the bounds of sense. Although Kant does not think we can ever stop making these kinds of fallacious inferences, we can at least recognize when we do so such that we are not deceived by them. In this way, Kant's project in the Transcendental Dialectic constitutes the *negative* phase of his critique of pure reason since it illustrates the kinds of errors that reason falls into once it ventures beyond the bounds of sense.

How does reason make these fallacious inferences? According to Kant, reason is governed by the legitimate logical maxim to find the unconditioned condition for conditioned cognitions.[5] This logical maxim, however, assumes the illegitimate principle that if the conditioned is given then so are all of its conditions including the unconditioned condition.[6] To say that something is conditioned is to say that it requires an explanation. The conditions provide this explanation. An unconditioned condition is something that provides an explanation for something but does not itself require any explanation. The logical maxim's demand that reason continually seek the unconditioned condition for conditioned cognitions is subjective and regulative, but the illegitimate principle's assertion that such an unconditioned condition is given is objective and constitutive. In order to avoid confusion, one should note that the sense in which Kant uses the term "regulative" here in the Transcendental Dialectic is different from the sense in which he uses the term in the Transcendental Analytic. Whereas in the former, a principle is regulative just in case it is a subjective imperative for human reason that has no constitutive application in experience, in the latter a principle is regulative just in case its constitutive application depends upon something being given in empirical intuition.

The illegitimate principle is a synthetic *a priori* existence claim, viz., that the unconditioned condition is *given*. As we will see below, such claims are themselves illegitimate since the existence of something cannot be established without appeal to experience. The illegitimate principle is natural and unavoidable, however, since the application of the logical maxim assumes the truth of the illegitimate principle. In seeking the unconditioned condition for conditioned cognitions, reason must assume that there is such an unconditioned condition to be found.[7] To use an example that Kant will discuss in the First Antinomy and which you have likely considered at some point in your life, it seems as if the universe (our cognitions of which are conditioned) must either have had a beginning in space and time (i.e., there is an unconditioned spatiotemporal starting point for the universe) or it has no beginning in space and time (i.e., there is no starting point for the universe and it is an unconditionally infinite spatiotemporal whole).[8] Regardless of which standpoint one takes, one is assuming that there is a determinate answer to the question. After all, why would we seek after an answer to the question of whether or not the universe had a beginning in space and time if we did not think there was an answer to be found?

In this respect, one might think of reason like a child who is always asking *why* something is the case. For example, a child might ask a parent why the sky is blue. Depending on the parent's knowledge (and patience), the parent might answer in terms of molecules of air, scattering effects, and light wavelengths. For each part of this answer, the child will likely ask *why* those are the case as well. The questions and the answers can, and often do, go on and on. As Kant puts it, for reason "the questions never cease."[9] In this respect, the child is acting quite rationally and certainly expects there to be answers to all the questions asked. As the parent knows, however, the series of questions usually leads to a point where one is sick of answering them or one does not know how to answer. The conversation typically ends with the parent saying "just because!" When it comes to some of the central questions of metaphysics, not only does Kant not know the answers but he will argue that there is no way of answering them.

The reasoning from conditioned to condition relies on syllogistic inference. There are three kinds of syllogism corresponding to the three judgments of relation: categorical, hypothetical, and disjunctive. The fallacious use of these syllogistic forms is what transforms the categories into "transcendental ideas," i.e., concepts that have no application within the bounds of sense but can only be understood as applying to things existing in themselves beyond these bounds.[10] Put most generally, the major premise offers a general rule of the understanding while the minor premise subsumes some cognition under the condition of this rule. In the conclusion, reason attributes the predicate of the rule to the cognition.[11] The classic example might be the categorical syllogism that: 1) All men are mortal (general rule), 2) Socrates is a man (cognition that falls under condition or subject of rule), 3) Socrates is mortal (predicate of general rule assigned to cognition). Although this inference is perfectly legitimate, when reason uses a general rule to make an inference beyond the bounds of sense, the rule is applied illegitimately. As we will see below, all of the Paralogisms have this form. As we saw above with regard to the conditions for applying the logical maxim by which reason operates, reason simply cannot help but make such fallacious inferences.

The three main sections of the Transcendental Dialectic are aimed at exposing the different kinds of fallacious inferences that generate the transcendental ideas and which are themselves associated with different branches of metaphysics. (1) The Paralogism is a form of transcendental illusion associated with rational psychology which infers from the categorical relation that every predicate must inhere in a subject, certain transcendental ideas concerning an immortal soul or unconditioned substance within which the activity of apperception inheres. (2) The Antinomy is a form of transcendental illusion associated with rational cosmology which infers from the hypothetical relation of ground (condition) to consequent (conditioned) transcendental ideas concerning the unconditioned basis for conditioned appearances in the natural world. As we will see, reason is always in conflict with itself when it comes to what the appropriate basis might be. (3) Finally, the Ideal of pure reason is a form of transcendental illusion associated with rational theology which infers from the disjunctive relation of possible judgments about a given thing the transcendental idea of God or an unconditioned being of all beings that contains within itself the sum total of all possibility.[12]

All of this might seem a bit arbitrary. Why should metaphysical reasoning be limited to the three syllogistic forms? Is Kant distorting the focus of metaphysics to spiritual ideas (e.g., the soul and God) at the expense of other important though non-theological concepts? In this respect, perhaps Kant's discussion in the Antinomies of the underlying metaphysical character of the natural world should be considered the real backbone of the Transcendental Dialectic.[13] It is important to note, however, that Kant does not consider his discussion of metaphysical positions to be exhaustive and makes clear that his primary focus is on how metaphysics tends to posit entities beyond the bounds of sense. Certainly, the soul and God are excellent examples of the latter. In addition, reason is not in conflict with itself when thinking of the unconditioned in these cases as it is with respect to the unconditioned in the Antinomies. As we will see, furthermore, the material simplicity under discussion in the Second Antinomy does not really capture the immaterial simplicity of the soul in the Paralogisms nor does the discussion of a necessary being in the Fourth Antinomy really capture the "most real being" Kant will discuss in the Ideal. Although the Antinomies are an important part of Kant's critique of metaphysics, they cannot deal adequately with the ideas of rational psychology or theology which is why the Paralogisms and Ideal are indispensible.[14]

The Paralogisms (chapter fifteen) are probably the clearest examples in the Transcendental Dialectic of how syllogistic reasoning can be used fallaciously to generate transcendental ideas. Since the syllogistic form of the Paralogisms is most explicit in the A edition, this is where we will focus our attention (though we will discuss the dramatically revised version of the Fourth Paralogism in the B edition as well). The Paralogisms are instances of fallacious reasoning which are fallacious by form but have as their ground the nature of human reason. The ground for this fallacious reasoning is the logical maxim that reason constantly seek for the unconditioned condition for any conditioned cognition which itself assumes that such an unconditioned is to be found. In this case, reason is seeking the unconditioned condition for the cognition of oneself which in its view is the immaterial soul. Rational psychologists (e.g., Descartes) believe that certain facts about the soul can be deduced from the *I think* that accompanies all of my representations, viz., that the soul is a substance, that it is simple, that it is a person, and that it exists independently of outer objects. They also think that all of these propositions can be known *a priori*. In sum, the Paralogisms attempt to establish the existence and properties of the soul which serves as the unconditioned basis for consciousness. Put slightly differently, rational psychologists try to *objectify* the *I think* without appeal to experience.[15] When it comes to the fallaciousness of the Paralogisms, the formal error is always the same. They are all categorical syllogisms that commit a fallacy of equivocation. For example:

1) All banks are financial institutions.
2) Some people fish from banks.

3)   Therefore, some people fish from financial institutions.

In the above example, the term "banks" is ambiguous in that it has more than one meaning, a financial institution and a hill descending into a body of water. This argument makes an equivocal use of the term "bank" since in the first premise it uses the word in the former sense and in the second premise it uses the word in the latter sense. In each of the Paralogisms, a concept related to a set of categories is used in two distinct senses. In the major premise, the concept will be used in an analytic proposition which has only logical significance whereas in the conclusion the concept will be used in a synthetic proposition that is supposed to have real significance (i.e., by claiming something exists and possesses certain properties). Besides involving a fallacy of equivocation, the conclusion will also involve a dialectical use of a concept since it will apply the concept beyond the bounds of sense.[16]

There are four Paralogisms corresponding to the four sets of categories. The First Paralogism attempts to establish the existence of the soul as substance (relation). The Second Paralogism tries to prove that this soul is simple (quality). The Third Paralogism attempts to establish that the soul is a person by arguing that it is identical or a unity over time (quantity). Finally, the Fourth Paralogism tries to prove that whereas the soul is actual, the existence of external objects is doubtful or merely possible (modality). By misapplying concepts that fall under these categories beyond the bounds of sense, however, the Paralogisms do not generate cognition of the soul, but only transcendental ideas of the soul.

The Antinomies (chapter sixteen) illustrate the conflict that reason has with itself when it tries to complete the series of conditions for something conditioned (whether events in time or substances in space). Although the Antinomies do not explicitly take the form of hypothetical syllogisms, the form of reasoning underlies all of them: 1) If a conditioned cognition is given, then the whole series of conditions for it is also given, 2) Objects of experience are given as conditioned cognitions, 3) Therefore, the whole series of conditions for them is also given.[17] If "given" is interpreted as being the logical maxim that reason is given the *task* to seek out the unconditioned condition for any conditioned cognition, then there is nothing wrong with the argument. However, the Antinomies view the "given" in the conclusion in light of the illegitimate principle that for any conditioned cognition the unconditioned condition is given as *something* that reason grasps. This equivocation transforms the categories into transcendental ideas understood, in this context, as "cosmological ideas" or "world-concepts."[18] They are *cosmological* ideas since reason is positing the unconditioned (that which assumes no other antecedent condition) that completes the series of conditions within the *world*. Again, Kant constructs an antinomy for each set of categories. The First Antinomy has to do with the whether the world is finite or infinite in space and time (quantity). The Second Antinomy concerns whether substance is ultimately simple or composite (quality). The Third Antinomy has to do with whether freedom exists or if all causation is in accordance with natural law (relation). The Fourth Antinomy concerns whether or not an absolutely necessary being exists (modality).

In order to illustrate the conflict that reason has with itself when it comes to each of these cosmological ideas, Kant constructs a seemingly sound thesis argument (e.g., in favor of a free cause that assumes no other cause) as well as a seemingly sound antithesis argument (e.g., in favor of natural causation being the only kind of causation which assumes no other kind of causation). Whereas the thesis argument assumes the conclusion of the antithesis and derives a contradiction (by *reductio ad absurdum* or indirect proof), the antithesis argument does the same though by assuming the conclusion of the thesis. The only exception to this is the first part of the thesis argument in the Fourth Antinomy which as a form of the cosmological argument has the structure of a direct rather than an indirect proof (an argument Kant will return to again in the Ideal). The thesis arguments are associated with traditional positions in rationalism, whereas the antithesis arguments are associated with traditional positions in empiricism.[19] In either case, however, reason generates a cosmological idea that is incongruent with what the understanding deems to be possible.[20] These seemingly contradictory positions will be equally justified from the perspective of reason which leaves reason in conflict with itself.[21]

Kant does not, however, characterize all of the antinomal conflicts in the same way. Kant calls the first two Antinomies *mathematical* and the last two Antinomies *dynamical*.[22] Although this should remind one of how Kant describes the distinction between the first two sets of principles (corresponding to the categories of quantity and quality) and the last two sets of principles (corresponding to the categories of relation and modality) in the Transcendental Analytic, Kant means the distinction to mark something somewhat different in the Transcendental Dialectic. Kant argues that if one accepts transcendental idealism, then though both the thesis and the antithesis of the First and Second Antinomies will be false (mathematical), there is a way in which both the thesis and antithesis of the Third and Fourth Antinomies can be true (dynamical). The main reason why is that in the mathematical Antinomies, both thesis and antithesis are operating within the same domain (the world of experience), but rely on the common assumption of transcendental realism (i.e., that the world of experience and the objects within it are things-in-themselves), which when rejected, renders both positions false. In the dynamical Antinomies, however, the thesis arguments posit objects that transcend the world of experience while the antithesis arguments operate squarely within it. If one accepts the transcendentally idealist distinction between the world as it appears and as it is in itself (an assumption that the transcendental realist does not accept), both the thesis and the antithesis can be true. Consequently, transcendental idealism offers us an escape, not open to transcendental realism, from all four antinomal conflicts, though the escape offered in the dynamical antinomies will be different from the one offered in the mathematical antinomies. Above all, this will have important implications for the possibility of human freedom which, as mentioned above, Kant sees as one of the central ideas of metaphysics and will be indispensable for his practical (moral) philosophy.

The Ideal of pure reason (chapter seventeen) is the result of taking a transcendental idea and thinking an individual thing that is "determined through the idea alone."[23] In this case, the idea of the sum total of all reality is posited as an individual having the highest degree of reality (God). Of the three main sections of the Transcendental Dialectic, it is probably most difficult to see how the Ideal reflects the use of disjunctive syllogism. Seeing this requires examining how Kant thinks the thoroughgoing determination of finite things occurs. For any given finite thing (e.g., an apple) and for any possible predicate (e.g., red or square), the thoroughgoing determination of this thing requires that it have either the positive predicate or its negation (e.g., the apple is either red or not red, square or not square) predicated of it (e.g., an apple is red but not square). This process follows the form of a disjunctive syllogism. According to Kant, however, the thoroughgoing determination of finite things which possess both positive and negative predicates requires us to think of something which possesses only positive predicates (the opposite is not the case since determinate negations can only be thought by negating the affirmation). This would be the idea of the most real being or God.[24] In other words, God serves as the unconditioned condition for thoroughgoing determination. In this way, the Ideal commits an error common to all sections of the Transcendental Dialectic. Operating according to the legitimate logical maxim to *seek* the unconditioned condition for any conditioned thing, reason assumes the illegitimate principle that if the conditioned is given then the whole series of conditions including the unconditioned is *given* (in this case, God).

Unlike the Paralogisms or the Antinomies, Kant does not construct arguments corresponding to each of the four sets of categories. Kant thinks there are only three arguments for God: 1) an argument that depends on no experience whatsoever (the ontological argument), 2) an argument that depends on only an indeterminate experience (the cosmological argument), or 3) an argument that depends on a determinate experience (the physico-theological or design argument). The ontological argument is wholly *a priori* since it proceeds from the concept of most real being (God) alone. The cosmological argument is *a posteriori* insofar as it requires that something be given in experience that is contingent. The design argument is also *a posteriori* but requires not only that what is given in experience is contingent but also that it exhibit purposiveness. In this way, the design argument requires an experience that is more determinate than the cosmological argument.[25] Although Kant discusses all three arguments, he also tries to show that the cosmological argument presupposes the ontological argument and likewise the design argument presupposes both of the others. Consequently, the ontological argument is "the only possible argument" for God's existence.[26] Even though Kant thinks that both the cosmological argument and the design argument fail in their own right, his main objections are reserved for the ontological argument since it is presupposed by both of the other arguments.

Notes

1. *CPR* A63-64/B88.
2. Kant describes these ideas of reason as the "proper end" of metaphysical investigation. See *CPR* B395.
3. Kant contrasts this "transcendent" use of the categories with the perfectly appropriate and necessary "transcendental" use of the categories for the possibility of experience in the Principles of Pure Understanding. See *CPR* A296/B352-53. Kant does not, however, always use the terms consistently. See, for example, our discussion at the beginning of the last chapter and *CPR* A238-39/B298.
4. *CPR* A297-98/B354.
5. *CPR* A307/B364.
6. *CPR* A307-8/B364. Michelle Grier describes the situation in this way. See Michelle Grier, *Kant's Doctrine of Transcendental Illusion* (Cambridge: Cambridge University Press, 2001), 117-130.
7. *CPR* A651/B679.
8. To see how our cognitions of events in the natural world are always conditioned, just consider the lesson of the Second Analogy. In order for one to cognize an event (conditioned), this cognition presupposes another event (condition) from which it follows in accordance with natural law.
9. *CPR* Aviii. This example was inspired by Rohlf's discussion in Michael Rohlf, "The Ideas of Pure Reason," in *The Cambridge Companion to Kant's Critique of Pure Reason*, 195-96.
10. *CPR* A321-28/B378-385.
11. *CPR* A304/B361.
12. See *CPR* A334-36/B391-93. Altman has a helpful table summarizing the architectonic of the Transcendental Dialectic. See Altman, *A Companion to Kant's Critique*, 170.
13. For these criticisms see Jonathan Bennett, *Kant's Dialectic* (Cambridge: Cambridge University Press, 1974), 258 and 283 as well as Strawson, *The Bounds of Sense*, 159-160.
14. This is Allison's response to the criticisms. See Allison, *Kant's Transcendental Idealism*, 320-22.
15. Buroker puts the point this way. See Buroker, *Kant's Critique*, 213.
16. *CPR* A403-4.
17. *CPR* A498-500/B526-28. See also Rosenberg's helpful discussion of the syllogism. Rosenberg, *Accessing Kant*, 286-87.
18. *CPR* A408/B434-35.
19. *CPR* A466/B494.
20. *CPR* A486/B514.
21. *CPR* A406-7/B433-34.
22. *CPR* A528-532/B556-560.
23. *CPR* A568/B596.
24. *CPR* A575-76/B603-4.
25. *CPR* A590-91/B619-620.
26. *CPR* A625/B653.

Chapter Fifteen
Paralogisms

First Paralogism: The soul is a substance.

Quote

That the representation of which is the *absolute subject* of our judgments, and hence cannot be used as the determination of another thing, is *substance*.

I, as a thinking being, am the *absolute subject* of all my possible judgments, and this representation of Myself cannot be used as a predicate of any other thing.

Thus I, as thinking being (soul), am *substance*. [A348]

Synopsis

As mentioned in the previous chapter, the four Paralogisms reflect the core positions of rational psychology which infers the substantiality of the soul, along with all the characteristics of this substance, from the *I think* (transcendental apperception for Kant).[1] Although each Paralogism employs a different set of categories, they are all categorical syllogisms that commit fallacies of equivocation. The First Paralogism is an attempt to prove the substantiality (relation) of the soul. The first premise says that any absolute subject of judgment is a substance. This is the general rule provided by the understanding and the conception of substance it offers goes back to Aristotle who claimed that a subject of predication which cannot be predicated or "used as the determination" of anything else is a substance.[2] The second premise states that I represent myself as the absolute subject of my judgments. This premise subsumes the representation of myself under the condition (subject) of the general rule given in the first premise. It boils down to the idea that my thoughts or judgments are attributed to myself and I cannot be predicated or be an attribute of anything. It follows then that I, as a thinking being, am a substance. In the conclusion, reason attributes the predicate of the general rule to the representation of myself since the latter falls under the subject of the general rule. As mentioned above, all of the Paralogisms will involve the same form of categorical inference.

Kant points out that this paralogism has both a valid and an invalid version.[3] The argument is valid if "substance" in the conclusion means the same thing as "substance" in the major premise, namely a logical subject of predication. This conception of substance, however, is quite uninformative.[4] According to Kant, that the *I think* is a logical subject of predication is an analytic claim since "I am always the determining subject of that relation that constitutes the judgment."[5] In order to draw the conclusion the rational psychologist requires, the First Paralogism must equivocate between the two senses of "substance." In the first premise, "substance" is the absolute subject of predication, i.e., a logical subject or concept which is never a predicate but always a subject. The conclusion, however, concerns a real substance (a soul) which has properties (being a thing that endures, is simple, etc.). This equivocation makes for an invalid argument. Although being a real subject of inherence (substance with properties) is sufficient for being a logical subject of predication (subject of a proposition), the reverse is not true. Being a logical subject of predication is not sufficient to be a real subject of inherence. Real subjects of inherence may underlie logical subjects of predication, but they need not. For example, in the proposition that "2 is a number," even though "2" is the logical subject of predication, nevertheless, it does not follow that the number 2 is a real substance with qualities (like the textbook in your hands). If we analyze the pure concept of substance what we get is some logical subject of predication, but we cannot conclude based on that analysis that there is some real object or a "subject subsisting for itself" corresponding to this logical subject.[6]

That the *I think* is a real substance that has properties is a synthetic claim and requires that an object correspond to the concept of substance. In order to establish that an object does correspond to the concept, however, one needs a sensible intuition of that object. As the First Analogy argues (see chapter eleven), substance is the persistent in appearance.[7] Yet there is nothing persistent given in inner sense.[8] In the Refutation of Idealism (see chapter twelve), Kant claims that introspection never reveals anything persistent, but only fleeting thoughts. This is why Kant argues, in the Refutation, that a determination of my own consciousness in time is possible only through the existence of objects outside of me that persist.[9] There is no intuition of the *I think*. It is not an object of experience but rather a condition of experience itself. The representation of the *I think* is thought though not intuited.[10] Rational psychologists mistake this *form* of representation for the representation of an *object*.[11]

It is important to note, however, that Kant is not claiming to prove that there is no subject subsisting in itself. A proof of the latter (e.g., Hume's position)

would pose just as much a problem for Kant as a proof that the subject does subsist in itself (e.g., Descartes' position). Either proof would require cognition
beyond the bounds of sense which Kant thinks is illegitimate. In other words,
although the synthetic conclusion of the First Paralogism cannot be proven
within the bounds of sense, it also cannot be proven or disproven outside these
bounds.[12] As we will see below, furthermore, the possibility of an immortal soul
from the theoretical perspective will be absolutely vital for Kant's practical philosophy.

Reconstruction

1) Any absolute subject of judgment (i.e., cannot be predicated of other things)
   is a substance.
2) I, as a thinking being, am the absolute subject of my judgments.
3) From (1) and (2), therefore, I am, as a thinking being (soul), a substance
   (categorical syllogism).

Second Paralogism: The soul is simple.

Quote

> That thing whose action can never be regarded as the concurrence of many acting
> things, is *simple*.
>   Now the soul, or the thinking I, is such a thing.
>   Thus etc. [A351]

Synopsis

The Second Paralogism attempts to determine the *quality* of the soul and concludes that the soul, or the thinking I, is simple. The major premise states, "That
thing whose action can never be regarded as the concurrence of many acting
things, is *simple*."[13] A composite substance is made up of many parts and so an
action of the composite is made up of the concurring actions of the parts, just
like the action of the entire body is made up of the concurring actions of its
parts.[14] For example, when somebody jumps into the air, this action of jumping
is composed of the knees bending and straightening, the arms swinging, the feet
pushing, and many muscles contracting. Thus, if the action of something is not
the concurrence of many acting parts, then it is not a composite but a simple
(i.e., indivisible) thing. The minor premise states that the actions of the soul are
not the concurrence of many acting parts. Why is this? Because if the soul, being
a thinking thing, were made up of parts (a composite), then every part of the
soul would have only a part or piece of the thought inhering in it and the whole
thought could never be thought together. When playing devil's advocate, Kant

illustrates the problem using the example of a (poetic) verse which is composed of different words. If the different words that go to constitute the verse are known by different people, but no one knows all the words, then no one would know the whole verse. In the same way, if the different representations that go to constitute a thought are represented by different substances, but no substance represents all of them, no substance would be conscious of the whole thought. Since we are conscious of thoughts made up of different representations, the soul must be a simple substance.[15]

Similarly to the First Paralogism, the Second Paralogism fails to distinguish between *logical* simplicity and *real* simplicity.[16] Logical simplicity refers to the absolute unity of the *I think* as the formal condition of all experience, whereas real simplicity refers to the absolute unity of the *I think* as an object of experience. The former is the analytic claim that "I am simple" and merely refers to the fact that the "I" which thinks cannot be a plurality of thinking subjects.[17] The latter is a synthetic claim that concerns a substance without parts. As Kant points out, however, the representation of the "I" is "not an experience" and is "wholly empty of content."[18] Although apperception is required to unify the manifold of representations, apperception is not itself a manifold of representations that would require such unity. While Kant presupposes that the *I think* is an undivided absolute unity, it is a "merely subjective condition" of experience in general. Kant does not claim to have cognition of the "real simplicity of my subject."[19] Although a valid version of the argument would interpret "simple" in both the major premise and conclusion as referring to the *I think* as the formal condition of all experience, this interpretation of "simple" does not allow the rational psychologist to attribute simplicity to a substance that underlies the activity of apperception.

Kant also offers a criticism of the verse analogy explained above. Although thoughts are collective unities of representations, whether this collective unity is the result of multiple substances (each providing representations) or only one substance (providing all the representations) cannot be settled simply on the basis of the concept of "thought" alone.[20] Either explanation is consistent with the concept of thought as a collective unity of representations. In this respect, Kant seems to endorse Locke's criticisms of Descartes. Besides there being no epistemic access to whatever substance might underpin consciousness, there is no inconsistency in the substance of the *I think* being composite.[21] As you might recall, we offered a similar example in order to illustrate the unity of consciousness in chapter seven. The idea, in the present context, is that although a unity of consciousness is necessary for the consciousness of the whole verse/thought, this unity could be instantiated by multiple substances or a single substance. It is the unity of apperception that is important regardless of what might underpin this unity ontologically. The claim that a thought can only be caused by a simple thinking substance is a synthetic claim. To move from the logical subject of thinking, thinking predicated of a single "I" (analytic) to a simple substance underlying the *I think* (synthetic) requires a sensible intuition.[22] Much like the First Paralogism, however, this is an intuition that we do not have.

Reconstruction

1) Anything whose actions are not the concurrence of many acting things is simple.
2) The actions of the soul (thinking I) are not the concurrence of many acting things.
3) From (1) and (2), therefore, the soul is simple (categorical syllogism).

Third Paralogism: The soul is a person

Quote

> What is conscious of the numerical identity of its Self in different times is to that extent a *person*.
>> Now the soul is etc.
>> Thus it is a person. [A361]

Synopsis

The Third Paralogism attempts to determine the *quantity* of the soul concluding that the soul, or the *I think*, is a person. A person being, "What is conscious of the numerical identity of its Self in different times."[23] In other words, the Third Paralogism determines the quantity of the soul by claiming it is a *unity* over time.[24] The first premise states anything that is conscious of the numeric identity of itself through time is a person. In other words, if it (whatever *it* is) is conscious of itself being the same thing through time, then *it* is a person. The next premise states that the soul, or the I that thinks, is conscious of the numerical identity of itself over time. For example, I recognize the "I" that I referred to yesterday, last month, or even ten years ago, is the same "I" that I refer to when I use that personal pronoun today. When I say, "I drank coffee at breakfast," I do not add the qualification, "and the drinking coffee at breakfast 'I' is a different 'I' than myself." "I's" are always unitary, thus the "I" cannot be many "I's." It follows then, from these two premises that the thinking I (soul) is a person.

Just like the previous Paralogisms, the argument involves an equivocation, this time on the meaning of "person." To see this equivocation, notice that the first premise identifies a person as what is conscious of the numerical identity of itself. This can be interpreted in two different ways, first, as a logical subject which is numerically identical to itself, and second, as a real subject of inherence which is also numerically identical to itself. If "person" in the first premise is meant to be taken as a logical subject, and "person" in the conclusion means a real subject of inherence, then there is an equivocation within the argument which renders it invalid.[25] A valid version of the argument would be to interpret "person" in both the major premise and conclusion as a logical subject of thought. This interpretation of "person," however, does not allow us to predicate of it things such as substantiality, persistence, or continued existence after death.[26] Propositions which make use of these kinds of predicates are synthetic since they are statements about an object (e.g., person as a real subject) corresponding to a concept (e.g., person as logical subject), in which case intuition is required to establish the truth of these propositions. The first premise can be understood as an analytic proposition, however, when "person" is interpreted in the logical subject sense. In this case, being a person just is being self-conscious in time.[27] Consistent with the B edition Transcendental Deduction (chapter eight), "person" in this analytic sense is the *I think* that accompanies all of my representations over time and without which there would be representations that could not be thought at all, a result which Kant considers self-contradictory.[28] From an analytic proposition, however, no synthetic proposition follows without appeal to sensible intuition.

Kant offers an analogy with elastic balls to help explain why the Third Paralogism is invalid.[29] The Third Paralogism argues that given the unity of consciousness there must be some underlying substance which also remains identical. Kant's elastic ball analogy is meant to show that the unity of consciousness (i.e., the *I think* along with all of its representations) through time can be preserved even if the identity of the underlying substance changes. The analogy is as follows: motion is a mode which can be transferred from one elastic ball to another upon contact. Similarly, it seems possible for the unity of consciousness as a modification of the soul (understood as a real substance) to be transferred from one soul to another while preserving its identity. In other words, contrary to the Third Paralogism, the substance (soul) may change even though the unity of consciousness remains the same. In another example of Locke's influence, his example of the prince and the cobbler helps to illustrate Kant's point (an example reworked by Hollywood every generation or so). In Locke's example, the unity of consciousness of the prince is transferred to the body of the cobbler and vice versa. The substance changes, yet the unity of consciousness continues to be the same after the switch. As Locke remarks, "self depends on consciousness, not on substance. Self is that conscious thinking thing,—whatever substance made up of, (whether spiritual or material, simple or compounded, it matters not)."[30] Since one can conceive of the identity of consciousness without the identity of substance, one simply cannot infer the latter from the former as the Third Paralogism attempts to do.

Reconstruction

1) Anything that is conscious of the numeric identity of itself at different times is a person.
2) The soul (thinking I) is conscious of the numeric identity of itself at different times.
3) From (1) and (2), therefore, the soul is a person (categorical syllogism).

Fourth Paralogism: The soul exists independently of outer objects.

Quote

> That whose existence can be inferred only as a cause of given perceptions has only a *doubtful existence*:
>
> Now all outer appearances are of this kind: their existence cannot be immediately perceived, but can be inferred only as the cause of given perceptions:
>
> Thus the existence of all objects of outer sense is doubtful. The uncertainty I call the ideality of outer appearances, and the doctrine of this ideality is called *idealism*, in comparison with which the assertion of a possible certainty of objects of outer sense is called *dualism*. [A366-67]

Synopsis

The Fourth Paralogism from the A edition of *CPR* (quoted above) gets replaced by a completely new argument in the B edition. Both arguments are, however, concerned with the relationship between the mind and body. In the A edition, one of the main points is that the existence of outer objects can only be inferred based on the fact that they are the cause of our (the soul's) perceptions (which, of course, presupposes the existence of this soul). In the B edition, the argument concludes that it is possible for the soul to exist without outer objects. It is this concern with the relationship between mind and body that separates the arguments from the other three Paralogisms. As Kant tells us, since the Fourth Paralogism makes an attempt at "explaining the community of the soul with the body," it does not properly belong to the field of rational psychology, whose subject is simply the soul itself.[31] Even so, like the other Paralogisms, the Fourth Paralogism involves the misuse of a set of categories. The Fourth Paralogism is concerned with the categories of *modality* insofar as it attempts to establish, in the A edition, that the existence of external objects is merely doubtful or *possible* while at the same time insisting upon the *actuality* of the soul.[32]

In the A edition Fourth Paralogism, the case being made is that since we can only infer that outer objects exist, based on their causal relationship with our perceptions, their existence is not certain but rather doubtful. Our perceptions mediate between us and the object, and so any belief in outer objects can only be based on the inference that because our perceptions must have a cause, that cause is objects outside of us. This inference from an effect to its cause will always be doubtful "since the effect can have arisen from more than one cause."[33] Kant, however, rejects this skepticism about objects since, for Kant, objects simply are appearances in space.[34] As a transcendental idealist, Kant holds that these objects are appearances in space and time and are nothing without the subject and her forms of intuition. As an empirical realist, however, Kant affirms the reality of these objects in space and time without inference.[35]

The problem for transcendental realists is that they take space and time, and thus the objects within space and time, to be things-in-themselves beyond appearances. Consequently, they are forced to make an inference to the existence of outer objects based on those appearances, an inference which is always doubtful. Kant's dual positions of transcendental idealism/empirical realism allow him to avoid transcendental realism and the doubtful inference on which the Fourth Paralogism relies.

Kant radically reworked the Fourth Paralogism in the B edition of *CPR*, changing it into an argument that mirrors Descartes' argument for the real distinction between mind and body from the Sixth Meditation.[36] The A edition version of the argument is largely replaced and supplemented by the Refutation of Idealism added in the B edition. In the B edition, the Fourth Paralogism argues that because I can distinguish between myself (as a thinking being) and outer objects, such as my body, I am therefore really distinct from my body. My existence is independent from my body as well as outer objects. Kant replies to this argument by maintaining that we cannot know if the subject exists independently of objects simply by virtue of the fact that one distinguishes between subjects and objects. Kant affirms the analytic proposition that there is a distinction to be drawn between myself and "other things" outside of me.[37] It is analytic because whenever I think of *other* things I automatically think of them as different from me. If I did not think of them as different I would not be thinking of them as *other* things. I would just be thinking of myself. If the argument went no further than to unpack this analytic truth (e.g., by claiming that there is a *conceptual* distinction between myself and outer objects), then it would be valid. The conclusion that I could exist independently of my body and other outer objects, however, is synthetic. It requires showing that we really could (real possibility) exist independently of those objects or that those objects really could exist independently of us. Kant does not think these propositions can be established through concepts alone. As with the other Paralogisms, the B edition Fourth Paralogism rests on a fallacy of equivocation, confusing a logical distinction (analytic) for a real distinction (synthetic). For Kant, nothing follows ontologically from the distinction between outer (bodies in space including one's own body) and inner sense (mental states in time). Both have simply to do with appearances in one single spatiotemporal framework. Kant can avoid the problems that plague Descartes' mind-body interactionism. Once one abandons the ontological distinction, the problem of how substances of different ontological types can causally interact (mind and body) dissolves into the question of how representations in inner sense are conjoined with the modifications of outer sense according to constant laws in one experience.[38] Given the fact that one is dealing simply with law-governed appearances, there seems to be little problem explaining this relationship in accordance with the Analogies of Experience.

Although there are differences between the Fourth Paralogism in the A and B editions of *CPR*, the solutions given to the problems raised in both are answered by Kant's duel positions of empirical realism and transcendental idealism. These two positions must be taken together. One could never affirm the existence of objects in space and time (empirical realism) if one did not already believe that objects simply were appearances in space and time (transcendental idealism). By recognizing that objects simply are appearances in space and time (transcendental idealism), one is likewise compelled to immediately affirm their existence (empirical realism).

Reconstruction

1) Anything whose existence can only be inferred as the cause of given perceptions has a doubtful existence.
2) The existence of outer objects can only be inferred as the cause of given perceptions.
3) From (1) and (2), therefore, the existence of outer objects is doubtful (categorical syllogism).

Notes

1. *CPR* A341-48/B399-407.
2. *CPR* A147/B186 and A348/B406.
3. *CPR* A350-51.
4. *CPR* A349.
5. *CPR* B407.
6. *CPR* B413.
7. *CPR* B224-25.
8. *CPR* A349-350.
9. *CPR* B275-76.
10. Kant makes this point at *CPR* B157. See also Altman's discussion in Altman, *A Companion to Kant's Critique*, 172.
11. This is how Rosenberg puts it. See Rosenberg, *Accessing Kant*, 263.
12. Both Burnham and Young as well as Rosenberg make similar points. Rosenberg makes the further point that Hume himself must assume the idea of a subject in order to generate the bundle of perceptions that constitute oneself (i.e., some way of identifying these perceptions as *mine*), but at the same time he denies the legitimacy of such an idea. As mentioned in chapter seven, Hume himself seems to recognize the shortcomings of his bundle theory in the appendix to the *Treatise*. See Burnham and Young, *Kant's Critique*, 145-46 and Rosenberg, *Accessing Kant*, 259.
13. *CPR* A351.
14. *CPR* A351-52.
15. *CPR* A352.
16. *CPR* A356.
17. *CPR* A355.
18. *CPR* A354-55.
19. *CPR* A354 and A356.
20. *CPR* A352-53.

21. See Locke, *Essay*, II.27.11-19. See also Buroker's and Rosenberg's discussions of this weakness in Descartes' argument. Buroker, *Kant's Critique*, 222 and Rosenberg, *Accessing Kant*, 264-65.

22. *CPR* B407-8.

23. *CPR* A361.

24. *CPR* A344/B402.

25. *CPR* A363.

26. *CPR* A365-66.

27. *CPR* A362.

28. *CPR* B131-32.

29. *CPR* A363-64.

30. Locke, *Essay*, II.27.17. For the prince/cobbler example, see Locke, *Essay*, II.27.15. It should be noted that Locke's example preserves the souls along with their consciousnesses and just changes the bodies. Likewise, Kant's elastic ball analogy seems most fit to illustrate a transfer of consciousness between bodies. Neither Kant nor Locke thinks, however, that much hinges on whether the substances are material (bodies) or immaterial (souls). In either case, the modification of substance (unity of consciousness) seems to be something that can be preserved irrespective of the substance that is being modified.

31. *CPR* B427.

32. *CPR* A344/B402, A404.

33. *CPR* A368.

34. *CPR* A26-30/B42-45, A369-376.

35. *CPR* A370.

36. Descartes, *Meditations*, 2:54.

37. *CPR* B409.

38. *CPR* A386.

Chapter Sixteen
Antinomies

First Antinomy

Quote

Thesis

The world has a beginning in time, and in space it is also enclosed in boundaries.

Proof

For if one assumes that the world has no beginning in time, then up to every given point in time an eternity has elapsed, and hence an infinite series of states of things in the world, each following another, has passed away. But now the infinity of a series consists precisely in the fact that it can never be completed through a successive synthesis. Therefore an infinitely elapsed world-series is impossible, so a beginning of the world is a necessary condition of its existence; which was the first point to be proved.

Regarding the *second* point, again assume the opposite: then the world would be an infinite given whole of simultaneously existing things. Now we can think of the magnitude of a quantum that is not given as within certain boundaries of every intuition in no other way than by the synthesis of its parts, and we can think of the totality of such a quantum only through the completed synthesis, or through the repeated addition of units to each other. Accordingly, in order to think the world that fills all space as a whole, the successive synthesis of the parts of an infinite world would have to be regarded as completed, i.e., in the enumeration of all coexisting things, an infinite time would have to be regarded as having elapsed, which is impossible. Accordingly an infinite aggregate of actual things cannot be regarded as a given whole, hence cannot be regarded as given *simultaneously*. Consequently, a world is *not infinite* in its extension in space, but is rather enclosed within its boundaries, which was the second point. [A426-29/B454-57]

Synopsis

An "antinomy" is a "contradiction in the laws of pure reason."[1] As we discussed in the opening chapter of Part Three, Kant believes that reason contradicts itself when it tries to complete the series of conditions for conditioned things in the world. To illustrate this, Kant constructs four antinomies that consider the world through the four sets of categories. Our present concern, the First Antinomy, considers the world through the categories of quantity and asks whether it is bounded (finite quantity) or unbounded (infinite quantity) in space and time. Kant constructs seemingly sound arguments for both sides of the question at issue. Since both the "thesis" as well as the "antithesis" positions are equally justified from the perspective of reason, it is left in conflict with itself, unable to resolve the issue. Below we will offer synopses and reconstructions of all the thesis and antithesis arguments. We will follow each antinomy with a synopsis of Kant's resolution of the antinomy.

The thesis for the First Antinomy argues first, that the world had a beginning in time, and secondly, that the world is enclosed in spatial boundaries. Like most of the arguments in the Antinomies, the thesis uses a *reductio ad absurdum*, the indirect proof strategy through which one reduces the position argued against to absurdity. In such an argument, the philosopher assumes what she is arguing against to be true, and then from that assumption derives a contradiction. Since a contradiction follows from the original assumption, it follows that that assumption must be false and the negation of that assumption true. The first part of the thesis says that the world had a beginning in time, and so for the indirect proof the thesis assumes that the world did not have a beginning in time. If the world did not have a beginning then it has always existed. Put another way, if there is no time in which the world did not exist, then the world must have existed for an infinite amount of time into the past. Accordingly, there would have needed to have been an infinite series of events leading up to the present event, or as the thesis says, "an infinite series of states of things in the world, each following another, has passed away." As a result, to have reached the present state, an infinite number of events must have been traversed, or as the thesis puts it, "completed though a successive synthesis." The key claim comes in premise four. An infinite series cannot be traversed since for a series to be infinite, it must be the case that it cannot, in fact, be traversed. No matter how many points in the series are crossed, if the series is actually infinite, then there will always be another point in the series to cross. For Kant, this is a logical, not an epistemological or a psychological point.[2] There is simply no sense in which an infinite whole could ever be considered *complete*.[3] In fact, according to Kant, that such an infinite series could never be completed through successive synthesis is the "true (transcendental) concept of infinity."[4] Since the assumption that the world did not have a beginning in time leads to a contradiction between the claim, in premise three, that an infinite series has been traversed and the claim, in premise four, that it is impossible to traverse an infinite series, the proponent of the thesis can negate the original assumption and conclude by indirect proof, in premise six, that the world did have a beginning in time.

The second part of the thesis states that the world is enclosed in spatial boundaries and so for indirect proof it assumes the contrary, viz., that the world is a spatially infinite given whole of simultaneously existing things. In order to think something that is not bounded in intuition (an indeterminate representation) as an actually infinite whole (a determinate representation) requires the successive synthesis of its parts (i.e., of the simultaneously existing things in space). Such a successive synthesis, however, would need to be completed. As explained above, however, it is impossible to complete a successive synthesis that is infinite. Just as the first part of the argument hinges on the idea that it is impossible to traverse an infinite series, so too does the second part of the argument hinge on this same idea. Much as with the first part of the argument, here the assumption, in premise seven, that world is a spatially infinite given whole of simultaneously existing things leads to a contradiction between the idea, in premise eleven, that an infinite successive synthesis of its parts is completed and the claim, in premise twelve, that completing such an infinite successive synthesis is impossible.[5] Putting the conclusions of the two indirect proofs together, it follows that "The world has a beginning in time, and in space it is also enclosed in boundaries" which is the thesis of the First Antinomy.

Reconstruction

1) [Assume for reductio] The world has no beginning in time.
2) If the world has no beginning in time, then an infinite number of moments have passed until now and so an infinite series has been traversed.
3) From (1) and (2), an infinite number of moments have passed until now and so an infinite series has been traversed (modus ponens).
4) It is impossible to traverse an infinite series.
5) From (3) and (4), contradiction.
6) From (1) – (5), the world has a beginning in time (indirect proof).
7) [Assume for reductio] The world is a spatially infinite given whole of si-multaneously existing things.
8) If the world is a spatially infinite given whole of simultaneously existing things, then it is not bounded in intuition and must be thought by construct-ing it through the successive synthesis of its parts.
9) From (7) and (8), the world is a spatially infinite given whole of simultane-ously existing things that is not bounded in intuition and must be thought by constructing it through the successive synthesis of its parts (modus ponens).

10) If the world is a spatially infinite given whole of simultaneously existing things that is not bounded in intuition and must be thought by constructing it through the successive synthesis of its parts, then an infinite series has been traversed through this successive synthesis.

11) From (9) and (10), an infinite series has been traversed through this successive synthesis (modus ponens).

12) It is impossible to traverse an infinite series.

13) From (11) and (12), contradiction.

14) From (7) – (13), the world is not a spatially infinite given whole of simultaneously existing things and so is enclosed in spatial boundaries (indirect proof).

15) From (6) and (14), the world has a beginning in time and in space it is also enclosed in boundaries (conjunction introduction).

Quote

Antithesis

The world has no beginning and no bounds in space, but is infinite with regard to both time and space.

Proof

For suppose that it has a beginning. Since the beginning is an existence preceded by a time in which the thing is not, there must be a preceding time in which the world was not, i.e., an empty time, because no part of such a time has, in itself, prior to another part, any distinguishing condition of its existence rather than its non-existence (whether one assumes that it comes to be of itself or through another cause). Thus many series of things may begin in the world, but the world itself cannot have any beginning, and so in past time it is infinite.

As to the second point, first assume the opposite, namely that the world is finite and bounded in space; then it exists in an empty space, which is not bounded. There would thus be encountered not only a relation between things in *space*, but also a relation of things *to space*. Now since the world is an absolute whole, besides which there is encountered no object of intuition, and hence no correlate of the world to which the world could stand in relation, the relation of the world to empty space would be a relation of the world to *no object*. Such a *relation*, however, and hence also the boundedness of the world by empty space, is nothing; therefore the world is not bounded at all in space, i.e., in its extension it is infinite. [A427-430/B455-58]

Synopsis

The antithesis of the First Antinomy seeks to prove the opposite of the thesis, viz., that the world has existed for an infinite amount of time and is spatially infinite. First, the antithesis assumes for indirect proof that the world had a beginning in time in which case it follows that there must have been a time preceding its beginning. This is what the antithesis calls an "empty time." There is nothing in an empty time, however, and so no event to which the beginning of the world could be temporally related. As the fifth premise notes, if this is true, then the beginning of the world must be related to nothing at all. To understand the problem with this view, consider the difference between reflexive and non-reflexive relations. The proposition that "The textbook is identical to itself" denotes a reflexive relation since there is only one relatum (the textbook) which stands in a relation with itself (i.e., being identical to). In contrast, the proposition that "The textbook is to the left of the pen" denotes a non-reflexive relation since there are two relata (the textbook and the pen) which bear a relationship to one another (being to the left of). Whereas reflexive relations have only one relatum, non-reflexive relations must have at least two relata. The thesis argument is not merely claiming that the world is temporally related to itself (a reflexive temporal relation) but rather that the world is temporally related to nothing at all (a non-reflexive temporal relation). Any non-reflexive relation, however, must have at least two relata. Since "nothing" does not denote *something* that can serve as a relata in this temporal relation, non-reflexive temporal relations between something (e.g., an event) and nothing at all are impossible. In other words, a non-reflexive relation with only one relatum is impossible. As premise six notes, the beginning of the world (an event) cannot be temporally related to nothing at all.[6] Therefore, the original assumption that the world has a beginning and is finite in time leads to a contradiction between the fifth premise and the sixth premise. As a result, it must be the case that the world did not have a beginning in time and is therefore infinite with regard to time.

The second part of the antithesis starts in premise nine by assuming that the world is finite and bounded in space. If so, then the world must exist in an empty space that is not bounded. Yet, for the world to be related to empty space is the same as being spatially related to nothing at all. Again, the thesis argument is not claiming that the world is related only to itself (reflexive relation). The relation must be non-reflexive since it requires the relation of something to nothing. The problem here is much like the problem with time above, *viz.,* a non-reflexive relation with only one relatum is impossible. As the antithesis claims near the end of the above quote, a relation between the world and nothing is itself nothing. Put slightly differently, the thesis requires that empty space and time serve as the *boundary* of the world. A boundary is where something differs from something else (e.g., the ocean and the coastline) and so there must be *something* with which we can contrast the world at that boundary. Since empty space and time are not objects of possible experience, there is *nothing* with which we could contrast the world at that boundary. Consequently, it makes little sense to talk about a boundary at all.[7] These considerations lead to a contradiction between the claim, in premise thirteen, that the world is spatially related to nothing at all and the claim, in premise fourteen, that the world cannot be spatially related to nothing at all. Since a contradiction results from the assumption that the world is finite and bounded in space, it follows that the world must be infinite and unbounded in space. Putting the conclusions of the two indirect proofs together, it follows that "The world has no beginning and no bounds in space, but is infinite with regard to both in time and space" which is the antithesis of the First Antinomy.

Reconstruction

1) [Assume for reductio] The world has a beginning and is finite in time.
2) If the world has a beginning, then the beginning of the world is preceded by an empty time.
3) From (1) and (2), the beginning of the world is preceded by an empty time (modus ponens).
4) If the beginning of the world is preceded by an empty time, then the beginning of the world is temporally related to nothing at all.
5) From (3) and (4), the beginning of the world is temporally related to nothing at all (modus ponens).
6) The beginning of the world cannot be temporally related to nothing at all.
7) From (5) and (6), contradiction.
8) From (1) – (7), the world has no beginning and is infinite with regard to time (indirect proof).
9) [Assume for reductio] The world is finite and bounded in space.
10) If the world is finite and bounded in space, then the world exists in an empty space that is not bounded.
11) From (9) and (10), the world exists in an empty space that is not bounded (modus ponens).
12) If the world exists in an empty space that is not bounded, then the world is spatially related to nothing at all.
13) From (11) and (12), the world is spatially related to nothing at all (modus ponens).
14) The world cannot be spatially related to nothing at all.
15) From (13) and (14), contradiction.
16) From (9) – (15), the world is infinite and unbounded in space (indirect proof).
17) From (8) and (16), the world has no beginning and no bounds in space, but is infinite with regard to both in time and space (conjunction introduction).

Resolution Synopsis

Assuming that both arguments are valid and arguably sound, reason is in conflict with itself when it comes to the spatiotemporal magnitude of the world. Kant's solution to this antinomal conflict comes in two steps. The first step is to recognize that both sides are assuming that the world has a *determinate* spatiotemporal magnitude. In other words, both sides are assuming that the world either is or is not in itself bounded in space and time. If this background assumption is denied, however, then it is possible to reject both thesis and antithesis without contradiction. Consider the claim that "You either love me or you hate me." Both options assume that the person to whom the claim is directed feels *something* toward the person making the claim. Assuming that the person to whom the claim is directed feels *nothing* at all toward the person making the claim, however, then both disjuncts of the original claim would be false. Kant believes his theory of transcendental idealism offers a way of understanding how both thesis and antithesis of the First Antinomy might be false.

He begins by arguing against the thesis that the world has a beginning in time and is enclosed in spatial boundaries. For the thesis to be true there would have to be both a temporal and spatial boundary for the world, in which case there must exist both empty time and empty space beyond this boundary. If one accepts transcendental idealism, and with it the view that the world is given only as appearance and not as it is in itself, there could be no bounding of appearance by nothing at all. Experience of either empty time or space is impossible according to Kant. Some of Kant's central arguments against the experience of empty space/time come in the Analogies (see chapter eleven). The Second Analogy establishes that every event presupposes *something* from which it follows in accordance with a rule.[8] Events arising from *nothing* at all would violate this causal principle.[9] Likewise, in the Third Analogy, if one assumes the experience of empty space, appearances would be broken off from one another, but this is contrary to our experience of one unified space.[10]

Next, Kant shifts his focus to the antithesis which claims that the world is both spatially and temporally infinite. In each case, there must be an empirical regress from the conditioned to conditions that continues to infinity. The question that Kant asks is, if there is no boundary to the world as it appears (i.e., the world is not finite), then is the regress through the series of appearances going to be infinite or indefinite? Although the antithesis argues that the regress is infinite, Kant claims that it is actually going to be indefinite. It cannot be infinite because the members of the series (appearances) are determined and incorporated into one experience through acts of synthesis (proceeding through the empirical regress) on the part of the subject.

If the world does not exist in itself but only insofar as it appears, then its magnitude can only be constructed through the successive synthesis of appearances. It is only through this successive synthesis that events in time or objects in space are generated and incorporated into one world of experience. One cannot claim that the magnitude of the world is either a finite whole (thesis) or an infinite whole (antithesis), but only that the magnitude of the world extends indefinitely since it extends as far as the successive synthesis of appearances itself extends. For any event, we can always look for another event from which the former event follows in accordance with natural law. Likewise, for anything existing in space we can always look toward something else existing in another spatial location related to the previous one. If the world were given as a thing-in-itself, then either the thesis or antithesis would be true. Assuming transcendental idealism, however, the magnitude of the world is not determinate but rather *indeterminate* since it depends upon the subject and her synthetic activities.[11] Even though we must always seek a "more remote member" of the series (of events in time or objects in space), it would be a mistake to infer from this that a most remote member actually exists (finite series) or that there is no most remote member (infinite series).[12] Although reason is naturally drawn toward making this mistaken inference, transcendental idealism cautions us against it.

Second Antinomy

Quote

Thesis

Every composite substance in the world consists of simple parts, and nothing exists anywhere except the simple or what is composed of simples.

Proof

For assume that composite substances do not consist of simple parts: then, if all composition is removed in thought, no composite part, and (since there are no simple parts) no simple part, thus nothing at all would be left over; consequently, no substance would be given. Thus either it is impossible to remove all composition in thought or else after its removal something must be left over that subsists without any composition, i.e., the simple. In the first case, the composite would once again not consist of substances (because with substances composition is only a contingent relation, apart from which, as being persisting by themselves, they must subsist). Now since this case contradicts the presupposition, only the second case is left: namely, that what is a substantial composite in the world consists of simple parts.

From this it follows immediately that all things in the world are simple beings, that composition is only an external state of these beings, and that even though we can never put these elementary substances completely outside this state of combination and isolate them, reason must still think of them as the primary subjects of all composition and hence think of them prior to it as simple beings. [A434-36/B462-64]

Synopsis

The thesis of the Second Antinomy is that all composite substances are made up of simple parts, and that these simple parts are all that exists or compose all that exists. As in the First Antinomy, the thesis argument begins by assuming the opposite, viz., that composite substances are not made up of simple parts. If this is the case, then an object can always be divided without reaching something simple, i.e., something that cannot be divided. Under this assumption, if we remove composition from the thought of a substance then no substance would be given since substance is essentially complex. The argument for the thesis holds that there are two possibilities, either the removal of composition from thought is impossible or, after the removal of composition, there must be something left that is not composite.[13] The thesis argument is predicated on transcendental realism which would reject the first option (holding it really is possible to remove all composition in thought) because composition is a contingent relation between substances that otherwise persist. Composition is contingent insofar as substances can either participate or not participate in this relation. For example, hydrogen and oxygen can participate in the relation of composition resulting in H_2O, but they need not do so. They can exist as elements independently of the composite. If all substances were ultimately composite, however, then there would be no relata to participate in the relation of composition since the substances would themselves consist wholly of relations (the hydrogen and oxygen atoms in our example). Transcendental realism would hold that it is absurd to think that something could consist wholly of relations without relata. All relations are ultimately reducible to the relata that participate in these relations where the relata essentially possess only non-relational properties, i.e., they must be capable of existing on their own independently of their relationship to other things.[14] Consequently, although substances as relata are necessary for the relation of composition, the reverse is not true.

From the original assumption, it follows in premise three that if we take away composition then nothing is left. This contradicts, however, the claim in premise six that taking away composition does not take away substance. Since the assumption that composite substances are not composed of simple parts leads to a contradiction, this assumption can be denied from which it immediately follows not only that "Every composite substance in the world consists of simple parts" but also that "nothing exists anywhere except the simple or what is composed of simples." These two claims together constitute the thesis of the Second Antinomy.

Reconstruction

1) [Assume for reductio] composite substances do not consist of simple parts.
2) If composite substances do not consist of simple parts, then it is impossible to remove all composition in thought and for a substance to still be given.
3) From (1) and (2), it is impossible to remove all composition in thought and for a substance to still be given (modus ponens).
4) Composition is a contingent relation between substances that otherwise persist.
5) If composition is a contingent relation between substances that otherwise persist, then it is possible to remove all composition in thought and for a substance to still be given.
6) From (4) and (5), it is possible to remove all composition in thought and for a substance to still be given (modus ponens).
7) From (3) and (6), contradiction.

8) From (1) – (7), composite substances do consist of simple parts (indirect proof).
9) If composite substances do consist of simple parts, then every composite substance in the world consists of simple parts, and nothing exists anywhere except the simple or what is composed of simples.
10) From (8) and (9), every composite substance in the world consists of simple parts, and nothing exists anywhere except the simple or what is composed of simples (modus ponens).

Quote

Antithesis

No composite thing in the world consists of simple parts, and nowhere in it does there exist anything simple.

Proof

Suppose a composite thing (as substance) consists of simple parts. Because every external relation between substances, hence every composition of them, is possible only in space, there must exist as many parts of space as there are parts of the composite thing occupying it. Now space does not consist of simple parts, but of spaces. Thus every part of the composite must occupy a space. But the absolutely primary parts of the composite are simple. Thus the simple occupies a space. Now since everything real that occupies a space contains within itself a manifold of elements external to one another, and hence is composite, and indeed, as a real composite, it is composed not of accidents (for they cannot be external to one another apart from substance), but therefore of substances; thus the simple would be a substantial composite, which contradicts itself.

The second proposition of the antithesis, that in the world nothing at all exists that is simple, is here supposed to signify only this: The existence of the absolutely simple cannot be established by any experience or perception, whether external or internal, and the absolutely simple is thus a mere idea, whose objective reality can never be established in any possible experience, and hence in the exposition of appearances it has no application or object. For if we assumed that this transcendental idea could find an object in experience, then empirical intuition of some such object would have to be recognized, an intuition containing absolutely no manifold whose elements are external to one another and bound into a unity. Now since there is no inference from our not being conscious of <such a manifold to its> complete impossibility in any intuition of an object, but this intuition is definitely required for absolute simplicity, it follows that this simplicity cannot be inferred from any perception, whatever it might be. Since, therefore, nothing can ever be given as an absolutely simple object in any possible experience, but the world of sense must be regarded as the sum total of all possible experiences, nothing simple is given anywhere in it.

This second proposition of the antithesis goes much further than the first since the first banishes the simple only from the intuition of the composite, while the second, on the other hand, does away with the simple in the whole of nature; hence also it could not have been proved from the concept of a given object of outer intuition (of the composite), but only from its relation to a possible experience in general. [A435-38/B463-66]

Synopsis

The antithesis of the Second Antinomy is that no composite substance is made up of simple parts and that simple substances do not exist. As with the First Antinomy, the antithesis of the Second Antinomy starts by assuming the thesis, viz., that composite substances consist of simple parts. If we consider an object in space, such as an apple, every part of that apple is going to occupy a space because anything that occupies space is going to have parts which are external to one another in space. If, as was assumed, the apple is made up of simple parts, then those simple parts will each occupy a space. This is the case because the apple is a composite substance and composition of substances can only happen in space. As the antithesis points out, anything that occupies space is composite because it has parts which are external to each other. An object (or part of an object) in *space* is minimally going to have a left and a right hand side which are distinct external parts. For example, imagine three objects: A, B, and C. Objects A and C are separated by B which is adjacent to A on its left and C on its right. Now if B does not have right and left hand sides then A and C would in fact be adjacent. B would not be in space at all if simple! Assuming that an object is made up of simple parts leads to a contradiction. In premise three, it is claimed that composite substances consist of simple parts that do not have external parts, but because they are in space these parts must have parts which are external to one another as premise eight notes. Therefore, the original assumption that composite substances consist of simple parts must be false.

The second part of the antithesis argues that simple substances do not exist anywhere in the world.[15] It begins by inferring from the conclusion of the indirect proof, in premise ten, that no composite thing in the world consists of simple parts, in premise twelve. Although one can immediately infer from the fact that composite substances do consist of simple parts to the conclusion that nothing exists anywhere except the simple or what is composed of simples in the thesis, one cannot immediately infer from the fact that no composite thing in the world consists of simple parts to the conclusion that simple substances do not exist anywhere in the world in the antithesis. After all, there could be simple substances that are not parts in any composite substance. The second part of the antithesis hinges on the idea that simple substances are not things of which we can have experience. As Kant established in the Axioms of Intuition (see chapter ten), every object of experience must be given in empirical intuition and everything given in empirical intuition has extensive magnitude, i.e., consists of parts.[16] A simple substance, by definition, does not have an extensive magnitude and so cannot be given in empirical intuition. As premise fourteen notes, if it cannot be given in empirical intuition, then it is not an object of experience. In the above quote, the antithesis assumes that the world is just the "sum total of all possible experiences." This idea is reflected in premise sixteen and it follows from this assumption that simple substances are not a part of the world. Putting premises twelve and eighteen together, one can conclude that "No composite thing in the world consists of simple parts, and nowhere in it does there exist anything simple" which is the antithesis of the Second Antinomy. Although this line of argumentation might seem to assume the conditions of possible experience that Kant has established in *CPR*, one should understand both the thesis and the antithesis of the Second Antinomy as making claims about the nature of substance in itself. If space is infinitely divisible in itself, then substances in space must be constituted by an infinite number of parts in themselves. This is a position that Kant will ultimately reject in his resolution to the Second Antinomy.

Reconstruction

1) [Assume for reductio] composite substances ultimately consist of simple parts.
2) If composite substances ultimately consist of simple parts, then composite substances ultimately consist of parts that do not have external parts.
3) From (1) and (2), composite substances ultimately consist of parts that do not have external parts (modus ponens).
4) Composition is an external relation that is possible only in space.
5) If composite substances ultimately consist of simple parts and composition is an external relation that is possible only in space, then the simple parts of composite substances must each occupy a space.
6) From (3), (4), and (5), the simple parts of composite substances must each occupy a space (modus ponens).
7) If the simple parts of composite substances must each occupy a space, then composite substances ultimately consist of parts that do have external parts.
8) From (6) and (7), composite substances ultimately consist of parts that do have external parts (modus ponens).
9) From (3) and (8), contradiction.
10) From (1) – (9), composite substances do not consist of simple parts (indirect proof).
11) If composite substances do not consist of simple parts, then no composite thing in the world consists of simple parts.
12) From (10) and (11), no composite thing in the world consists of simple parts (modus ponens).
13) The simple cannot be given in empirical intuition.
14) If the simple cannot be given in empirical intuition, then the simple is not an object of possible experience.
15) From (13) and (14), the simple is not an object of possible experience (modus ponens).
16) The world is the sum total of the objects of possible experience.

17) If the simple is not an object of possible experience and the world is the sum total of the objects of possible experience, then nowhere in the world does there exist anything simple.
18) From (15), (16), and (17), nowhere in the world does there exist anything simple (modus ponens).
19) From (12) and (18), no composite thing in the world consists of simple parts, and nowhere in it does there exist anything simple (conjunction introduction).

Resolution Synopsis

In the resolution to the First Antinomy we saw that the regress to prior conditions of a given conditioned (appearance in space and time) is an indeterminate regress. For any given conditioned we know that there is some prior condition but we cannot know whether this regress goes on to infinity or if it stops at some unconditioned condition. This is because the conditions for the conditioned must be found *outside* of the conditioned (time prior to the beginning of time or space outside the place where the world began). This is different from the resolution of the Second Antimony in which the conditions (parts) of a given conditioned (substance in empirical intuition) are already given *within* the conditioned. We know that a substance in empirical intuition can be divided to infinity because that substance is an appearance in space and so must always have extensive magnitude. Kant holds, in the Axioms of Intuition, that all appearances are intuited as aggregates.[17] Consequently, unlike the resolution to the First Antinomy, the regress from conditioned to conditions in the Second Antinomy is infinite rather than merely indefinite.[18] Even so, we are not entitled to say that the substance has an infinite number of parts since the parts of the appearance are "given and determined only through the subdivision" where this subdivision is itself an act of the understanding.[19] In this respect, there is a strong similarity between the resolution of the First Antinomy and the resolution of the Second Antinomy. Just as the spatiotemporal extent of the world is indeterminate, so too is the total number of parts that constitute a given substance indeterminate. It is only through successive synthesis that the parts of a substance are determined and incorporated into a unified whole of experience. Just as with the First Antinomy, if the world existed in itself, then either the thesis or the antithesis of the Second Antinomy would have to be true. Since reason is drawn naturally to each of the two positions, it is in conflict with itself. Transcendental idealism, however, allows us to see how both thesis and antithesis could be false which offers reason an escape from this conflict.

Third Antinomy

Quote

Thesis

Causality in accordance with the laws of nature is not the only one from which all
the appearances of the world can be derived. It is also necessary to assume another
form of causality, i.e., causality through freedom, in order to explain them.

Proof

Assume that there is no other causality than that in accordance with the laws of nature: then everything *that happens* presupposes a previous state, upon which it follows without exception according to a rule. But now the previous state itself must be
something that has happened (come to be in a time when it previously was not),
since if it had been at every time, then its consequence could not have just arisen,
but would always have been. Thus the causality of the cause through which something happens is always something *that has happened*, which according to the law of
nature presupposes once again a previous state and its causality, and this in the same
way a still earlier state, and so on. If therefore, everything happens according to
mere laws of nature, then at every time there is only a subordinate but never a first
beginning, and thus no completeness of the series on the side of the causes descending one from another. But now the law of nature consists just in this, that nothing
happens without a cause sufficiently determined *a priori*. Thus the proposition that
all causality is possible only in accordance with laws of nature, when taken in its unlimited universality, contradicts itself, and therefore this causality cannot be assumed to be the only one.

Accordingly, a causality must be assumed through which something happens
without its cause being further determined by another previous cause, i.e., an *absolute* causal *spontaneity* beginning *from itself* a series of appearances that runs according to natural laws, hence transcendental freedom, without which even in the
course of nature the series of appearances is never complete on the side of the causes. [A444-46/B472-74]

Synopsis

The thesis of the Third Antinomy argues that there must be some other kind of
causation besides causality in accordance with natural law. This other kind of
causation is what the thesis calls "causality through freedom" or "transcendental
freedom" which does not presuppose any prior event or cause from which it
follows. As with the earlier arguments in the Antinomies, the thesis is an indirect proof. It assumes that the only kind of causality is naturally deterministic
causation or causation in accordance with natural law. This is the kind of causation that Kant describes in the Second Analogy (see chapter eleven) where each
event presupposes something else from which it follows "without exception
according to a rule."[20] This conception of causation in the natural world is, fur-

thermore, accepted by both proponents of the thesis and the antithesis.[21] When causality is in accordance with the laws of nature, no matter what the event, that event must have been caused by one that came before it, and this earlier cause must have been caused by a prior event, and so on.

The key to the argument comes in recognizing that if the only kind of causality is naturally deterministic causation, then it must be sufficient to itself. In other words, it must not require another form of causation (i.e., transcendental freedom) in order to explain a causal series. As premise three puts it, naturally deterministic causation must provide the complete sufficient condition for any causal series. In other words, it must provide a complete explanation of the existence of a causal series. In this respect, the thesis argument is making implicit appeal to the principle of sufficient reason, viz., that there must be a sufficient reason for the existence of a causal series as a whole.[22]

It is easy to see how naturally deterministic causation can give the necessary conditions for any causal series, insofar as each prior event in the series is necessary for the event which follows from it, but the prior event is not sufficient in itself to bring about the subsequent event since the prior event itself presuppose another event from which it follows. For example if event E_3 follows from E_2 in accordance with natural law, then E_2 is necessary for E_3 insofar as E_3 presupposes E_2. Even so, E_2 is not sufficient in itself for E_3 insofar as E_2 itself presupposes some other event E_1 from which E_2 follows in accordance with natural law. What is true of E_2 is likewise true of E_1 and so on to infinity. If causality in accordance with natural law must be able to give the complete sufficient conditions for any causal series, however, then there must be an end to the series of antecedent causal conditions. Put in terms of the example, there must be a sense in which the series of conditions for E_3 is complete.

As has already been said, however, if naturally deterministic causation is the only kind of causation, then every event necessarily presupposes another event from which it follows in accordance with natural law. With naturally deterministic causation, the presupposing of antecedent events goes on to infinity. Consequently, as premise seven notes, naturally deterministic causation cannot give the complete sufficient conditions for any causal series. This contradicts, however, the claim in premise three that naturally deterministic causation can give the complete sufficient condition for any causal series. Therefore, the original assumption in premise one must be false, from which it follows that there must be another kind of causation which gives the complete sufficient condition for any causal series, viz., causality through freedom.[23] One can conclude that "Causality in accordance with the laws of nature is not the only one from which all the appearances of the world can be derived. It is also necessary to assume another causality through freedom in order to explain them" which is the thesis of the Third Antinomy.

Reconstruction

1) [Assume for reductio] there is only naturally deterministic causation.
2) If there is only naturally deterministic causation, then it gives the complete sufficient condition for any causal series.
3) From (1) and (2), naturally deterministic causation gives the complete sufficient condition for any causal series (modus ponens).
4) If there is only naturally deterministic causation, then every event presupposes (necessary condition) another event from which it follows according to natural law *ad infinitum*.
5) From (1) and (4), every event presupposes another event from which it follows according to natural law *ad infinitum* (modus ponens).
6) If every event presupposes another event from which it follows according to natural law *ad infinitum*, then it is not the case that naturally deterministic causation gives the complete sufficient condition for any causal series.
7) From (5) and (6), it is not the case that naturally deterministic causation gives the complete sufficient condition for any causal series (modus ponens).
8) From (3) and (7), contradiction.
9) From (1) — (9), it is not the case that naturally deterministic causation is sufficient to itself (indirect proof).
10) If it is not the case that naturally deterministic causation is sufficient to itself, then causality in accordance with the laws of nature is not the only one from which all the appearances of the world can be derived. It is also necessary to assume another causality through freedom in order to explain them.
11) From (9) and (10), causality in accordance with the laws of nature is not the only one from which all the appearances of the world can be derived. It is also necessary to assume another causality through freedom in order to explain them (modus ponens).

Quote

Antithesis

There is no freedom, but everything in the world happens solely in accordance with laws of nature.

Proof

Suppose there were a *freedom* in the transcendental sense, as a special kind of causality in accordance with which the occurrences of the world could follow, namely a faculty of absolutely beginning a state, and hence also a series of its consequences; then not only will a series begin absolutely through this spontaneity, but the determination of this spontaneity itself to produce the series, i.e., its causality, will begin absolutely, so that nothing precedes it through which this occurring action is determined in accordance with constant laws. Every beginning of action, however, presupposes a state of the not yet acting cause, and a dynamically first beginning of action presupposes a state that has no causal connection at all with the cause of the previous one, i.e., in no way follows from it. Thus transcendental freedom is contrary to the causal law, and is a combination between the successive states of effective causes in accordance with which no unity of experience is possible, which thus cannot be encountered in any experience, and hence is an empty thought-entity.

Thus we have nothing but *nature* in which we must seek the connection and order of occurrences in the world. Freedom (independence) from the laws of nature is indeed a *liberation* from *coercion*, but also from the *guidance* of all rules. For one cannot say that in place of the laws of nature, laws of freedom enter into the course of the world, because if freedom were determined according to laws, it would not be freedom, but nothing other than nature. Thus nature and transcendental freedom are as different as lawfulness and lawlessness; the former burdens the understanding with the difficulty of seeking the ancestry of occurrences ever higher in the series of causes, because the causality in them is at every time conditioned, but it promises in compensation a thoroughgoing and lawful unity of experience, while the mirage of freedom, on the contrary, though of course offering rest to the inquiring understanding in the chain of causes by leading it to an unconditioned causality that begins to act from itself, since it is itself blind, breaks away from the guidance of those rules by which alone a thoroughly connected experience is possible. [A445-47/B473-75]

Synopsis

The antithesis of the Third Antinomy concludes that everything happens in accordance with the laws of nature and that there is no transcendental freedom. The antithesis assumes for the indirect proof a central claim of the thesis, viz., that transcendental freedom is "a special kind of causality in accordance with which the occurrences of the world could follow." Put in terms that parallel our reconstruction of the thesis argument, the antithesis assumes that transcendental freedom can provide the complete sufficient condition of a naturally deterministic causal series. Transcendental freedom is a kind of causality that is spontaneous and begins absolutely. As the above quote notes, "nothing precedes it through which this occurring action is determined in accordance with constant laws." This free cause will not be determined by anything that came before it in accordance with natural law, and is thus not governed by natural law. This is noted in the third premise and reflects the antithesis' claim that "transcendental freedom is contrary to the causal law."

The problem shows up in the fourth premise. The complete sufficient condition for a naturally deterministic causal series must be governed by natural law otherwise the causal series would no longer be naturally deterministic. For example, if event E_1 is the spontaneous cause of E_2 and E_2 is supposed to be the naturally deterministic cause of E_3, then E_2 must presuppose an event from which it follows in accordance with natural law in order for it to be the naturally deterministic cause of E_3. Being subject to natural law, however, contradicts the assumption that the cause of E_2 (i.e., E_1) is spontaneous. In other words, the fact that E_1 is a spontaneous cause renders the causal series which purportedly follows from it indeterministic.[24] Whereas the thesis argument deploys the principle of sufficient reason with respect to the sufficient condition for a casual series as a whole, the antithesis deploys the principle with respect to the individual deterministic connections within a causal series. As noted in the above quote, furthermore, if there are indeterministic causal series within experience, then "no unity of experience is possible" since the unity of our experience is predicated upon events being subject to natural law (a point Kant makes in the Second Analogy).[25] Since the third and fourth premises of the antithesis argument contradict one another, its original assumption must be false. If transcendental freedom cannot provide the complete sufficient condition for a naturally deterministic casual series, however, then the central claim of the thesis is false. As the antithesis would have it, "There is no freedom, but everything in the world happens solely in accordance with laws of nature." It is important to note that the antithesis argument only denies the existence of freedom "in the world." Since both the thesis and antithesis arguments are predicated on a transcendental realist conception of the world, this is where the story would end. Kant even concedes that if appearances are things-in-themselves, then the antithesis argument would have to be granted.[26] Fortunately, as we will see below, Kant's transcendental idealism offers another way of resolving the antinomy.

Reconstruction

1) [Assume for reductio], transcendental freedom (an absolutely spontaneous cause) can provide the complete sufficient condition for a naturally deterministic causal series.

2) If transcendental freedom can provide the complete sufficient condition for a naturally deterministic causal series, then the complete sufficient condition for a naturally deterministic causal series would not be governed by natural law.

3) From (1) and (2), the complete sufficient condition for a naturally deterministic series would not be governed by natural law (modus ponens).

4) The complete sufficient condition for a naturally deterministic causal series must be governed by natural law.

5) From (3) and (4), contradiction.

6) From (1)—(5), transcendental freedom cannot provide the complete sufficient condition for a naturally deterministic causal series (indirect proof).

7) If transcendental freedom cannot provide the complete sufficient condition for a naturally deterministic casual series, then there is no freedom, but everything in the world happens solely in accordance with the laws of nature.

8) From (6) and (7), there is no freedom, but everything in the world happens solely in accordance with the laws of nature (modus ponens).

Resolution Synopsis

In the resolution of the Third Antinomy Kant tells us that we have two kinds of causation to choose from when explaining what happens: causality according to nature or causality from freedom.[27] Whereas the former is a cause which always presupposes a previous cause from which it follows according to a rule, the latter does not presuppose any other cause but rather begins from itself. Kant suggests that another difference between the two is that causality according to nature is "in the world of sense," while freedom is "a pure transcendental idea, which, first, contains nothing borrowed from experience, and second, the object of which also cannot be given determinately in any experience."[28] The main question now, according to Kant, is "whether freedom is possible anywhere at all," and if so does it exist together with nature, or can both happen at the same time yet "each in a different relation?"[29]

As mentioned above, Kant has already established in the Second Analogy that every event assumes something which it follows in accordance with a rule, so it would seem that granting transcendental freedom would violate that principle. As discussed earlier, Kant replies that if the world were a thing-in-itself, this would leave no room for freedom since every event and its condition would be contained in the series of events themselves and nature would be sufficient in itself. Although some compatibilists try to square free-will with determinism by claiming that the former is only a special case of the latter, Kant claims in his practical philosophy that this position amounts to no more than the "freedom of a turnspit."[30] For example, a compatibilist might claim that free actions are those which occur in accordance with natural law but whose proximate causes are the mental states of intentional agents. Since these mental states and their causes (which distally lie outside the agent and her mental states) are just as subject to natural law as their effects, however, it does not seem as if the agent is any more free than the turnspit which rotates over the fire according to these same laws. Kant takes determinism within the natural world very seriously and recognizes that within this world free causes (i.e., those that are absolute and spontaneous) are impossible. This is not to say that Kant thinks that free-will and determinism are incompatible with one another. Although Kant thinks that there is a way of applying both concepts, one will not be a special case of the other.[31]

For Kant, freedom must be possible if one is to defend the possibility of ethics and moral responsibility. If there is not some sense in which our actions could be considered free, it is unclear how we could be considered morally responsible for our actions. For example, if a murderer was determined by natural law to pull the trigger just as a rock was determined by natural law to fall on someone's head, then it does not seem as if the murderer can be held any more or less morally responsible than the rock. Although Hume and Kant are surely right to claim that just because something *is* the case (e.g., the murderer murders someone) this does not entail that it *ought* to be the case (e.g., the murderer ought not to have murdered someone), it seems likewise true that if something *ought* to be the case it seems important that it *could* be the case (e.g., that the murderer could not have murdered someone).[32] Only the possibility of freedom makes the latter intelligible.[33]

The resolution to the Third Antinomy is vitally important to Kant's overall philosophical project. If successful, it will show how transcendental idealism can serve as a bridge between the theoretical and practical philosophy. Unlike the First and Second Antinomies where transcendental idealism illustrates how both the theses and antitheses can be false (mathematical antinomies), Kant argues, in the Third and Fourth Antinomies, that transcendental idealism illustrates how both the theses and antitheses can be true (dynamical antinomies).[34] The key is that whereas both the theses and the antitheses of the mathematical antinomies stay within appearances, the theses of the dynamical antinomies go beyond appearances while only the antitheses stay within appearances. Since the theses and antitheses of the dynamical antinomies apply to different realms, both theses and antitheses can be true. In the dynamical antinomies, it is possible for the demands of reason and the understanding to both be met in a way in which they cannot be met in the mathematical antinomies.[35]

If the world is the sum total of all appearances, as transcendental idealism holds, then those appearances must be thought as having a basis that is not itself an appearance. When it comes to this basis, Kant compares freedom to the transcendental object which we must *think* of as grounding appearances but cannot be *cognized* as a thing-in-itself.[36] Although freedom is not given in experience, it is not unthinkable, but is at least intelligible. Just as the transcendental object must be thought as grounding the appearances of phenomenal objects, transcendental freedom must be thought as grounding the free actions of phenomenal subjects. For Kant, the practical concept of freedom (relevant to moral agency) presupposes the transcendental concept of freedom (absolute spontaneity) the intelligibility of which is defended in the resolution to the Third Antinomy.[37] When it comes to this moral aspect of freedom, a comparison can be drawn between transcendental freedom and the activity of apperception discussed in the Transcendental Analytic. The spontaneity of transcendental freedom can be viewed as the practical analogue of the spontaneity of apperception in the theoretical philosophy. Just as the spontaneity of transcendental freedom allows us to incorporate sensible inclinations under practical rules we endorse (maxims) resulting in free action, so too does the spontaneity of apperception allows us to incorporate sensible intuitions under rules of the understanding (categories) resulting in cognition.[38]

Considered most generally, the distinction between the intelligible and the phenomenal constitutes the heart of Kant's resolution to the Third Antinomy. In relation to an intelligible cause, events can be freely caused (thesis), and at the same time, in relation to appearances, these events occur in accordance with natural law (antithesis). Therefore, both the thesis and the antithesis can be true, but relative to different realms. Although there are many details of Kant's positive account that need to be worked out (e.g., how exactly one and the same event can be both free as well as fully determined by natural law), he does view the burden of proof as resting with the skeptic who tries to deny the existence of human freedom given the fact that we seem conscious of our freedom and the important implications that denying human freedom would have for moral responsibility and ethics more generally. To use a legal metaphor, Kant need only introduce "reasonable doubt" into the skeptic's case by presenting a plausible theory of how we might be free. By Kant's lights, distinguishing between an intelligible realm of free causes and a phenomenal realm governed by natural law is sufficient to introduce this doubt.[39]

Fourth Antinomy

Quote

Thesis

To the world there belongs something that, either as a part of it or as its cause, is an absolutely necessary being.

Proof

The world of sense, as the whole all appearances, at the same time contains a series of alterations. For without these, even the temporal series, as a condition of the possibility of the world of sense, would not be given to us. Every alteration, however, stands under its condition, which precedes it in time, and under which it is necessary. Now every conditioned that is given presupposes, in respect of its existence, a complete series of conditions up to the unconditioned, which alone is absolutely necessary. Thus there must exist something absolutely necessary, if an alteration exists as its consequence. This necessary being itself, however, belongs to the world of sense. For supposing it is outside it, then the series of alterations in the world would derive from it, without this necessary cause itself belonging to the world of sense. Now this is impossible. For since the beginning of a time-series can be determined only through what precedes it in time, the supreme condition of the beginning of a series of changes must exist in the time when the series was not yet (for the beginning is an existence, preceded by a time in which the thing that begins still was not). Thus the causality of the necessary cause of the alterations, hence the cause itself, belongs to time, hence to appearance (in which alone time is possible, as its form); consequently, it cannot be thought as detached from the world of sense as the sum total of all appearances. Thus in the world itself there is contained something absolutely necessary (whether as the whole world-series itself or as a part of it). [A452-54/B480-82]

Synopsis

The thesis of the Fourth Antinomy holds that an absolutely necessary being exists as either a part of the world or as its cause. This is the only argument from the Antinomies that does not begin as a *reductio ad absurdum*, but as a version of the cosmological argument it starts as a direct proof. The thesis begins by claiming that every alteration in the world presupposes something that brought about this alteration and through which it is necessary. As the above quote says, "every alteration, however, stands under its condition, which precedes it in time, and under which it is necessary." For example, a boat moves downstream. The change in the location of the boat is conditioned since it requires previous conditions for it to bring this change about, e.g., the current of the river. The current of the river is likewise conditioned since it also assumes previous conditions to bring it about, e.g., the melting of snow in the mountains. The above reasoning and the example we have chosen to illustrate it clearly reflect what Kant says in the Second Analogy. Again, just as with the Third Antinomy, both sides in the Fourth Antinomy likewise seem to accept the principle of the Second Analogy.

Although the idea that every alteration has a cause from which it follows reflects the principle of the Second Analogy, the claim, in the first premise, that every conditioned thing in time presupposes a complete series of conditions up to the unconditioned reflects the illegitimate principle through which reason makes existential claims beyond what is given in experience. This can be seen from the fact that the thesis immediately concludes from this reasoning that "thus there must exist something absolutely necessary." The reason why should, by this point, be fairly familiar. Whatever completes the series must be unconditioned otherwise the series would not be complete. If this being is unconditioned then it does not depend upon anything else for its existence and so is a necessary being. As the third premise puts it, a necessary being completes the series of conditions for any conditioned thing in time. Although the argument in the first part of the thesis of the Fourth Antinomy might seem to repeat Kant's reasoning in the thesis to the Third Antinomy, it is important to note that the Third Antinomy is concerned with the relational category of causation (establishing a free cause) whereas the Fourth Antinomy is concerned with the modal category of necessity (establishing a necessary being). Consequently, the target of each proof is quite different.[40]

At this point, the direct proof ends. The thesis adopts an indirect proof strategy in order to establish that this necessary being belongs to the world. Although Kant will return to the cosmological argument again in the Ideal (chapter seventeen), there he will reconstruct a version of the argument that places this necessary being outside the world. The second part of the current argument begins, however, by assuming the latter position for an indirect proof. If this necessary being does not belong to the world, then it does not exist in time. The key to the indirect proof comes in premise seven which claims that by not existing in time, this necessary being could not cause anything within time. For the necessary being to be the thing that causes the complete series of alterations in time, it must have existed *before* the series itself. As the thesis puts it in the above quote, "the beginning of a time-series can be determined only through what precedes it in time." In order for something to precede something else in time, the former must be in time as well, since without time there is no before and after. If the necessary being does not exist in time, then it could not, as premise eight notes, complete the series of conditions for any conditioned thing in time. This sets up a contradiction, however, between premise three (from the first part of the argument) and premise eight. This contradiction allows the proponent of the thesis to deny the original assumption of the second part of the argument which leads to the conclusion that "To the world there belongs something that, either as a part of it or as its cause, is an absolutely necessary being" which is the thesis of the Fourth Antinomy. Although this necessary being cannot exist beyond the world, we already know that since there are conditioned things in time (i.e., alterations), and these presuppose prior causes which themselves presuppose a complete series of causes, there must be a necessary being that completes the series. In order to complete the series, this necessary being must act in time and so must belong to the world.

Reconstruction

1) Every conditioned thing in time presupposes a complete series of conditions up to the unconditioned.
2) If every conditioned thing in time presupposes a complete series of conditions up to the unconditioned, then a necessary being completes the series of conditions for any conditioned thing in time.
3) From (1) and (2), a necessary being completes the series of conditions for any conditioned thing in time (modus ponens).
4) [Assume for reductio] This necessary being does not belong to the world.
5) If this necessary being does not belong to the world, then it is not in time.
6) From (4) and (5), this necessary being is not in time (modus ponens).
7) If this necessary being is not in time, then this necessary being cannot complete the series of conditions for any conditioned thing in time.
8) From (6) and (7), this necessary being cannot complete the series of conditions for any conditioned thing in time (modus ponens).
9) From (3) and (8), contradiction.
10) From (4) – (9), to the world there belongs something that, either as a part of it or as its cause, is an absolutely necessary being (indirect proof).

Quote

Antithesis

There is no absolutely necessary being existing anywhere, either in the world or outside the world as its cause.

Proof

Suppose that either the world itself is a necessary being or that there is such a being in it; then in the series of its alterations either there would be a beginning that is unconditionally necessary, and hence without a cause, which conflicts with the dynamic law of the determination of all appearances in time; or else the series itself would be without any beginning, and, although contingent and conditioned in all its parts, it would nevertheless be absolutely necessary and unconditioned as a whole, which contradicts itself, because the existence of a multiplicity cannot be necessary if no single part of it possesses an existence necessary in itself.

Suppose, on the contrary, that there were an absolutely necessary cause of the world outside the world; then this cause, as the supreme member in the *series of causes* of alterations in the world, would first begin these changes and their series. But it would have to begin to act then, and its causality would belong in time, and for this very reason in the sum total of appearances, i.e., in the world; consequently, it itself, the cause, would not be outside the world, which contradicts what was presupposed. Thus neither in the world nor outside it (yet in causal connection with it) is there any absolutely necessary being. [A453-55/B481-83]

Synopsis

The antithesis argues that there is no necessary being at all. There are three (and arguably only three) candidates for the necessary being that the argument considers and rules out through indirect proof: The world itself, something in the world, and something outside of the world. The first part of the argument considers the first two options together. Since the thesis of the Fourth Antinomy takes itself to have established that a necessary being exists in the world, the first part of the argument will be crucial to setting up the antinomal conflict. As the second premise notes, if either the world itself is a necessary being or a necessary being exists in the world, then either the whole series of alterations (events) that constitute the world is necessary or something uncaused exists in the world as the cause of this series of alterations. As the quote above notes, the problem with the first option is that the world is "contingent and conditioned in all its parts." Put differently, every alteration in the world is contingent and so the series of events that constitute the world through its entire history cannot be necessary. The contingency of every alteration in the world is illustrated in the Second Analogy. Every event in the natural world is contingent since every event presupposes something else which it follows in accordance with natural law. When it comes to modality, the whole cannot be greater than the sum of its parts. If the parts are contingent, then the whole must be contingent as well. As the antithesis puts it above, "the existence of a multiplicity cannot be necessary if no single part of it possesses an existence necessary in itself."

This leads to a disjunctive syllogism between the third and the sixth premises. If the whole series of events that constitute the world is necessary *or* something uncaused exists in the world as the cause of this series of alterations, but the whole series of alterations that constitute the world is not necessary, then it follows, in premise seven, that something uncaused exists in the world as the cause of this series of alterations. The problem, as premise eight notes, is that an uncaused cause cannot exist in time since this would seem to violate the principle of the Second Analogy. This is a point shared with the antithesis to the Third

Antinomy. If nothing uncaused can exist in time, however, then nothing un-caused can exist in the world as the cause of the series of alterations that consti-tute the world. The latter claim, made in premise ten, contradicts the result of the disjunctive syllogism in premise seven. This allows the proponent of the antithe-sis to deny the original assumption of the argument, concluding in premise twelve that neither the world itself is a necessary being nor does a necessary being exist in the world.

The last possibility remaining for the antithesis to deny through indirect proof is that the necessary being is something that does not exist in the world, but rather outside of it. In this case, the necessary being is on the outside looking in, yet is able to bring about the causal series of alterations in the world. As premise fifteen puts it, this necessary being acts outside of time when beginning any casual series in the world. This option was already ruled out in the second part of the thesis argument, and the reasoning in the antithesis is similar. The problem with this view, as premise sixteen notes, is that whatever *begins* a caus-al series in the world must act *in* time. This act of bringing something about pre-supposes that the necessary being is in time, since if it was not, then it could not *begin* its action. To begin an act there must have been a time previous to the act where the action had not yet taken place. Premises fifteen and sixteen contradict one another. A necessary being *outside* of time cannot begin a causal series *in* time, if whatever begins a causal series *in* time must be *in* time as well. Since the original assumption, that the necessary being is outside of the world, leads to a contradiction, that assumption must be false.

One might wonder whether the final indirect proof is able to establish that a necessary being cannot exist outside the world or just that a necessary being cannot exist outside the world as the cause of events in the world. Although Kant's concern clearly seems to be the latter, it is important to note that neither position is required in order to set up the antinomal conflict with the thesis. Since the thesis places this necessary being within the world, all the antithesis must establish is that this necessary being cannot exist within the world for which the first indirect proof is sufficient. As mentioned above, Kant will return to the question of whether a necessary being exists outside the world in the Ideal. By conjoining the conclusions of both indirect proofs, however, one can conclude that "There is no absolutely necessary being existing anywhere, either in the world or outside the world as its cause" which is the antithesis of the Fourth Antinomy.

Reconstruction

1) [Assume for reductio] Either the world itself is a necessary being or a nec-essary being exists in the world.
2) If either the world itself is a necessary being or a necessary being exists in the world, then either the whole series of alterations that constitute the

world is necessary or something uncaused exists in the world as the cause of this series of alterations.

3) From (1) and (2), the whole series of alterations that constitute the world is necessary or something uncaused exists in the world as the cause of this series of alterations.

4) Every alteration in the world is contingent.

5) If every alteration in the world is contingent, then the whole series of alterations that constitutes the world cannot be necessary.

6) From (4) and (5), the whole series of alterations that constitutes the world cannot be necessary (modus ponens).

7) From (3) and (6), something uncaused exists in the world as the cause of this series of alterations that constitute the world (disjunctive syllogism).

8) Nothing uncaused can exist in time.

9) If nothing uncaused can exist in time, then nothing uncaused can exist in the world as the cause of the series of alterations that constitute the world.

10) From (8) and (9), nothing uncaused can exist in the world as the cause of the series of alterations that constitute the world (modus ponens).

11) From (7) and (10), contradiction.

12) From (1) – (11), neither the world itself is a necessary being nor does a necessary being exist in the world (indirect proof).

13) [Assume for reductio] there is a necessary being outside the world that begins causal series in the world.

14) If there is a necessary being outside the world that begins causal series in the world, then this necessary being acts outside of time when beginning any causal series in the world.

15) From (13) and (14), this necessary being acts outside of time when beginning any casual series in the world (modus ponens).

16) Whatever *begins* a causal series in the world must act *in* time.

17) From (15) and (16), contradiction.

18) From (13) – (17), there is not a necessary being outside the world that begins causal series in the world (indirect proof).

19) From (12) and (18), there is no absolutely necessary being existing anywhere, either in the world or outside the world as its cause (conjunction introduction).

Resolution Synopsis

Like the Third Antinomy, in the resolution to the Fourth Antinomy, Kant holds that there is no conflict between the thesis and antithesis when considered from the standpoint of transcendental idealism. Each position can be true relative to a different realm. The antithesis is true of the world of appearances because every change in appearances (alteration) is going to be conditioned by prior events in accordance with natural law as shown in the Second Analogy. The thesis is a bit trickier. The indirect proof of the second part of the thesis argument attempts to establish that the necessary being belongs to the "world of sense." Although Kant's solution precludes this option, the conclusion of the direct proof in the first part of the thesis argument can be true insofar as it refers to a realm beyond appearances. The necessary being of the thesis is what Kant calls a "merely intelligible being."[41] We cannot know if it in fact exists, though this being is consistently thinkable. The logical possibility of a necessary being beyond appearances is not ruled out by the contingency of all appearances in the world since we can still conceive of a being which is outside of the conditioned series of causes and effects. So both thesis and antithesis can be true in so far as the latter refers to the empirical world of appearances and the former refers to an intelligible world beyond appearances. As mentioned above, Kant will return to the idea of a necessary being in the Ideal to which we will now turn.

Notes

1. *CPR* A407/B434.
2. Buroker makes this point in response to both Guyer's and Kemp Smith's claims to the contrary. See Buroker, *Kant's Critique*, 233, Guyer, *Kant and the Claims*, 407, and Kemp Smith, *A Commentary to Kant's Critique*, 485.
3. In response to objections by Bertrand Russell and Strawson, Allison notes that Kant's worry is not with the concept of infinity as such but rather with the thought of a completed infinite series. In addition, even if there were an infinite amount of time to traverse the members of the series, would there be any sense in which one might say that the series has been *completed*? See Allison, *Kant's Transcendental Idealism*, 367-372, Bertrand Russell, *Our Knowledge of the External World* (London: Open Court, 1914), 123 and Strawson, *The Bounds of Sense*, 176.
4. *CPR* A432/B460.
5. We are repeating this key premise in the argument since each *reductio* should be considered as its own sub-proof.
6. Bennett attempts to defend the intelligibility of a first event at a first time. Although Allison agrees that both concepts are *individually* intelligible, he does not believe that Bennett is successful in showing that the *conjunction* of the two concepts is intelligible. If an event is an alteration of something, it will always presuppose an earlier time where the thing existed in a different state. If one responds by saying that the first event is not subject to this temporal requirement, then one cannot say that the first event occurred at the first time. See Bennett, *Kant's Dialectic*, 160-61 and Allison, *Kant's Transcendental Idealism*, 375-76.
7. Rosenberg makes this point. See Rosenberg, *Accessing Kant*, 276.
8. *CPR* A189.
9. Kant explicitly precludes this possibility at *CPR* A191-92/B237.
10. *CPR* A212/B259.
11. For Kant's resolution of the First Antinomy, see *CPR* A517-523/B545-551. For a good summary of the solution, also see Gardner, *Kant and the Critique*, 248.
12. *CPR* A519/B547.

13. Although the rest of the argument is presented as a disjunctive syllogism, this has the effect of obscuring Kant's indirect proof strategy. Consequently, we will reconstruct the argument as an indirect proof where the original assumption leads to a contradiction allowing one to negate this assumption.

14. In the Amphiboly, Kant characterizes the Leibnizian position this way. See *CPR* A274/B330. Buroker holds that the validity of the argument for the thesis relies on this view. See Buroker, *Kant's Critique*, 241. Given its affinity to the Leibnizian position on substance, it is not surprising that Falkenstein argues that the thesis of the Second Antinomy is contrary to Newton's view on space and time. If self-substantial things must consist ultimately of simple parts, then space and time cannot be self-substantial since they are infinitely divisible. See Lorne Falkenstein, *Kant's Intuitionism: A Commentary on the Transcendental Aesthetic* (Toronto, University of Toronto Press, 1995), 183-85.

15. Buroker notes that this provides an independent line of argument against the claim, already attacked in the Paralogisms, that the soul is a simple substance. See Buroker, *Kant's Critique*, 243.

16. *CPR* A162/B202.

17. *CPR* A163/B204.

18. *CPR* A523-24/B551-52.

19. *CPR* A526/B554.

20. *CPR* A444/B472.

21. As Allison notes, since both sides assume the same conception of causation in the natural world, Kant cannot be accused of begging the question by using the causal principle of the Second Analogy in the Antinomies. See Allison, *Kant's Transcendental Idealism*, 383.

22. Allison makes this point which he believes reflects Leibniz' reasoning, viz., that the existence of the causal series is a positive fact that requires an explanation. In conjunction with the antithesis argument, the Third Antinomy generates a *reductio ad absurdum* of Leibniz' position. At the same time, however, it is not merely a *reductio* of Leibniz' reasoning insofar as any naturally deterministic view on causation cannot provide the complete sufficient condition for a causal series. See Allison, *Kant's Transcendental Idealism*, 380-81. For a similar point, see Buroker, *Kant's Critique*, 245.

23. For both sides of the debate, causality through freedom and causality through natural law are the only two options.

24. Sadik Al-Azm explains the argument this way. See Sadik Al-Azm, *The Origin of Kant's Arguments in the Antinomies* (Oxford: Oxford University Press, 1972), 103-105.

25. Buroker makes the last two points. See Buroker, *Kant's Critique*, 248.

26. *CPR* A536/B564.

27. *CPR* A532/B560.

28. *CPR* A533/B561.

29. *CPR* A536/B564.

30. Immanuel Kant, *Critique of Practical Reason*, 133-272 in *Practical Philosophy*, trans. Mary Gregor (Cambridge, Cambridge University Press, 1996), originally published 1788, 5.97.

31. Even if one admits that there are different forms of compatibilism, there are serious questions as to how free-will and determinism are to be squared with one another and to what extent Kant's account involves both compatibilist and incompatibilist aspects. For example, see Allen Wood, "Kant's Compatibilism," in *Kant's Critique of Pure Rea-*

son: Critical Essays, 239-263 as well as Allison's response in Henry Allison, *Kant's Theory of Freedom* (Cambridge: Cambridge University Press, 1990), 29-53.

32. For Hume's denial that the *ought* can be inferred from the *is*, see Hume, *Treatise*, 3.1.1. Kant makes a similar point when discussing the difference between moral and natural law. See Immanuel Kant, *Groundwork of the Metaphysics of Morals*, 37-108 in *Practical Philosophy*, originally published 1785, 4:387-88.

33. Although Kant does not think he can establish the *real* possibility of freedom (in accordance with the First Postulate), he does seem committed to the *logical* possibility of freedom. See *CPR* A558/B586.

34. *CPR* A529-530/B557-58.

35. *CPR* A531-32/B559-560.

36. *CPR* A539/B567, Bxxvi-xxvii.

37. *CPR* A533/B561. According to Allison, the presupposition should be taken as conceptual rather than real which mirrors our own description of how the presupposition of the transcendental object by appearances is conceptual rather than real. For more on the relationship between transcendental and practical freedom, see Allison, *Kant's Theory of Freedom*, 57.

38. This is Allison's view. See Allison, *Kant's Theory of Freedom*, 40.

39. Allen Wood brings up the legal metaphor. See Wood, "Kant's Compatibilism," 248 and 261.

40. Grier discusses this objection. See Grier, *Kant's Doctrine of Transcendental Illusion*, 219-27.

41. *CPR* A564/B592.

Chapter Seventeen
Ideal

Ontological Argument

Quote

> Against all these general inferences (which no human being can refuse to draw) you challenge me with one case that you set up as a proof through the fact that there is one and indeed only this one concept where the non-being or the canceling of its object is contradictory within itself, and this is the concept of a most real being. It has, you say, all reality and you are justified in assuming such a being as possible (to which I have consented up to this point, even though a non-contradictory concept falls far short of proving the possibility of its object). Now existence is also comprehended under all reality; thus existence lies in the concept of something possible. If this is cancelled, then the internal possibility of the thing is cancelled which is contradictory. [A596-97/B624-25]

Synopsis

As mentioned at the outset of Part Three, the Ideal of pure reason is the result of reason taking the transcendental idea of the sum total of all reality (assumed for the thoroughgoing determination of finite things) and positing this as an individual thing that possesses the highest degree of reality. Once this transcendental *idea* is thought of as having a particular entity that embodies it, it becomes a transcendental *ideal*. This "being of all beings" corresponds to the standard theological conception of God, and in the Ideal, Kant considers the three standard

arguments for God's existence (ontological, cosmological, and design) beginning with the ontological argument.[1]

The ontological argument attempts to prove the existence of God (understood as the "most real being" in the above quote) from the concept of God
alone. Saint Anselm (11th century) is widely credited with first formulating the
argument though it is also used by Descartes, in the Fifth Meditation, to prove
the existence of God.[2] Like both of these philosophers, Kant presents the argument as an indirect proof starting with the assumption that the most real being
does not exist. The proof then asks one to examine the concept of the most real
being, and consider if *existence* would be contained within this concept. Holding
all else equal, isn't something that exists *more* real than something that is alike
in all ways to the thing that does exist but which itself does not exist? Consider
$100. Isn't the existence of $100 in your hand more real (you can save it, spend
it, give it away) than simply the idea of $100 that you do not have (the latter
being all too often the case for a philosophy student)? Assuming that something
is more real if it exists, then, as premise three notes, the concept of the most real
being would have to contain existence within its concept otherwise it wouldn't
be the concept of the *most* real being. Unlike the concept of something that is
both P and not-P at the same time in the same manner, it does not seem as if the
concept of the most real being is self-contradictory. Whereas the former is the
concept of an *impossible* being (violates the law of non-contradiction), the latter
concept, as premise two notes, appears to be the concept of a *possible* being.
Although all impossible beings do not exist, possible beings can either exist or
not exist. Since the concept of the most real being is the concept of a possible
being and the concept of the most real being contains existence within its concept, the most real being must exist. If the most real being does not exist (as the
argument assumes), then the concept of the most real being could not contain
existence within its concept. This would, however, generate a contradiction
within the concept of the most real being itself (cancelling its "internal possibility" as the above quote puts it). It would both contain, as premise three asserts,
and could not contain, as premise five asserts, existence within its concept which
is contradictory. Since assuming the non-existence of the most real being leads
to a contradiction, the proponent of the argument is able to infer by indirect
proof that the most real being must exist.

Kant has a few problems with the argument. His first criticism echoes Gua-
nilo's early criticism of Anselm's version of the argument, viz., that the concept
of an "absolutely necessary being" outstrips our cognitive capacities. As Kant
argues in the Third Postulate, the understanding must always think of necessity
in accordance with certain *conditions*, but since the being described in the ontological argument is *unconditionally* necessary, one must "reject all the conditions that the understanding always needs in order to regard something as necessary."[3]

Kant's second criticism is more original. He rejects the idea that denying
the existence of such a being would be self-contradictory. For Kant, all existence
claims are synthetic and so can be consistently denied. There is a distinction,

according to Kant, between the necessity of judgments and the necessity of things. Borrowing an example from Descartes' Fifth Meditation, Kant admits the judgment that "a triangle has three angles" is absolutely necessary.[4] The absolute necessity of this judgment, however, does not entail that a triangle exists. If a triangle exists, then it must have three angles, but if one denies that the triangle exits one can likewise deny that it has three angles. There is no contradiction in judging that "Every triangle has three angles but there are no triangles." Likewise, although the judgment that "God is omnipotent" is absolutely necessary, this does not entail that God exists. If God exists, then God is omnipotent, but if one denies that God exists one can likewise deny that God is omnipotent. There is no contradiction in judging that "God is omnipotent but God does not exist." As Kant puts it, "If you cancel its existence, then you cancel the thing itself with all its predicates."[5] Just because a *judgment* is necessary, this does not entail that the *thing* that the judgment refers to in the subject of the judgment is likewise necessary.

This has an important implication for the analyticity of the judgment that "God exists." The judgment that "God exists" can be analytic only by begging the question, i.e., by assuming that such a being exists and then including this feature in the concept of the being from which the existence of the being is then ostensibly derived. In other words, the *judgment* that "God exists" is necessary only by already assuming the existence of the *thing*. Such a claim, however, would be nothing more than a "miserable tautology."[6] If the judgment is synthetic, however, then denying the judgment cannot result in the contradiction upon which the argument trades in premise six. Appeal to intuition is required in order to establish the existence of something that instantiates the subject concept and so denying that the concept is instantiated cannot, in any way, contradict that concept. Ultimately, Kant thinks the proponent of the ontological argument contradicts herself by treating a synthetic proposition as if it were analytic.[7]

Kant's final criticism is that existence is not a real predicate.[8] In order to understand Kant's criticism, it is important to distinguish between two senses of predication, logical and real predication. Although "existence" can serve as a logical predicate in the sense of occupying the predicate position in a sentence, in this context, it only indicates that the subject concept is instantiated by an object (i.e., the concept has an extension). This should not be taken to imply, however, that whenever "is" shows up in the predicate position of a sentence that it indicates the subject concept is instantiated. For example, saying "Oliver Twist is" implies something very different from "Oliver Twist is hungry." Although in both cases "is" logically occupies the predicate position, in the former case "is" denotes existence whereas in the latter "is" serves merely as the copula for judgment attaching the real predicate "hungry" to the concept "Oliver Twist."[9] Unlike the predicate "hungry," however, "existence" cannot serve as a real predicate in the sense of adding to the semantic content of a concept (i.e., enriching the intension of the concept). Kant holds that the ontological argument conflates these two different senses of predication.

In order to illustrate the point, Kant uses the example of $100 mentioned above.[10] Close your eyes and imagine a $100 bill. It is rectangular, made of paper, has a greenish hue, and a picture of Benjamin Franklin. All of these are real predicates. If I additionally asked you to imagine the $100 bill existing, have I added anything to your *concept* of the $100 bill? If the picture in your mind has not changed, then it does not seem that I have added anything to your concept of the $100 bill. There is no difference in the concept of an existing $100 bill vs. a non-existent $100 bill. The semantic content or intension of the concepts is identical. Unlike predicates like "rectangle" and "green," Kant believes that "existence" is not a real predicate. Again, it can only serve as a logical predicate denoting that a concept (e.g., the $100 bill) is instantiated or has an extension.[11] Consequently, to claim, in premise three, that existence is contained within the concept of the most real being is itself an error since existence is not the right kind of thing (a real predicate) to be contained within the concept of something. It cannot enrich the semantic content or intension of a given concept.[12] Existence claims are always synthetic and require appeal to sensible intuition in order to establish the existence of an object corresponding to the concept in question.

Reconstruction

1) [Assume for reductio], the most real being does not exist.
2) The concept of the most real being is the concept of a possible being.
3) The concept of the most real being contains existence within its concept.
4) If the most real being does not exist and the concept of the most real being is the concept of a possible being, then the concept of the most real being cannot contain existence within its concept.
5) From (1), (2) and (4), the concept of the most real being cannot contain existence within its concept (modus ponens).
6) From (3) and (5), contradiction.
7) From (1) - (6), the most real being does exist (indirect proof).

Cosmological Argument

Quote

It goes as follows: If something exists, then an absolutely necessary being also has to exist. Now I myself, at least, exist; therefore, an absolutely necessary being exists. The minor premise contains an experience, the major premise an inference from an experience in general to the existence of something necessary. Note: This inference is too well known for it to be necessary to expound it in detail here. It rests on the allegedly transcendental natural law of causality that everything contingent must have a cause, which, if it in turn is contingent must likewise have its cause, until the series of causes subordinated one to another has to end with an absolutely necessary cause, without which it would have no completeness. . . Thus the proof really starts from experience, so it is not carried out entirely *a priori* or ontologically; and because the object of all possible experience is called "world," it is therefore termed the *cosmological* proof. . . Now the proof further infers: The necessary being can be determined only in one single way, i.e., in regard to all possible predicates, it can be determined by only one of them, so consequently it must be *thoroughly* determined through its concept. Now only one single concept of a thing is possible that thoroughly determines the thing *a priori*, namely that of an *ens realissimum*: Thus the concept of the most real being is the only single one through which a necessary being can be thought, i.e., there necessarily exists a highest being. [A604-6/B632-34]

Synopsis

Kant's version of the cosmological argument is similar to Leibniz' argument for the existence of God in the *Mondadology* and Kant actually attributes the above argument to Leibniz.[13] The argument might also remind one of the thesis argument in the Fourth Antinomy (see the previous chapter). Kant notes that the main difference between this argument and the one from the Fourth Antinomy is that whereas the latter argues that the necessary being must be *within* the world (in time), the option is left open in the former argument that the necessary being could be *outside* the world (outside time).[14] As mentioned above, whereas the ontological argument is wholly *a priori* since it infers the existence of God simply from the concept of God, the cosmological argument is *a posteriori* insofar as it assumes the existence of contingent things. Although the above argument requires only *one* contingent thing (Kant uses the example of himself), we have reconstructed the argument using the series of all and only contingent things as an elliptical description of the world (to which "cosmological" refers). Everything in this series is contingent and so presupposes causes which if contingent are members of this series and so on. For example, Kant's existence as a contingent being is caused, at least initially, by his parents and their existence as contingent beings is caused by their parents, and so on. The key to understanding the argument is premise four. If the series of all and only contingent things is *complete* (which it must be if it includes *all* contingent things), then it presupposes something which completes the series that is necessary. If the latter were contingent, then it could not complete the series but would rather be a member of the series presupposing other things that cause it. As Kant puts it in the above quote, "the series of causes subordinated one to another has to end with an absolutely necessary cause, without which it would have no completeness."

The second part of the argument goes on to argue that this necessary being is the most real being. As the seventh premise notes, since it is absolutely necessary, this cause depends on nothing else for its determination. It is not caused by anything outside of itself and is in this respect very much unlike Kant or his parents. The argument infers the only thing that could thoroughly determine its own necessary existence is something whose concept possesses unlimited reality. If the concept were limited in some way, then its object would be logically contingent in the sense that one could not infer the existence of the being from its concept. If the concept were *a posteriori*, the being determined through that concept would likewise be contingent. Since the cause is necessary, however, the concept of this cause cannot be limited in any way. The only concept that seems to fit the bill is the *a priori* concept of the most real being, i.e., the concept of God that serves as the starting point of the ontological argument. As Kant puts it in the above quote, "the concept of the most real being is the only single one through which a necessary being can be thought." Consequently, the necessary being is the most real being, i.e., "there necessarily exists a highest being."

Kant's main worry with the argument is its second half starting in premise six. Specifically, Kant is concerned with the inference that the necessary being must be the most real being. This seems to assume that only the most real being could be a necessary being. It seems at least logically possible, however, that there could exist a necessary being that is limited in some fashion though its necessity could not be inferred from the concept of a limited being.[15] In order to make the inference that the cosmological argument aims to make, it must assume the ontological argument which establishes that the concept of the most real being contains the concept of a necessary being.[16] If the cosmological argument assumes the ontological argument, however, then the former faces all of the problems that the latter faced in the previous section. Consequently, the cosmological argument is faced with a dilemma. Either (1) it assumes the ontological argument and takes on all of the problems that the latter argument faces, or (2) it does not assume the ontological argument in which case it cannot make the inference from necessary being to most real being.[17]

Kant has worries with the first half of the cosmological argument as well.[18] Assuming that this necessary being lies outside of the world but still causes it, the argument applies the categories of causation and necessity beyond the bounds of sense which is an illegitimate use of the categories. This sets up an interesting dilemma when compared to the thesis of the Fourth Antinomy. Even assuming the impossibility of an infinite series of causes, Kant does not think one can infer a first cause either within the bounds of sense as the thesis of the Fourth Antinomy would have it (where such a cause is not given) or beyond the bounds of sense as the cosmological argument would have it (where causal inferences are illegitimate). Put slightly differently, Kant thinks that an uncaused cause is neither a possible object of experience nor a justifiable posit of reason. Since the idea of an uncaused cause lacks determinate content, reason finds false satisfaction in this idea. Finally, given the connection between the cosmological argument and the ontological argument, the cosmological argument must infer the real possibility of the most real being from its concept which is only logically possible.[19] Whereas real possibility requires that the most real being be *cognizable* (i.e., a possible object of experience), logical possibility requires only that the most real being be *thinkable* (i.e., its concept is not self-contradictory). There is a large gap, however, between something being thinkable and something being cognizable, a gap which neither the cosmological nor the ontological argument can bridge.

Reconstruction

1) There is a series of all and only contingent things (the world).
2) If there is a series of all and only contingent things, then the series of all and only contingent things is complete.
3) From (1) and (2), the series of all and only contingent things is complete (modus ponens).
4) If the series of all and only contingent things is complete, then the series of all and only contingent things has a cause which is itself necessary.
5) From (3) and (4), the series of all and only contingent things has a cause which is itself necessary (modus ponens).
6) If the series of all and only contingent things has a cause which is itself necessary, then this cause depends on nothing else for its determination (thoroughly determined through its own concept).
7) From (5) and (6), this cause depends on nothing else for its determination (modus ponens).
8) If this cause depends on nothing else for its determination, then this cause is the most real being.
9) From (7) and (8), this cause is the most real being (modus ponens).
10) If this cause is the most real being, then there necessarily exists a highest being.
11) From (9) and (10), there necessarily exists a highest being (modus ponens).

Physico-Theological (Design) Argument

Quote

The chief moments of the physico-theological proof we are thinking of are the following: 1) Everywhere in the world there are clear signs of an order according to determinate aim, carried out with great wisdom and, and in a whole of indescribable manifoldness in content as well as of unbounded magnitude in scope. 2) This purposive order is quite foreign to the things of the world, and pertains to them only contingently, i.e., the natures of different things could not by themselves agree in so many united means to determinate final aims, were they not quite properly chosen for and predisposed to it through a principle of rational order grounded on ideas. 3) Thus there exists a sublime and wise cause (or several), which must be the cause of the world not merely as an all-powerful nature working blindly through fecundity, but as an intelligence, through freedom. 4) The unity of this cause may be inferred from the unity of the reciprocal relation of the parts of the world as members of an artful structure, inferred with certainty wherever our observation reaches, but beyond that with probability in accordance with all principles of analogy. [A625-26/B653-54]

Synopsis

The physico-theological proof is a version of what we today call the "design argument." It attempts to infer the existence of God from the purposiveness that seems inherent in the world around us and which seems to indicate some design. As Kant puts it in the above quote, "Everywhere in the world there are clear signs of an order according to determinate aim." The design argument has the most contingent starting point of any of the three arguments for God's existence. As mentioned above, whereas the ontological argument proceeds wholly *a priori*, and the cosmological argument is *a posteriori* only insofar as it depends upon the existence of something contingent, the design argument requires not only that contingent things *exist* but also that they possess a certain kind of purposive *nature* that makes design the most reasonable explanation.

For evidence of this design, one might look at how so many things in the world are so well adapted to certain ends. For example, as William Paley observed in *Natural Theology* (which offers the classic nineteenth century version of the design argument), the eye seems specifically constructed to see things and depending upon what kind of creature has an eye (human, fish, insect), the eye is constructed so as to meet the specific needs of that creature in its environment.[20] If one does not consider specific examples of biological adaptation (which we now know to have a good evolutionary explanation), one might look at the fact that our planet seems placed in just the right location such that life is possible. If it were a little closer to the sun or a little further away, life would be impossible. At the level of the solar system, the orbits of the planets are such that they follow very simple mathematical laws (e.g., Kepler's laws of planetary motion). In other words, the world (considered generally or in detail) seems to exhibit purposiveness or the adaptation of means to ends. We know from looking at the artifacts that we create that their purposiveness (e.g., of a watch to tell time) depends upon intelligent design. As Paley noted, things like watches do not simply spring into existence, but rather depend upon the artifice of the maker. Much as the parts of the watch would not exhibit purposiveness were it not for the designer that puts them together in a specific way, matter does not exhibit purposiveness in itself, but rather, as premise three notes, purposiveness seems to be added to it. As Kant puts it in the above quote, "This purposive order is quite foreign to the things of the world, and pertains to them only contingently."

In premise seven, the argument holds, furthermore, that this purpose cannot be the result of blind fecundity because this kind of *aimless* productivity is not itself *purposive*. A copier on the fritz might very well produce a lot of blurry copies, but we consider this copier to be on the fritz since it is not producing these copies according to its intended purpose (viz., clear copies). If blind productivity cannot be the cause of the world's purposiveness, the argument infers, in premise eight, that it must be the result of intelligent design. To summarize this part of the argument, Kant says in the above quote, "Thus there exists a sublime and wise cause (or several), which must be the cause of the world not merely as an all-powerful nature working blindly through fecundity, but as an intelligence, through freedom."

As this quote makes clear, however, it is still an open question as to whether the design is the result of multiple designers or just one. Here, the argument points to the *unity* that is found among the purposes that the world exhibits. Organisms on earth are dependent on one another to meet their ends. Likewise they all depend on the fact that the earth is a certain distance from the sun and this depends upon the orbit of the earth which is itself describable by simple mathematical rules. In premise eleven, the argument holds that if the purposiveness of the world were the result of multiple designers, the world would not exhibit the unity of purpose that it does. For example, think about how work done by committee often lacks the focus and clarity of work done by a single person (this book, of course, being an exception). The unity of purpose that the world exhibits suggests a unity in designer, i.e., a single intelligence. As Kant puts it in the above quote, "the unity of this cause may be inferred from the unity of the reciprocal relation of the parts of the world as members of an artful structure."

Kant's main objection to the design argument is in the same spirit as his main objection to the cosmological argument. If the purpose of the design argument is to prove the existence of the most real being (God), it seems as if the argument is insufficient to this task. The argument only gives reason to think that the single designer has skills *proportional* to the design found in the world. Although these skills might be very great, there is no reason to think that the designer possess omnipotence, omniscience, or is wholly benevolent, i.e., the highest degree of reality with regard to any of these attributes.[21] One also cannot prove that the designer actually *created* the world, but rather, like human designers, the designer might have simply *arranged* matter as it already existed.[22] Proving the former would seem to require appeal to the cosmological argument. Likewise, if one wanted to prove that whatever created the world (necessary first cause) was also the most real being (God), this would require appeal to the ontological argument. This leads Kant to conclude that the ontological argument is the "only possible argument" for God's existence warts and all.[23]

Although Kant does not think that the existence of God can be proven theoretically, it is important to note that Kant also does not think that the existence of God can be disproven theoretically.[24] As Kant famously remarks in the B edition Preface to *CPR*, "I had to deny knowledge in order to make room for faith."[25] In fact, the theoretical possibility of God, the modal space that faith can occupy, is absolutely essential for Kant's practical philosophy. In the *Critique of the Power of Judgment*, Kant holds that the moral argument for God's existence can help to overcome the physico-theological proof's shortcomings. For example, God's benevolence insures that nature is designed in such a way as is fit for us to accomplish our moral ends.[26] In addition, the existence of a highest being would give us an objective basis for obeying the moral law considered as divine command.[27] He also thinks that the idea of God has an important regulative role when it comes to driving scientific inquiry. Viewing nature "as if" it is purposive sparks inquiry into the hidden mechanisms of nature, but in viewing nature this way we assume that its purposiveness reflects the design of a higher intelligence.[28]

Reconstruction

1) The world exhibits purposiveness which does not belong to the nature of the world.
2) If the world exhibits purposiveness which does not belong to the nature of the world, then the world's purposiveness is the result of an external cause.
3) From (1) and (2), the world's purposiveness is the result of an external cause (modus ponens).
4) If the world's purposiveness is the result of an external cause, then the world's purposiveness is the result of either (a) blind fecundity (productivity) or (b) intelligent design.
5) From (3) and (4), the world's purposiveness is the result of either (a) blind fecundity or (b) intelligent design (modus ponens).
6) If (a), i.e., the world's purposiveness is the result of blind fecundity, then the world would not exhibit purposiveness.
7) From (1) and (6), not (a), i.e., the world's purposiveness is not the result of blind fecundity (modus tollens).
8) From (5) and (7), therefore (b), i.e., the world's purposiveness is the result of intelligent design (disjunctive syllogism).
9) If the world's purposiveness is the result of intelligent design, then the world's purposiveness is the result of design either by (a) multiple intelligences or by (b) a single (unified) intelligence.
10) From (8) and (9), the world's purposiveness is the result of design either by (a) multiple intelligences or by (b) a single (unified) intelligence (modus ponens).
11) If (a), i.e., the world's purposiveness is the result of design by multiple intelligences, then the parts of the world would not exhibit unity in purpose.
12) The parts of the world exhibit unity in purpose.
13) From (11) and (12), not (a), i.e., the world's purposiveness is not the result of design by multiple intelligences (modus tollens).
14) From (10) and (13), therefore (b), i.e., the world's purposiveness is the result of design by a single (unified) intelligence (disjunctive syllogism).

Notes

1. *CPR* A334/B391.
2. Descartes, *Meditations*, 2:46.
3. *CPR* A593/B621.
4. *CPR* A593/B621.

5. *CPR* A594-95/B622-23.

6. *CPR* A597/B625.

7. This is how Altman puts Kant's point. See Altman, *A Companion to Kant's Critique*, 180.

8. Wood argues that both Descartes and Hume anticipate this point in similar ways. Given the fact that Descartes himself deploys the ontological argument, however, this is particularly surprising. For Descartes, the idea is that existence is a perfection that belongs to *any* nature that does not involve a contradiction. For Hume, there is no distinction between conceiving a thing and conceiving that thing existing. See Allen Wood, "Kant's Rational Theology," in *Kant's Critique of Pure Reason: Critical Essays*, 269.

9. William Rowe seems to make this mistake when claiming that Kant's view on predication entails that fictional objects must exist if anything is predicated of them. See William Rowe, *William L. Rowe on Philosophy of Religion: Selected Writings*, ed. Nick Trakakis (Burlington, VT: Ashgate Publishing, 2007), 13.

10. *CPR* A599/B627.

11. Buroker spends some time comparing Kant's view to modern logic's view on existential quantification while also discussing some problems associated with both. See Buroker, *Kant's Critique*, 273-74.

12. The argument based on this thought experiment seems to avoid the problems that philosophers have posed for a separate argument at *CPR* A600/B628 that seems to draw a stronger conclusion. In the latter, Kant asks us to consider something under concept C and then to predicate "existence" of C. He holds that "existence" cannot be a real predicate since if "existence" were a real predicate we would no longer be considering C but rather C′ (i.e., C + existence). He concludes from this that existence cannot be a real predicate of C. Of course, this same argument would work for any predicate. Wood raises this criticism. See Wood, "Kant's Rational Theology," 275 as well as Buroker's discussion of the problem in Buroker, *Kant's Critique*, 272-74. In the thought experiment, however, Kant only asks us to notice how some predicates (e.g., rectangle) enrich the semantic content of a concept, whereas other predicates (e.g., existence) do not. Kant calls the former real predicates and holds that the latter can be, at most, logical predicates.

13. See Gottfried Leibniz, *The Monadology* in *Monadology and Other Philosophical Essays*, trans. Paul Schrecker and Anne Martin Schrecker (New York: Macmillan Publishing, 1965), originally published 1714, §45. *CPR*, A604/B632.

14. *CPR* A456/B484. The first half of the thesis argument of the Fourth Antinomy, however, is consistent with the idea that this necessary being could exist outside the world of sense.

15. *CPR* A588/B617.

16. *CPR* A599/B636. Grier has argued, however, that there is an important way in which the ontological argument presupposes the cosmological argument. At *CPR* A604/B632, Kant suggests that the ontological argument appears persuasive insofar as it is motivated by the natural course reason whose demand for the unconditioned leads us to affirm the existence of a necessary being. The cosmological argument simply puts this natural course of reason in argumentative form. See Michelle Grier, "The Ideal of Pure Reason," in *The Cambridge Companion to the Critique of Pure Reason*, 283-84.

17. *CPR* A611/B639.

18. *CPR* A609-610/B637-38. See also Buroker's summary of these problems in Buroker, *Kant's Critique*, 275-77.

19. Grier notes that Kant is again attacking Leibniz here. Leibniz claims that Descartes' ontological argument can only get off the ground if God is really possible. Leibniz argues that God is really possible since the concept of God is not contradictory. Kant argues, however, that the latter is only sufficient for logical possibility but not real possibility. See Grier, "The Ideal of Pure Reason," 276-77.

20. William Paley, *Natural Theology* (Cambridge: Cambridge University Press, 2009), originally published 1803, chapter three.

21. *CPR* A627-28/B655-56. Several of Kant's objections are shared with Hume. See Hume, *Dialogues on Natural Religion* (Indianapolis, IN: Hackett, 1998), originally published 1779, part II.

22. *CPR* A627/B655.

23. *CPR* A625/B653.

24. Burnham and Young make this point. See Burnham and Young, *Kant's Critique*, 160.

25. *CPR* Bxxx.

26. Immanuel Kant, *Critique of the Power of Judgment*, trans. Paul Guyer and Eric Matthews (Cambridge: Cambridge University Press, 2000), originally published 1790, 5:448.

27. Kant, *Critique of Judgment*, 5:481.

28. Kant, *Critique of Judgment*, 5:398-400.

Chapter Eighteen
Conclusions from the Transcendental Dialectic

Whereas the Transcendental Analytic argued that cognition is confined to the bounds of sense, the Transcendental Dialectic reaffirms the same position by bringing to light the illusion that reason fall into when it oversteps these bounds. Given reason's natural tendency to cross the bounds of sense, it must continuously guard itself from being deceived by this illusion. Transcendental ideas, Kant says, are just as natural to reason as the categories are to the understanding. As Kant argues in the appendix to the Transcendental Dialectic, however, the transcendental ideas are not wholly pernicious but can also serve an indispensable role as *regulative* ideas. In other words, we must approach nature "as if" the transcendental ideas are objectively valid. As regulative ideas, they function as a *"focus imaginarius"* for the understanding, pushing it to both unify as well as expand its cognitions in the hopes of reaching a goal that can never be reached.[1] The speculative interest that reason has in finding the unconditioned condition for any conditioned thing sparks the understanding's enquiry into nature. Although we can never cognize what lies beyond the bounds of sense, the transcendental ideas can inspire us to understand as much as we can within these bounds.

Additionally, reason supplies methodological principles that the understanding uses in constructing empirical theories and unifying its cognitions. These methodological principles include that the simplest explanation for natural phe-

nomena is the best explanation (principle of parsimony), that species of phenomena must have subspecies (principle of specification), and that there is a
continuous transition between species and within species (principle of affinity),
i.e., there are no gaps in nature.[2] Put most generally, reason is constantly striving
for the systematic unification of natural phenomena through concepts.

Kant even goes so far as to say that if there is to be a "sufficient mark of
empirical truth" for understanding's cognitions, then reason must assume the
"systematic unity of nature as objectively valid and necessary."[3] The idea seems
to be that in order for empirical propositions to have truth-conditions, the events
that these propositions describe must be incorporated into a unified system. Take
any empirical proposition that describes an event in the natural world. According to the Second Analogy, in order for something to be an event, it must assume another event from which it follows in accordance with natural law. The
same is true of the latter event, and so on. Consequently, in order for the empirical proposition to be true, it must assume that the event it describes is part of a
complete network of events connected with one another in accordance with natural law. In other words, the truth of the individual empirical proposition assumes the systematic unity of nature. Although this systematic unity cannot be
demonstrated constitutively but can only be assumed regulatively, it must be
assumed nonetheless.[4]

In addition to reason's important regulative role within the theoretical philosophy, reason's transcendental ideas have an indispensible role within the context of Kant's practical philosophy. Although one must look to works like the
Groundwork of the Metaphysics of Morals (1785) and the *Critique of Practical
Reason* (1788) for a full development of Kant's ethical theory, in the latter parts
of *CPR* he sketches the outlines of his practical philosophy and explains how it
connects up with the theoretical philosophy. In the Canon of Pure Reason, Kant
asks three questions: "What can I know? What should I do? What may I hope?"[5]
The first question is theoretical and is answered by what has preceded in *CPR*. I
can only cognize objects within the bounds of sense. The second question is
practical and Kant answers that I am obligated to obey the moral law. The final
question, according to Kant, is both practical and theoretical. As we will see,
although the question is itself motivated by practical concerns, the answer to the
question involves three of the theoretical philosophy's most important transcendental ideas: the immortal soul (Paralogisms), human freedom (Antinomies),
and God (Ideal).[6]

Kant believes that all hope concerns happiness and that although what
makes us *happy* is the satisfaction of our inclinations what makes us *worthy* to
be happy is obedience to the moral law. If I am worthy to be happy, then may I
hope to be happy? For the practical antecedent of this conditional to be true, it
must be possible for me to obey the moral law. This is where the transcendental
idea of freedom comes into the picture. As we saw above, the concept of practical freedom assumes the concept of transcendental freedom where the former is
"independence of the power of choice from necessitation by impulses of sensibility."[7] If we are practically free then we can do what we ought to do (obey the

moral law) even if it conflicts with what we want to do (through sensible inclination). Given the moral consciousness of our practical freedom, we must *believe* that we are transcendentally free. The question is now whether I can hope for happiness within morality, i.e., can I hope for the satisfaction of my inclinations insofar as they are commensurate with what the moral law demands?

If I am worthy to be happy, Kant believes I may hope for a world where happiness is apportioned according to everyone's free obedience to the moral law.[8] Since the sensible world in which we all live is a world where the inclinations of the immoral are often satisfied (the unjust are rewarded), what I may hope for is a "moral world" which we can only hope to attain in a *future* life. This is where the immortal soul comes into the picture. We must *believe* that we possess an immortal soul in order to hope for the kind of happiness that only a moral world can provide.

Finally, we must *believe* that there is a "highest reason" a "highest original good" that created both a natural world where we may demonstrate our worthiness to be happy and a moral world where we may hope to be happy.[9] In other words, the natural world must be designed so that we can freely obey the moral law and the moral world must be designed such that we can hope for a future state where happiness is apportioned in accordance with obedience to the moral law. This ideal of a highest good is, of course, the idea of God, the final transcendental idea that Kant thinks is absolutely indispensible to his practical philosophy. As mentioned above, Kant offers a related justification for belief in God in the *Critique of Judgment* and in other works he further develops the role that the immortal soul, human freedom, and God play in the practical philosophy.[10] Kant uses the term "belief" or "faith" [*Glaube*] to describe the epistemic attitude that the subject must adopt toward these transcendental ideas. Although it may well be subjectively necessary to *believe* in the immortal soul, human freedom, and God from the practical standpoint, one nevertheless cannot claim *cognition* of them from the theoretical perspective.[11]

In the conclusions to the Transcendental Aesthetic and Transcendental Analytic, we saw how Kant's arguments go to collectively support his overall theory of transcendental idealism. It is only appropriate that we close this final chapter by examining how Kant's arguments in the Transcendental Dialectic might go to support transcendental idealism as well. At one point, in the Antinomies, Kant suggests that the mathematical antinomies provide indirect support for transcendental idealism.[12] As mentioned above, since both thesis and antithesis of the mathematical antinomies stay within the world of experience, they cannot both be true. Either reason is left in conflict with itself or both the conclusions of the thesis and the antithesis are false. Since transcendental idealism allows one to avoid the conflict that reason naturally has with itself in the mathematical Antinomies, one can also view the latter as offering a proof for transcendental idealism independent of his arguments in the Transcendental Aesthetic and Transcendental Analytic. Kant puts the proof in terms of the First Antinomy, though what he says would work equally well for the Second Antinomy:

1) Either transcendental realism is true or transcendental idealism is true.[13]
2) If transcendental realism is true, then the world is either spatiotemporally finite or infinite.
3) It is not the case that the world is either spatiotemporally finite or infinite (established by the thesis and antithesis arguments).
4) From (2) and (3), transcendental realism is false (modus tollens).
   From (1) and (4), transcendental idealism is true (disjunctive syllogism).

The key to the proof comes in premise three. If the thesis argument is sound, then the world is spatiotemporally *finite*. If the antithesis argument is sound, then the world is spatiotemporally *infinite*. Transcendental realism provides no reason to prefer one argument to the other and so they seem to undermine one another taking transcendental realism along with them. By Kant's lights, transcendental idealism provides the only way out of this conflict, since it allows one to say that the spatiotemporal extent of the world is *indefinite*. If the world is just the sum total of appearances, and the extent of this world is only determined through the successive synthesis of these appearances, there is no way of saying whether or not this successive synthesis will ever come to an end.

One might object that the arguments Kant constructs in the First Antinomy make implicit appeal to arguments in support of transcendental idealism and so it would be circular for Kant to then hold that these arguments provide indirect support for transcendental idealism. For example, in the antithesis to the First Antinomy, Kant argues that empty space and time are not objects of possible experience, but this is something that he also argues for in the Analogies (see chapter eleven) where the Analogies are in direct support of transcendental idealism. In response, it is important to note that Kant is not making explicit appeal to *transcendental idealism* in the antithesis of the First Antinomy but rather to the *arguments* of the Transcendental Analytic that go to *support* transcendental idealism. Although the former strategy would be circular, the latter most certainly is not.[14]

Even though the above argument from the Transcendental Dialectic builds a *negative* case for transcendental idealism by showing how the only alternative (transcendental realism) is untenable, Kant's *positive* case for transcendental idealism comes in the Transcendental Aesthetic and Transcendental Analytic. The Transcendental Aesthetic proves that we cannot cognize objects as they might exist in themselves but only insofar as they appear to us spatiotemporally where space and time are themselves contributions of the subject to her experience of these objects. The Transcendental Analytic completes the positive case for transcendental idealism by proving that we can only cognize these objects as they appear in accordance with our concepts of them where these concepts are likewise contributions of the subject to her experience of these objects.

Returning to the opening metaphor of this book, the *Critique of Pure Reason* is meant to show not only how reason is subject to errors and falsehoods (negative comments), but also to show how reason can be both useful and necessary (positive comments). The Transcendental Aesthetic and Transcendental

Analytic offer many positive comments. Reason, in its broad sense, is useful and necessary in supplying the principles of cognition *a priori* both of sensibility (Transcendental Aesthetic) and the understanding (Transcendental Analytic) which are the two sources of our cognition. Cognition is limited to the bounds of sense, however, and so reason, in its narrow sense, is misused when it feigns cognition beyond these bounds. Although the Transcendental Dialectic offers many negative comments by illustrating the kinds of errors and falsehoods to which reason is subject once reason transcends the bounds of sense, its comments are not wholly negative. As we have seen, in the appendix to the Transcendental Dialectic, Kant argues that reason has an indispensible *regulative* role in systematizing cognition and driving scientific inquiry. Likewise, after the Transcendental Dialectic, in the Canon of Pure Reason, Kant suggests that the boundaries that constrain reason from the theoretical perspective no longer do so from the practical perspective. What is impossible for cognition is made possible through faith.

Notes

1. *CPR* A644/B672. For a diagram illustrating the metaphor, see Burnham and Young, *Kant's Critique*, 163.
2. *CPR* A652-58/B680-86. See also Buroker's helpful discussion of these three principles and how they are assumed in empirical concept formation. Buroker, *Kant's Critique*, 286-87.
3. *CPR* A651/B679.
4. Philip Kitcher suggests an explanation along similar lines. See Philip Kitcher, "Projecting the Order of Nature," in *Kant's Critique of Pure Reason: Critical Essays*, 219-238.
5. *CPR* A804-5/B832-33.
6. Although we will focus on the use of these ideas within the context of practical reason, Frederick Rauscher discusses how the ideas of God, the soul, and the world can have an important role to play both for theoretical as well as practical reason. See Frederick Rauscher, "The Appendix to the Dialectic and the Canon of Pure Reason: The Positive Role of Reason," in *The Cambridge Companion to Kant's Critique of Pure Reason*, 290-309.
7. *CPR* A534/B562.
8. *CPR* A811/B839.
9. *CPR* A810/B839.
10. Altman has a nice discussion of how the ideas from the Canon of Pure reason are developed in the *Critique of Practical Reason*. See Altman, *A Companion to Kant's Critique*, 184-87.
11. *CPR* A828-29/B856-57.
12. *CPR* A506-7/B534-35.
13. One might wonder if empirical idealism is another option. In the A edition Paralogisms, however, Kant claims that transcendental realism and empirical idealism are two

aspects of the same position much as transcendental idealism and empirical realism are two aspects of the contrary position. See *CPR* A369-372.

14. Wood makes this response to the objection. Even so, he does think there are deeper problems with Kant's indirect proof of transcendental idealism. He argues that Kant can claim, at most, that the antinomies provide an indirect proof for the illegitimacy of reason's principle that if the conditioned is given then so are all of its conditions including the unconditioned conditioned. He claims, however, that the transcendental realist could simply reject this illegitimate principle while still adhering to the logical maxim that reason must seek the unconditioned condition for its conditioned cognitions. See Allen Wood, "The Antinomies of Pure Reason," in *The Cambridge Companion to Kant's Critique of Pure Reason*, 252-53 and 259-261. Allison responds to this criticism by holding that the illegitimate principle cannot be rejected since it is a condition for the application of the logical maxim, but that it ceases to be deceptive when separated from transcendental realism. Although we cannot avoid transcendental illusion we can at least avoid being deceived by it if we reject transcendental realism. In other words, although one cannot deny that the unconditioned condition is subjectively necessary for the use of one's reason (i.e., application of the logical maxim), one can reject that the unconditioned condition is objectively necessary if one rejects transcendental realism. For the debate between Wood and Allison on this issue, see Allen Wood et. al., "Debating Allison on Transcendental Idealism," *Kantian Review* 12, no. 2 (April, 2007): 1-39, especially 1-10 and 24-31.

Appendix
Advice for the Student Reader

The *Arguments of Kant's Critique of Pure Reason* is meant to relieve your anxiety. We understand your uneasiness about tackling such a large complex work, and if your initial reaction after trudging through a few pages is to retreat back to those old familiar Platonic dialogues or Descartes' comparatively pleasant *Meditations*, do not worry, we were once there. It has taken much time, effort, and instruction (the most valuable intellectual goals require all three), but our diligence has paid off. Reading *CPR* has also required some intellectual humility on our part. We just mean that when the time came when we had read the same passage multiple times and had only succeeded in becoming more confused, we had to be willing to say to both ourselves and our professor, "We just do not understand." It is often difficult to admit one's own ignorance but it is only in doing so that it can be overcome. We would like for you to know that reading and understanding *CPR*, while difficult, is not an impossible task. At last, Kant's personal lexicon no longer boggles our minds, and instead of a hurdle, *CPR* has become a bridge between the modern and contemporary periods of philosophy. Moreover, making sense of *CPR* is important for all students of philosophy. Kant's insights into epistemology and metaphysics are still valuable today. In addition, *CPR* is an essential piece of that impressive puzzle called the history of philosophy. Without a basic understanding of it, a huge gap will remain in one's knowledge of philosophy's history in general.

Maybe you understand the importance of *CPR* and are willing to put forth the effort to study it, but you are having difficulty. This book is meant to help. By reading it along with *CPR*, you will be able to follow Kant's arguments step by step. We have given definitions to key terms in a glossary near the end of the

211

book. These are terms that we, as undergrads reading *CPR* for the first time, had difficulty with and also those that are essential to understanding Kant's arguments. Furthermore, we tried to define these terms in a way which is at the same time helpful to new readers while still technically precise, so that one is able to not only understand the term being defined but also be confident it the definition.

Throughout this project we came across our own difficulties in understanding *CPR* that we had to work through and overcome in various ways. In this appendix, we would like to share with you some of those rough spots and how we were able to overcome them. We would also like to offer some general advice when it comes to reading *CPR* for the first time, such as study habits that we found helpful. We hope that the things we have gathered from our experience in studying *CPR* will benefit you as well. We understand that these hints, tips, and lessons will not work for everybody, since study methods and learning styles are specific to individuals. If we can offer at least one piece of advice that is useful to you, however, this appendix will have been worth the writing. It is our hope that by learning from our mistakes, and applying the advice given here, your study of *CPR* will be a more enjoyable and less stressful learning experience.

The knowledge and skills of your professor will be of great help in understanding *CPR*. We feel confident in saying that anyone who is teaching a course in which Kant's philosophy is the subject will have struggled with this material during their own studies. This will make them an invaluable resource and we recommend that you consult them at every opportunity. Your professors may also assign or recommend supplemental material which can aid in your study. But keep in mind that any supplemental text, including the one you hold in your hands now, are just that and they will not and cannot replace an in-depth study of the primary text.

The first thing you may notice when reading *CPR* is its old-fashioned language and tedious style of writing. It is true that Kant is no poet. His purpose for writing *CPR*, however, was not for it to be aesthetically pleasing to our ears, but rather to be an intellectual challenge for our minds. His style of writing will take some getting used to and also some work. To keep things as tidy as possible, we will keep distinct three related linguistic issues that should not be confused. Those issues are style, general vocabulary, and philosophical vocabulary. Each of these may require a different approach. First we will deal with the writing style of *CPR*. What we found helpful was to break up certain sentences in order to look at them in more detail. We used a number of methods, such as reordering sentences, removing unnecessary terms, and linking pronouns such as "it," "they," "that," "these" and "which," with the nouns they stand for. For example, the very first sentence from the Transcendental Aesthetic states that "In whatever way and through whatever means a cognition may relate to objects, that through which it relates immediately to them, and at which all thought as a means is directed as an end, is intuition."[1]

If you were like us, after reading this for the first time, you still did not know what an intuition is. What we recommend is to take a closer and slower look at the sentence, piece by piece. It is easy to realize that he is defining what an intuition is, but not so easy to understand how he is defining an intuition. We understand definitions better if the term being defined is at the beginning and not at the end. So we simply rephrase the sentence as, "An intuition is. . ." and move on from there. The first clause of the sentence, "In whatever way and through whatever means a cognition may relate to objects," gives us a part of the framework for the definition Kant is providing. The sentence is like a sandwich, in that the first clause tells us that cognitions relate to objects, the last one tells us that intuition is a way in which cognitions relate to objects, and everything in the middle explains the details of that relation. He is in essence saying: Although there might be other ways in which cognition will relate to objects, nevertheless, intuition is one of those ways. The second clause then states, "that through which it relates immediately to them." Within these eight words Kant has used four pronouns! We must figure out what noun each pronoun is referring to in order to make the statement more understandable. "That through which," is clearly referring to an intuition. Since the previous clause stated, "a cognition may relate to objects," Kant is probably keeping the same form when he says, "it relates immediately to them," "it" referring to cognitions and "them" referring to objects. Thus, the definition can be modified further to say, "An intuition is that through which cognitions relate immediately to objects." The last part states, "and at which all thought as a means is directed as an end," and offers us a second characteristic of intuition, but also something about concepts as well. According to Kant, concepts are the way in which we think about objects, just like intuitions are the way in which objects are given to us. What is confusing here is the means/ends language. It seems Kant is saying that thought, when directed at intuition, is the means by which cognition, the end, is possible. This would also fit Kant's view of cognition in *CPR*, viz., that since intuition provides the content, i.e., objects are given to us through intuition, thought must be directed at intuition, otherwise thought will not have any content. In other words, we would not be thinking about anything in particular. Our final definition looks something like this: An intuition is (1) that through which cognitions relate immediately to objects and (2) at which all thought is directed. Compared to the definition given in the quote, this version is much simpler and direct. This is just one example of how a complicated sentence in *CPR* can be turned into a straightforward statement. Though a step by step process of re-ordering of words and linking or replacing pronouns with the nouns they refer to, the fog may begin to clear.

The second linguistic issue is Kant's general vocabulary in *CPR*. There is not much that needs to be said about this second issue since a dictionary would probably solve most problems you may run into. In fact, we actually thought this was a bigger problem until we started looking through *CPR* for terms that were difficult but were not technical philosophical terms. To our surprise, we could not find many. If you do run into any words that just do not seem to make sense and a dictionary does little to help, remember to keep the context in mind when trying to determine the meaning. If you have two competing definitions for a term, definition A may make more sense in light of what is surrounding the term then definition B. If the term is part of Kant's philosophical vocabulary, the glossary of this book should be helpful. When a term is not defined in the glossary, however, keep an eye out for other places in *CPR* where Kant uses the same term to see if any of these additional uses might aid in figuring out the definition. Most of all, try not to get hung up on a term to the point that it keeps you from moving on after a few minutes of thought. Sometimes the answers to your questions come to you in an epiphany when you do not even expect it. Something just clicks. This was our experience after we had spent nearly an hour or more discussing the meaning of the word "determination." It now seems somewhat silly looking back that such a common term caused us so much difficulty.

We should warn you, however, not to be too presumptuous when it comes to terms that you are already familiar with. One such example would be the word "intuition." If you feel comfortable with this term before reading *CPR* and think you already know what it means, then we advise you to make yourself uncomfortable with it. Within *CPR*, "intuition" is one of those general terms with a technical philosophical meaning. To understand it, you must find out what Kant means by "intuition." You will not be able to look this term up in a dictionary and hope to find Kant's meaning. *The Merriam-Webster Dictionary Eleventh Edition* gives these two definitions of "intuition": (1) quick and ready insight (2) the power or faculty of knowing things without conscious reasoning. If you look again at Kant's definition of intuition given above, you will see that neither of these fully captures the meaning that he gives the term. See the difference? Once again, we hope our glossary will aid in your study of *CPR*.

The third linguistic issue is philosophical vocabulary. We can confidently assert that you will not be able to get a handle on *CPR* without a basic understanding of the technical terms included within it. If you are not familiar with terms such as "*a priori*" and "*a posteriori*," "analytic" and "synthetic," much of what Kant says in *CPR* will be gibberish to you. However, there are many ways to overcome this problem. First, Kant does define many of his terms in *CPR* for us. For example, at the beginning of the Transcendental Aesthetic, Kant defines "intuition," "sensibility," "concepts," and "appearance."[2] It is important to focus on the definitions given within *CPR* because Kant is defining his terms in a particular way for the project he is working on. If you went to a philosophical dictionary on the internet and looked up "intuition," it may give any number of definitions, but only Kant's definition works the way he has intended it to within the rest of *CPR*. Also, the secondary material on *CPR* was helpful when trying to understanding Kant's technical language. Some of these books include their own glossaries and may contain examples to help illustrate what a word means. For a few examples of these kinds of secondary sources, see the works mentioned at the end of our glossary. Next, try coming up with your own examples for philosophical terms and concepts. For instance, an analytic proposition is one whose predicate concept is contained within its subject concept or whose denial is logically or conceptually self-contradictory.[3] An example would be that "Bachelors [subject] are unmarried [predicate]." If you know what "bachelor" means, then you know a bachelor is unmarried. You need only examine the subject of the proposition to discover the predicate within it. The latter concept is contained in the former. Likewise, to deny that bachelors are unmarried would contradict the concept of what it is to be a bachelor. When you are able to come up with accurate examples, that is a pretty good sign that you know what the term means.

Another thing which makes *CPR* so difficult to decipher is the compact way in which Kant presents his arguments. For example, the first two arguments from the Metaphysical Exposition of space, which argue that space is an *a priori* representation, are only three sentences each. Our reconstructions of these arguments, however, are five and six steps long respectively. He manages to give his arguments in such a compact manner through a prodigious use of compound sentences. You will see these throughout *CPR* and they are often difficult to comprehend. To illustrate this point, the second sentence of the first argument from the Metaphysical Exposition of space (B38) contains sixty-one words, three commas, one set of parentheses, and one set of angle brackets. Working through this sentence requires multiple readings. This is true of *CPR* as a whole. You will not be able to read through it one time and comprehend the full meaning of what is being said. One must submerse themselves in the language of *CPR*. Some ways this may be accomplished are reading paragraphs over and over again, memorizing definitions so that you do not have to continuously return to the glossary, and reading *CPR* every day. What you are aiming for is familiarity with the text which will inevitability lead to a better understanding of it. The more you read and think about this material, the more familiar the language will become, and soon, to the annoyance of your friends and family, you will be speaking Kantian.

No philosopher throughout history philosophized in a bubble. Their work was not done in isolation from history or the world around them. Kant is no different. In fact, many of the arguments within *CPR* are direct responses to philosophers who came before him. In light of this, it is helpful to be familiar with the modern period of philosophy. Major players of the modern period include René Descartes, John Locke, Gottfried Leibniz, George Berkeley, and David Hume. An understanding of their positions will make dealing with many of Kant's arguments much easier. For example, Kant's "Refutation of Idealism" includes a rejection of Descartes' idealism from the First Meditation, which Kant calls "problematic idealism."[4] If you already know what Descartes' idealism is, you will not have to try and figure it out when you come to that argument. Likewise, with Leibniz' view on space and time, which Kant argues against in the Transcendental Aesthetic.[5] In the same way that being familiar with ancient philosophy aids in understanding the philosophers from the medieval era, having a working knowledge of modern philosophy can help you to understand *CPR*.

If you have tried all of these things and you still are finding yourself confused, your puzzlement may not be directly related to the details of the language or the other modern philosophers, but the bigger picture. After doing all of this reading while thinking about words, definitions, and sentence structure, you still may be unsure what exactly Kant is talking about. This is where we found ourselves early on, asking ourselves if we have missed the forest for the trees. Clearly, there is a lot going on in *CPR*, from space and time as *a priori* forms of intuition, to the cognition of objects being limited to how they appear. Very soon, one starts to wonder what exactly is going on that would require such complex arguments and technical terminology. Our quick and easy solution to this problem was the secondary source material. Please see the endnotes of each chapter for secondary sources that deal with the material covered in that chapter. Kant's preface and introduction to *CPR*, however, are also great for setting up what is to come. All it took was a little background, and a basic understanding of the problem Kant was working to solve, and we were able to read *CPR* with far more perspective.

As with most subjects one might study, taking notes while reading *CPR* may be the first thing you would think of doing. While this is not a bad idea, we have found that it can cause problems starting out. When we began reading *CPR*, we would keep a notebook and pen by our book and write down all the questions and important concepts that we wanted to remember. Of course we barely understood anything we were reading and so the result was pages full of notes, with very few pages of *CPR* getting read. Every point seemed important enough to write down, and each one sparked more questions. Eventually, to make some progress, we forced ourselves to put the notebook away. Now that we are more familiar with *CPR*, we can bring our notebook back out and take more productive notes and ask more significant questions. This also was a better choice for us since many of the initial questions we had were eventually answered through reading more of *CPR*, the secondary sources, and discussions with Dr. Hall.

Understanding the arguments of *CPR* is a worthy and attainable goal. We hope that this book and the personal insights we have shared will provide you with a few stepping stones toward that end.

Notes

1. *CPR* A19/B33.
2. See *CPR* A19-20/B33-34.
3. In this book, we will give you another way of understanding analyticity that avoids some common objections to the above criteria. See the introduction for more on this issue.
4. See *CPR* B274-79.
5. See *CPR* A19/B33.

Glossary[1]

A posteriori: See "A priori."

A priori: *A priori* propositions are known without appeal to experience. Since they do not depend upon experience, according to Kant, all *a priori* propositions are necessarily true. *A priori* propositions can be either "pure" or "impure" (B3). Pure *a priori* propositions contain nothing which has been derived from experience (e.g., that $2 + 2 = 4$). Impure *a priori* propositions have empirical content (e.g., involve empirical concepts). Such propositions are still *a priori*, however, as long as one need not appeal to experience in order to combine the concepts in a proposition. For example, in the proposition that "Every alteration has a cause" although alteration is an empirical concept while cause and effect is a category, the proposition itself can be formed without appeal to experience. *A posteriori* propositions, in contrast, cannot be known without appeal to experience. All *a posteriori* propositions are contingent since they depend on the way the world is which could have turned out otherwise (B2).

Analytic: An analytic proposition is one whose predicate concept is contained within its subject concept or whose denial is logically or conceptually self-contradictory. For example, the statement, "Bachelors are unmarried, adult, males" is analytic because the concept "unmarried" is contained within the concept "bachelor," i.e., part of what it means to be a bachelor is to be unmarried. All one needs to do is analyze the subject concept to find the predicate concept. Denying that bachelors are unmarried would contradict the concept of what it is to be a bachelor. Analytic propositions stand in contrast to synthetic propositions whose predicate concepts are not contained in their subject concepts and whose denials are logically or conceptually consistent. For example, in the proposition that "Bachelors are messy," the concept "messy" is not contained within the concept "bachelor." Denial of the former does not contradict the latter concept. One can, in principle, be a tidy bachelor (A6-7/B10-11, A151/B190). Additionally, one need not appeal to intuition (either pure or empirical) in order to form analytic propositions. One need only possess the relevant concepts. Consequently, all analytic statements are *a priori* according to Kant and so are necessarily true. In contrast, with synthetic propositions, one must appeal to intuition (either pure or empirical) in order to form them. If the appeal is to pure intuition, then the proposition is synthetic *a priori*. If the appeal is to empirical intuition, then the proposition is synthetic *a posteriori*. Whereas the former are necessary, the latter are contingent.

Antinomy: An antinomy is a "contradiction in the laws of pure reason" (A407/B434). It is a paradox whereupon on the assumption of the thesis, *P*, a contradiction can be derived; and on the assumption of the antithesis, ~ *P*, another contradiction can be derived. Hence the defender of the thesis can "prove" his claim by a *reductio ad absurdum* of the antithesis; and the defender of the antithesis can "prove" her claim by a *reductio* of the thesis.

Apodictic: When a proposition is necessary because it is demonstrated as holding universally (A31/B47). Thus, Kant's statement that "geometrical propositions are all apodictic" (B41) can be restated as "geometrical propositions are necessarily true."

Appearance: For Kant, an appearance is the "undetermined object of an empirical intuition" (A20/B34). An appearance is undetermined in that it has not been brought under concepts. It is an object of empirical intuition insofar as intuition is immediately related to it through sensation. There is, however, also a way of understanding appearances as relations between subjects and objects (B66-67). Appearances are not illusions for Kant. The former are empirically real and we experience the world only insofar as it appears.

Apperception: Transcendental apperception is the consciousness of one's own identity or the "I think" which must accompany all of my representations. Attaching the "I think" to representations is what unifies them under one consciousness and allows me to recognize myself as the same subject over time. This stands in contrast to empirical apperception which is consciousness at a time but not consciousness of the one's own identity over time (A106-7 and B131-32).

Axiom: Axioms are basic principles that can only be exhibited in intuition. For example, that time has only one dimension (B47) is a principle concerning the intuition of time. In the Principles, Kant introduces the Axioms of Intuition which hold that all intuitions are extensive magnitudes (B202).

Categories: See "Concept."

Cognition: This is Kant's term for how we come to know things. Generally, Kant claims that cognition requires the unification of concepts, the way we think about objects, and intuitions, the way that objects are given to us sensibly (A51/B75). Intuitions and concepts are unified through judgment (A68/B93). The cognition is *a priori* when it results from the unification of categories and formal intuition *a priori*. The cognition is empirical when it results from the unification of categories and empirical intuition *a posteriori*. Kant also calls the latter "experience" (B147-48).

Concept: Concepts are the representations by which we think about objects. Concepts are general in that they can pick out more than one object. They are mediate because they refer to their object only indirectly through characteristics that the object shares with other objects that fall under the same concept. Concepts come in three forms: empirical concepts, categories, and transcendental ideas (A320/B376-77). (1) An empirical concept is a concept which is derived from experience. Empirical concepts are formed when we recognize shared characteristics between objects and then subtract from those objects anything which is not common to them all. The result is a "common mark" that all the objects falling under the concept share. (2) Categories, or pure concepts of the understanding, contain nothing which has been derived from experience and are thus *a priori*. Pure concepts contain the form of thinking about objects in general. They are derived from the logical table of judgments which contains the form of thinking in general. (3) Transcendental ideas, or pure concepts of reason, are the result of reason taking the categories, which the understanding applies legitimately to objects in sensible intuition, and attempting to apply them illegitimately beyond the bounds of sense.

Condition: Something is a condition if it makes something else possible or actual. The condition provides the *explanation* for something conditioned. For example, space, time, categories, and apperception are all conditions for the possibility of experience. Something is conditioned if it requires something else for it to be possible or actual. For example, the objects of experience are all conditioned. Something is unconditioned if it does not require anything else for it to be possible or actual. For example, God (as described in the Ideal) would be unconditioned.

Deduction: A deduction is a reasoned attempt to show not that something is the case, but that something is lawful or justified (A84-85/B116-17). In *CPR*, Kant is concerned with justifying our possession of the categories as well as their employment with respect to the objects of experience. Whereas the Metaphysical Deduction justifies our possession of the categories by deriving them from the logical table of judgments, the Transcendental Deduction justifies our employment of the categories by showing how they are *a priori* conditions for the possibility of objects of experience.

Determination: To "determine" something is to set, fix, or characterize the properties of that thing. To be a "determination" is to be a property of that which is determined. To be "determinate" is to be something which has its properties set, fixed, or characterized.

Dialectic: Dialectical illusion results from reason applying the categories beyond the bounds of sense. The Transcendental Dialectic enumerates the kinds of errors that reason falls into once it transcends these bounds (A61-64/B85-88).

Discursive: This term derives from the Latin "*discursus*" which means to run through something. In the Transcendental Analytic, Kant describes how understanding runs through the diverse representations offered by sensibility classifying them under the concepts of the understanding. This requires judgment applying understanding's concepts to what is given in intuition resulting in cognition (A68/B93).

Empirical Concept: See "Concept."

Empirical Idealism: See "Transcendental Idealism."

Empirical Realism: See "Transcendental Idealism."

Experience: See "Cognition."

Imagination: Kant describes it as "the faculty for representing an object even without its presence in intuition" (B151). It mediates between the sensibility and the understanding by synthesizing sensible representations in accordance with the categories. Imagination drives the three-fold synthesis of the A edition Transcendental Deduction (A124-25). It also produces the schemata of the categories (A140/B179).

Intuition: Intuitions are that through which cognitions relate immediately to objects and at which all thought is directed if it is to produce cognition. They are singular in that they pick out individual objects. They are immediate because they directly refer to their objects. Intuitions come prior to thought and for creatures like us are always sensible. Sensible intuitions can be either empirical or pure (A20-21/B34-35). (1) Empirical intuitions are the means by which objects are given to us, i.e., objects appear to subjects via intuition. Empirical intuitions are related to their objects *a posteriori* through the matter of appearance (sensation) though their form (space and time) are *a priori*. The object of an empirical intuition produces sensation by affecting the subject through the five senses. (2) Pure intuitions are representations of space and time *a priori* without any content derived from sensation *a posteriori*. Kant also discusses two forms of nonsensible intuition that creatures like us do not possess: (1) God possesses a divine intuition that is *productive*. Given his omnipotence, God can simply think objects into existence (B145). 2) Intellectual intuition is the kind of intuition that rationalists think we possess. It is cognition through reason alone. Although the rationalist cannot think things into existence, reason alone is supposed to provide the immediate representation of an individual through concepts (B307).

Judgment: Judgment is a faculty of the understanding whereby different representations are unified. Judgments produce propositions which are truth evaluable and deal with the relations between concepts and intuitions, one concept and another, or the relation between a set of judgments (A68/B93, A73/B98).

Logic: General logic deals only with the form of thought in general without regard to the content of thought. All thinking is judging for Kant and the necessary rules for thought are given in the logical table of judgments (A70/B95). General logic stands in contrast to transcendental logic which deals with the form of thinking about objects in general and how these forms of thought relate to objects *a priori* (A55-57/B79-82). The necessary rules for thinking about objects in general are given in the table of categories (A80/B106).

Manifold: A manifold contains unsynthesized representational content. A manifold can be either pure or empirical. A pure manifold contains nothing which has been derived from experience, e.g., the space in which we construct geometrical objects. An empirical manifold contains the appearances that we receive through empirical intuition *a posteriori*. The manifold is synthesized through the application of the categories to its representational content (A77-78/B102-4).

Metaphysical Deduction: See "Deduction."

Metaphysical Exposition: A metaphysical exposition "contains that which exhibits the concept as given *a priori*" (B38). In the metaphysical expositions of space and time, Kant is concerned with examining what characteristics space and time exhibit *a priori*. The first two metaphysical expositions argue that space and time are *a priori* rather than *a posteriori* representations and the second two metaphysical expositions argue that space and time are intuitions rather than concepts.

Noumena: See "Things in Themselves."

Paralogism: A paralogism has the form of a categorical syllogism but commits a fallacy of equivocation (A402). Each paralogism corresponds to the dialectical use of a different set of categories (A404). Kant associates the paralogisms with fallacious arguments in rational psychology

Phenomena: Objects of experience. They are objects insofar as they appear to us in space and time and in accordance with the categories (B306).

Practical: See "Theoretical."

Reason: Reason is the innate faculty for logical inference (in particular through syllogistic reasoning) and the systematic organization of cognition (A302-5/B359-361). There are two senses of "reason" that are important to distinguish. In its broad sense, reason supplies the principles of cognition *a priori* (A11/B24-25). Understanding and sensibility are the two sources of cognition (A50-51/B74-75). The Transcendental Aesthetic enumerates the principles of sensibility *a priori* while the Transcendental Analytic enumerates the principles of the understanding *a priori*. The Transcendental Aesthetic and Analytic also establish that cognition is possible only within the bounds of sense. In its narrow sense, reason is considered as a separate faculty that is prone to error when it uses these principles to make inferences beyond the bounds of sense (A308-9/B365-66). Kant enumerates these errors in the Transcendental Dialectic. Kant also distinguishes between theoretical and practical (moral) reason. What we have described above has to do with theoretical reason. One of the positive results of *CPR*, however, will be to open up a separate role for practical reason by constraining the role of theoretical reason (Bxxiv-xxv). For more on the theoretical/practical distinction, see "Theoretical" below.

Representation: This is a broad term which refers to anything of which the subject is conscious. Representations can be divided into sensations (referring to the subject) as well as cognitions (referring to objects). The components of cognition (concepts and intuitions) are likewise representations (A320/B376-77).

Schemata: The transcendental schemata mediate between the categories and the manifold of sensible intuition. Kant characterizes them as "transcendental time-determinations" of the categories and it is only the schema of a given category that applies directly to the manifold of sensible intuition. They perform this function by serving as conceptual procedures for the production of sensible images in time (A139-140/B178-79).

Sensibility: Sensibility is the faculty through which objects are given to us in intuition. It is a completely passive faculty in that it is merely the capacity to receive representations (A50-51/B74-B75). That sensibility has two *a priori* forms, i.e., space and time, is shown in the Transcendental Aesthetic.

Substance: There are two definitions of substance corresponding to the unschematized and schematized versions of the category. The unschematized version holds that substance is "something that can be though as subject (without being predicate of something else" (A147/B186). The schematized version holds that substance is "the persistence of the real in time" (A143-44/B183). In other words, substance is what persists in empirical intuition.

Synthesis: Synthesis is the act of combining different representations together in such a way that they come to be regarded as a whole (A77/B102-3). In the A edition Transcendental Deduction, Kant describes three ways in which representations are synthesized (apprehension, reproduction, and recognition) through the imagination in accordance with the categories (A124-25).

Synthetic: See "Analytic."

Theoretical: Whereas theoretical philosophy has to do with what *is* the case (objects of possible experience), practical philosophy concerns what *ought* to be the case (A633/B661). Practical philosophy is moral philosophy. Whereas Kant thinks that we can *cognize* objects within the bounds of sense from the theoretical perspective, we may only *think* of objects that fall beyond the bounds of sense from the theoretical perspective. The latter is the speculative use of reason (Bxxiv-xxvi). From the practical perspective, however, certain objects (such as God, the soul, and human freedom) that fall beyond these bounds demand our *faith* (A828-29/B856-57). It is for the sake of the practical that Kant "had to deny knowledge in order to make room for faith" (Bxxx).

Things-in-themselves: Objects can either be understood insofar as they appear spatiotemporally and in accordance with our concepts of them, or as they are independently of these conditions. The latter are things-in-themselves (A42/B59). Whereas objects insofar as they appear are phenomena (sensible), things-in-themselves are noumena (non-sensible). Noumena come in two flavors. *Positive* noumena possess their own essences and exist independently of their relationship to other things beyond the bounds of sense. They can be cognized only by God or a being with a capacity for intellectual intuition, but not by creatures like us that possess only sensible intuition. The *negative* noumenon, in contrast, delineates the limits of experience and serves as that which corresponds to the non-sensible ground of appearances (B306-7). Kant sometimes refers to the latter as the transcendental object (A288/B344-45).

Transcendent: See "Transcendental."

Transcendental: Transcendental principles describe the *a priori* conditions for the possibility of objects of experience and as such are principles of cognition *a priori*. A system of such principles is transcendental philosophy (A11-12/B25). There are transcendental principles both of sensibility (space and time) as well as of the understanding (categories). These principles should be contrasted with *transcendent* principles which result from reason illegitimately extending understanding's concepts beyond the bounds of possible experience to make objective claims (A295-96/B352-53).

Transcendental Deduction: See "Deduction."

Transcendental Exposition: A transcendental exposition is an explanation of how a concept can be used as a foundation on which to ground the possibility of synthetic *a priori* propositions (B40). In the case of the Transcendental Expositions of space and time, Kant wants to show how the synthetic *a priori* propositions of geometry and mathematics are possible only under the assumption that space and time are *a priori* intuitions.

Transcendental Idealism: The central position of *CPR* which holds that we cannot cognize objects as they might exist in themselves but only insofar as they appear to us spatiotemporally and in accordance with our concepts of them, where not only these concepts but space and time themselves are contributions of the subject to her experience of these objects. Transcendental idealism is intimately connected to Kant's theory of empirical realism. Since the transcendental idealist holds that the objects of experience, as appearances, are nothing independently of the subject's cognitive contribution to her experience, she is also an empirical realist who can immediately affirm the reality of the objects of experience without going beyond the subject's consciousness of them (non-skeptical). The dual position of transcendental idealism/empirical realism is opposed to the dual position of transcendental realism/empirical idealism (A369-372). Since the transcendental realist holds that objects of experience are things-in-themselves distinct from our representations, she is also an empirical idealist who denies that our representations are sufficient to establish the reality of these objects (skeptical).

Transcendental Ideas: See "Concepts."

Transcendental Object: See "Things-in-Themselves."

Transcendental Realism: See "Transcendental Idealism."

Understanding: The understanding is the faculty for actively thinking about objects in sensible intuition through concepts. This can be contrasted with sensibility which is the passive faculty by which objects are given to us in sensible intuition (A50-51/B74-75). The Transcendental Analytic establishes that there are certain *a priori* concepts (categories) that are conditions for the possibility of objects of experience.

Note

1. In formulating definitions for the glossary, we consulted Caygill, Howard, *A Kant Dictionary* (Oxford: Blackwell, 1995) as well as the glossaries in Altman, *A Companion to Kant's Critique* and Burnham and Young, *Kant's Critique*.

Bibliography

Al-Azm, Sadik. *The Origin of Kant's Arguments in the Antinomies*. Oxford: Oxford University Press, 1972.

Allison, Henry. *The Kant-Eberhard Controversy*. Baltimore: Johns Hopkins University Press, 1973.

——. *Kant's Theory of Freedom*. Cambridge: Cambridge University Press, 1990.

——. *Kant's Transcendental Idealism: An Interpretation and Defense*. 2nd ed. New Haven, CT: Yale University Press, 2004.

Altman, Matthew. *A Companion to Kant's Critique of Pure Reason*. Boulder, CO: Westview Press, 2007.

Anderson, R. Lanier, "Introduction to the Critique: Framing the Question." Pp. 75-92 in *The Cambridge Companion to Kant's Critique of Pure Reason*. Edited by Paul Guyer. Cambridge: Cambridge University Press, 2010.

Aristotle. *Selections*. Translated by Terence Irwin and Gail Fine. Indianapolis, IN: Hackett Publishing, 1995.

Beck, Lewis White. "Did the Sage of Königsberg Have no Dreams?" Pp. 103-16 in *Kant's Critique of Pure Reason: Critical Essays*. Edited by Patricia Kitcher. Lanham, MD: Rowman & Littlefield, 1998.

Bennett, Jonathan. *Kant's Analytic*. Cambridge: Cambridge University Press, 1966.

——. *Kant's Dialectic*. Cambridge: Cambridge University Press, 1974.

Berkeley, George. *The Works of George Berkeley, Bishop of Cloyne*. Edited by A.A. Luce and T.E. Jessop. 9 vols. London: Thomas Nelson and Sons, 1948-1954.

Buchdahl, Gerd. *Kant and the Dynamics of Reason: Essays on the Structure of Kant's Philosophy*. Oxford: Blackwell Publishing, 1992.

Burnham, Douglas and Harvey Young. *Kant's Critique of Pure Reason*. Bloomington, IN: Indiana University Press, 2001.

Buroker, Jill Vance. *Kant's Critique of Pure Reason: An Introduction*. Cambridge: Cambridge University Press, 2005.

Caygill, Howard. *A Kant Dictionary*. Oxford: Blackwell Publishing, 1995.

Descartes, René. *The Philosophical Writings of Descartes*. Translated by John Cottingham, Robert Stoothoff, and Dugald Murdoch, vol. 3 including Anthony Kenny. 3
vols. Cambridge: Cambridge University Press, 1988.

Dicker, Georges. *Kant's Theory of Knowledge: An Analytical Introduction*. New York:
Oxford University Press, 2004.

Falkenstein, Lorne. *Kant's Intuitionism: A Commentary on the Transcendental Aesthetic*.
Toronto, University of Toronto Press, 1995.

——. "Was Kant a Nativist?" Pp. 21-44 in *Kant's Critique of Pure Reason:
Critical Essays*. Edited by Patricia Kitcher. Lanham, MD: Rowman & Littlefield,
1998.

Friedman, Michael. *Kant and the Exact Sciences*. Cambridge, MA: Harvard University
Press, 1992.

Gardner, Sebastian. *Routledge Philosophy Guidebook to Kant and the Critique of Pure
Reason*. London: Routledge, 1999.

Gibbons, Sarah. *Kant's Theory of Imagination: Bridging Gaps in Judgment and Experience*. Oxford: Oxford University Press, 1994.

Grice H.P. and P.F. Strawson. "In Defense of a Dogma." *Philosophical Review* 65, no. 2
(April, 1956): 141-158.

Grier, Michelle. "The Ideal of Pure Reason." Pp. 266-289 in *The Cambridge Companion
to Kant's Critique of Pure Reason*. Edited by Paul Guyer. Cambridge: Cambridge
University Press, 2010.

——. *Kant's Doctrine of Transcendental Illusion*. Cambridge: Cambridge University
Press, 2001.

Guyer, Paul, ed. *The Cambridge Companion to Kant's Critique of Pure Reason*. Cambridge: Cambridge University Press, 2010.

——. "The Deduction of the Categories: The Metaphysical and Transcendental Deductions." Pp. 118-150 in *The Cambridge Companion to Kant's Critique of Pure Reason*. Edited by Paul Guyer. Cambridge: Cambridge University Press, 2010.

——. *Kant and the Claims of Knowledge*. Cambridge: Cambridge University
Press, 1987.

Hall, Bryan. "Appearances and the Problem of Affection in Kant." *Kantian Review* 14,
no. 2 (January, 2010): 38-66.

——. "A Dilemma for Kant's Theory of Substance," *British Journal for the History of
Philosophy* (forthcoming).

——. "Kant and Quine on the Two Dogmas of Empiricism," *Proceedings of the 11th
International Kant Congress* (forthcoming).

Hanna, Robert. *Kant and the Foundations of Analytic Philosophy*. Oxford: Oxford
University Press, 2001.

Hogan, Desmond. "Kant's Copernican Turn." Pp. 21-40 in *The Cambridge Companion to
Kant's Critique of Pure Reason*. Edited by Paul Guyer. Cambridge: Cambridge University Press, 2010.

Hume, David. *Dialogues on Natural Religion*. Edited by Richard Popkin. Indianapolis,
IN: Hackett, 1998.

——. *Enquiries Concerning Human Understanding and Concerning the Principles of Morals*. Edited by L. A. Selby-Bigge, 3rd ed. revised by P. H. Nidditch.
Oxford: Oxford University Press, 1975.

——. *A Treatise of Human Nature*. Edited by L. A. Selby-Bigge, 2nd ed. revised by P.H.
Nidditch. Oxford: Oxford University Press, 1975.

Jacobi, F.H. *David Hume über den Glauben, oder Idealismus und Realismus. Ein
Gespräch*. Breslau: Gottlieb Löwe. 1787.

James, William. *Principles of Psychology*, 2 vols. New York: Henry Holt, 1890.
Kant, Immanuel. *Critique of the Power of Judgment*. Translated by Paul Guyer and Eric Matthews. Cambridge: Cambridge University Press, 2000.
——. *Critique of Pure Reason*. Translated by Paul Guyer and Allen Wood. Cambridge: Cambridge University Press, 1999.
——. *Lectures on Metaphysics*. Translated by Karl Ameriks and Steve Naragon. Cambridge: Cambridge University Press, 1997.
——. *Practical Reason*. Translated by Mary Gregor. Cambridge, Cambridge University Press, 1996.
——. *Prolegomena to Any Future Metaphysics*. Translated by James Ellington. Indianapolis, IN: Hackett Publishing, 2001.
Katz, Jerrold. *Cogitations: A Study of the Cogito in Relation to the Philosophy of Logic and Language and a Study of Them in Relation to the Cogito*. Cambridge: Cambridge University Press, 1988.
Kemp Smith, Norman. *A Commentary to Kant's Critique of Pure Reason*. New York, Humanities Press, 1962.
Kitcher, Patricia, ed. *Kant's Critique of Pure Reason: Critical Essays*. Lanham, MD: Rowman & Littlefield, 1998.
Kitcher, Philip. "Projecting the Order of Nature." Pp. 219-238 in *Kant's Critique of Pure Reason: Critical Essays*. Edited by Patricia Kitcher. Lanham, MD: Rowman & Littlefield, 1998.
Langton, Rae. *Kantian Humility: Our Ignorance of Things in Themselves*. Oxford: Oxford University Press, 2001.
Leibniz, Gottfried. *G.W. Leibniz and Samuel Clarke: Correspondence*. Translated by Roger Ariew. Indianapolis, IN: Hackett Publishing, 2000.
——. *Monadology and Other Philosophical Essays*. Translated by Paul Schrecker and Anne Martin Schrecker. New York: Macmillan Publishing, 1965.
——. *New Essays on Human Understanding*. Translated by Peter Remnant and Jonathan Bennett. Cambridge: Cambridge University Press, 1981.
Lewis, C.I. *Mind and the World Order: Outline of a Theory of Knowledge*. Mineola, NY: Dover, 1956.
Locke, John. *An Essay Concerning Human Understanding*. Edited by P.H. Nidditch. Oxford: Oxford University Press, 1975.
Maaß, J.G. "Über den höchsten Grundsatz der synthetischen Urtheile; in Beziehung auf die Theorie von der mathematischen Gewissheit." *Philosophische Magazin* 2, no. 2, (1789-1790): 186-231.
Melnick, Arthur. *Kant's Analogies of Experience*. Chicago: University of Chicago Press, 1974.
Newton, Isaac. *Mathematical Principles of Natural Philosophy*. Translated by Andrew Motte, revised by Florian Cajori. Berkeley: University of California Press, 1934.
Paton, H.J. *Kant's Metaphysic of Experience*. 2 vols. New York: Macmillan Publishing, 1936.
Plato. *Five Dialogues*, Translated G.M.A Grube, 2nd ed. revised by John Cooper. Indianapolis, IN: Hackett Publishing, 2002.
Quine, W.V. "Two Dogmas of Empiricism." *Philosophical Review* 60, no. 1 (January, 1951): 20-43.
Rauscher, Frederick. "The Appendix to the Dialectic and the Canon of Pure Reason: The Positive Role of Reason." Pp. 290-309 in *The Cambridge Companion to Kant's Critique of Pure Reason*. Edited by Paul Guyer. Cambridge: Cambridge University Press, 2010.

Rohlf, Michael. "The Ideas of Pure Reason." Pp. 190-209 in *The Cambridge Companion to Kant's Critique of Pure Reason*. Edited by Paul Guyer. Cambridge: Cambridge University Press, 2010.

Rosenberg, Jay. *Accessing Kant: A Relaxed Introduction to the Critique of Pure Reason*. Oxford: Oxford University Press, 2005.

Rowe, William. *William L. Rowe on Philosophy of Religion: Selected Writings*. Edited by Nick Trakakis. Burlington, VT: Ashgate Publishing, 2007.

Russell, Bertrand. *Our Knowledge of the External World*. London: Open Court, 1914.

Savile, Anthony. *Kant's Critique of Pure Reason: An Orientation to the Central Theme*. Oxford: Blackwell Publishing, 2005.

Strawson, P.F. *The Bounds of Sense*. London: Methuen & Co, 1966.

———. *Entity and Identity: and Other Essays*. Oxford: Oxford University Press, 1997.

Trendelenburg, Friedrich Adolf. *Logische Untersuchungen*. Leipzig: Hinzel, 1862.

Van Cleve, James. *Problems from Kant*. New York: Oxford University Press, 1999.

Watkins, Eric. *Kant and the Metaphysics of Causality*. Cambridge: Cambridge University Press, 2005.

———. *Kant's Critique of Pure Reason: Background Source Materials*. Cambridge: Cambridge University Press, 2009.

Westphal, Kenneth. *Kant's Transcendental Proof of Realism*. Cambridge: Cambridge University Press, 2004.

Winkler, Kenneth. "Kant, the Empiricists, and the Enterprise of Deduction." Pp. 41-72 in *The Cambridge Companion to Kant's Critique of Pure Reason*. Edited by Paul Guyer. Cambridge: Cambridge University Press, 2010.

Wolff, Robert P. *Kant's Theory of Mental Activity*. Cambridge, MA: Harvard University Press, 1963.

Wood, Allen. "The Antinomies of Pure Reason." Pp. 245-265 in *The Cambridge Companion to Kant's Critique of Pure Reason*. Edited by Paul Guyer. Cambridge: Cambridge University Press, 2010.

—— Paul Guyer and Henry Allison. "Debating Allison on Transcendental Idealism." *Kantian Review* 12, no. 2 (April, 2007): 1-39

———. "Kant's Compatibilism." Pp. 239-263 in *Kant's Critique of Pure Reason: Critical Essays*. Edited by Patricia Kitcher. Lanham, MD: Rowman & Littlefield, 1998.

———. "Kant's Critique of Three Theistic Proofs." Pp. 265-282 in *Kant's Critique of Pure Reason: Critical Essays*. Edited by Patricia Kitcher. Lanham, MD: Rowman & Littlefield, 1998.

Index

a posteriori/a priori, 4-5, 23-27, 39-42, 46-47, 115, 151, 198, 217; impure/pure a priori, 12n20
actuality, 102-3, 128, 131. *See also* modality
aesthetic, 17
affection, 60, 88, 102-3, 136, 138
alteration, 109, 111-18, 183-89. *See also* causation; event
analogy, 108. *See also* causation; substance
analytic/synthetic, 5-6, 8, 52-53, 69-70, 149, 154, 156, 158, 160, 194-95, 214-15, 217-18
Anselm, 194
antinomy, 149-51, 164, 218; dynamical/mathematical, 150, 182, 207
appearance, 3-4, 8, 17, 20n5, 63n18, 93, 95, 102-3, 108, 110, 122-23, 136-38, 150, 160-61, 169, 175, 182, 188-89, 208, 218. *See also* form; matter
apperception, 72n15, 82n22, 136, 147, 182, 218; empirical, 82n17, 85; pure, 78-79, 85-86, 88-89, 140n13, 143. *See also* consciousness; I think
apprehension, 78-79, 86, 109, 111, 112-14, 117-18, 120, 123
argument: cosmological, 184, 196-99, 201; ontological, 193-96, 198, 201; physico-theological (design), 199-

202; progressive, 21n10, 61, 98, 108, 113, 117; reductio ad absurdum, 150, 164; regressive, 18, 21n10, 32, 61
Aristotle, 20n6, 47n2, 58, 70, 154
axioms, 46-47, 97-101, 174, 175, 218

Berkeley, George, 2, 11n11, 21n17, 58, 61, 76, 80, 93, 109, 129-30, 132n16, 137. *See also* empiricism
Boole, George, 70

categories. *See* concepts, pure
causation, 6, 12n31, 61, 68-69, 94, 103, 111-18, 120-21, 128-29, 159, 161, 176-83, 198. *See also* alteration; event
cognition, 1, 3, 9, 50, 53, 58, 88, 94, 135-36, 139, 182, 208-9, 219
compatibilism, 181
complexity/simplicity, 155-57, 170-175
concept, 18, 27-31, 42-45, 51-52, 57-58, 78, 92-93, 135, 138, 182, 194-96, 197-98, 219; contrast with intuition, 27-31, 42-45; empirical, 23-5, 39-40, 62n7, 93, 209n2; pure, 8, 57, 59-61, 66-71, 78-80, 81, 84, 86-89, 92-95, 98, 103, 131, 135, 139, 145, 149-50, 198

About the Author

Bryan Hall is an Assistant Professor of Philosophy at Indiana University Southeast. He earned his Ph.D. in Philosophy from the University of Colorado at Boulder. Hall is a two-time Fulbright Scholar who wrote his dissertation at the Philipps-Universität Marburg in Germany during his first Fulbright award. He is the author of several articles on Kant's philosophy which have appeared in journals such as *The British Journal for the History of Philosophy*, *Kantian Review*, and *Kant-Studien*. Mark Black and Matt Sheffield are recent graduates from Indiana University Southeast who helped work on this book as upperclassmen. They are both currently pursuing graduate degrees.

CPSIA information can be obtained at www.ICGtesting.com
Printed in the USA
LVOW101806221211

260676LV00003B/1/P